Endorphins, Eating Disorders and Other Addictive Behaviors

HANS F. HUEBNER, M.D.
Clinical Assistant Professor of Psychiatry
Cornell University Medical College, New York

W. W. NORTON & COMPANY • NEW YORK • LONDON

A NORTON PROFESSIONAL BOOK

Copyright © 1993 by Hans Huebner

All rights reserved.

Printed in the United States of America.

First Edition

Library of Congress Cataloging-in-Publication Data

Huebner, Hans F.
 Endorphins, eating disorders, and other addictive behaviors / Hans
F. Huebner.
  p.   cm.
 "A Norton professional book"—P. facing t.p.
 ISBN 0-393-70156-5
 1. Compulsive behavior—Physiological aspects. 2. Endorphins—
Psychological aspects. 3. Anorexia nervosa—Physiological aspects.
I. Title.
 [DNLM: 1. Anorexia Nervosa—therapy. 2. Bulimia—therapy.
3. Endorphins—adverse effects. 4. Endorphins—therapeutic use.
5. Psychotherapy. 6. Substance Dependence.   WM 175 H887e 1993]
RC533.H84 1993
616.85'26—dc20
DNLM/DLC   92-48431 CIP
for Library of Congress

W.W. Norton & Company, Inc., 500 Fifth Avenue, New York, N.Y. 10110
W.W. Norton & Company, Ltd., 10 Coptic Street, London WC1A 1PU

1 2 3 4 5 6 7 8 9 0

For my children
Nils and Julia

Acknowledgments

M OST OF ALL I wish to thank my anorectic and bulimic patients and their parents, especially those who participated in my initial study 13 years ago but also those whom I have had the privilege of treating since then. Without their open-minded collaboration in what was a very novel idea and their honesty in reporting their experiences, this book would not exist.

A special thanks goes to the many individuals at the New York Hospital-Cornell University Medical Center who made the study possible. I particularly thank Dr. Maria New, Dr. Lenore Levine, and the staff of the Pediatric Clinical Research Center for their support in every step of the complex research protocol. I am also most grateful to Dr. Robert Michels and Dr. William Frosch from the Department of Psychiatry for their personal interest in this project and for their valuable advice. Of the staff and trainees of the Division of Pediatric Mental Health, I wish to thank Dr. Charles Silberstein for his clinical contributions and Dorothy Hilpman and Christine Sinclair-Prince for their tireless clerical help.

I also wish to express my gratitude to Susan Barrows Munro at Norton Professional Books for her superb editorial contributions and patient counsel.

Finally, my thanks goes to the radio station WQXR-FM for keeping me company during my days and nights at the computer.

Contents

Introduction

THE POPPY PLANT has played a remarkable role in the workings of
the human body and mind. In the form of opium, or its alka-
loid, morphine, the poppy plant has provided us for thousands
of years with the greatest blessing, but also with the greatest
scourge: a blessing in its medical use to relieve physical pain; a
scourge in its nonmedical use to alleviate mental pain, to dull
emotional and spiritual misery. Whether taken for pain or ''pleasure,'' morphine's tendency to produce addiction is its major disadvantage. The ever increasing doses needed to achieve its desired effect inevitably lead to the profound mental and physical
changes of addiction.

Endorphins would not have been discovered if it weren't for
the addictive property of morphine. Since morphine fit so well into the pain-perceiving system of our body, scientists reasoned that
the body might produce a similar pain-killing substance that might
not be addictive. Their search led to the discovery of endorphins,
which, like morphine, turn out to have far-reaching functions in
the body and mind.

This book will be a struggle and a revelation at the same time,
not only for mental health professionals and persons with anorexia nervosa or bulimia, but for many who have never thought
about the deeper motives for their habits and life-styles. The
reader will struggle with the concept that many dear and comfort-

ing habits and customs are motivated by the pursuit of endorphins. Therefore, many will feel as if deserted by a dear old friend, especially when the behavior has become addictive and has to be relinquished. The revelation will come from the application of this new knowledge of endorphin-mediated behavior to the understanding of some of our deepest motives and will point the way to recovery for those who have become addicted.

This book gives an account of my research, clinical work, and thoughts on the role of endorphins as a motivating force of human behavior. My work began 15 years ago when I developed the first notion of endorphin involvement in anorexia nervosa and bulimia. Since then the concepts have undergone many evolutionary changes, eventually leading to a cohesive understanding of these conditions as endorphin addictions. While further research needs to be done on the biochemical aspects of endorphin mediation of these conditions, I have tested this theory many times in clinical situations while treating patients with anorexia nervosa and bulimia.

Over time I have realized that the concept of endorphin addiction has implications far beyond eating disorders. This book will give an account of my thinking on the relevance of the endorphin addiction concept to these other aspects of human behavior, be they normal forms of human behavior and customs or clinical conditions that bear the hallmarks of psychiatric illness. The analogies between these behaviors and anorexia nervosa are so striking that they can be understood in entirely new ways by extrapolating from the anorexia nervosa model.

This book was written for the professional therapist. However, it initially was conceived in response to many requests by patients, their parents, and other nonprofessionals for a written summary of my research and clinical experiences on the subject of eating disorders. Therefore, great pains have been taken to avoid medical and psychological terminology and concepts without first explaining them in terms understandable by readers who are not professionally trained. As the scope of the book has expanded to include many other forms of addictive behavior, it is hoped that any interested reader will find the material readable—the nonmedical therapist, someone afflicted by addictive behavior conditions, or anyone merely curious about the role of endorphins in human behavior.

To illustrate clinical and theoretical concepts, much use has been made of actual case material and vignettes. It should be noted, however, that all clinical illustrations presented are composites of several case histories and the names are fictitious.

*Endorphins, Eating Disorders
and Other Addictive Behaviors*

"It is as if you were slowly poisoned, something like being under the chronic influence of something like alcohol or dope."

A patient of Hilde Bruch,
quoted in *The Golden Cage*, 1978

1

What Is Anorexia Nervosa?
Tascha's Story

Tascha is a bright and perceptive college junior. We meet her at a moment of crisis and turmoil, when she is very confused about her feelings and thoughts.

If Tascha were aware of all her inner feelings and thoughts and how they have been influenced by events in her environment, from early childhood on, she would be able to understand her experiences and articulate them clearly. Many aspects of her life are observable facts and events; however, her story will be told by describing the inner workings of her mind, as ultimately revealed in therapy.

THE PAST

Tascha has had it! She has to stop all this eating to calm herself down while all this is going on. The scale shows that again she has gained two pounds and she feels really fat. Tascha feels nervous and upset; she could burst out of disgust with herself. Her mind is full of angry thoughts, memories from recent days and months and from the past.

Tascha is considering how she got to this point.

Her life at college seems to be caving in. Her grades are bad even though she has been studying obsessively, virtually day and

1

night. She feels exhausted. It's mid October, junior year, and she is already burnt out. She had moved all her easier subjects up so that she had credits to show. Now comes the horror part, the more academically oriented courses, such as math and natural sciences. No matter how hard she tries, these theoretical subjects defy her; she does not grasp them, and if she did, the material would not stay in her head. And she has lots of math and science yet to take.

Then there is Tom, her brother. He started at the same college one month ago. Tom seems to love it; he has plunged right into the social life, is popular and outgoing, likes to get drunk at parties, and is having a good time. Even in class, Tom does not seem to be afraid of teachers; he goes to them when he can't keep up and asks for help. He has friends, both male and female. Tom also seems to be able to sit down and study when he has to; he leaves things to the last minute, but he always gets them done, and his grades are alright, at least so far.

Why, Tascha laments, did Tom have to pick this college? Tascha does not want him here. Aren't there enough other colleges? Starting a life of her own, getting away from Tom—actually, getting away from the whole family—was a goal in going to college. Tom was "bad" at home, gave parents a lot to worry about; in high school he was "selfish," only looking out after himself, rude to their parents, would not abide by rules, curfew, not call from parties when late or the location changed. Yet, the parents, especially the mother, seemed always to take greater pleasure in Tom than in Tascha. Tom and mother have much in common; they understand each other, often even without words. Sometimes Tascha would overhear them chat in the kitchen, laughing together over the most trivial things.

Tom makes their mother happy, makes her feel that everything goes well in the family, that she is a good mother. And mother needs to be made happy, because she worries a lot. Ever since father and mother met as high school sweethearts, mother has been easily discouraged, hesitant to speak up for herself, and dependent on others. Father has tried to help her feel better, feeling that he was responsible for her unhappiness, even though he is a good man. He has worked very hard and became very successful.

Actually, how did mother and father manage? They both came from well-to-do families, growing up in a wealthy neighborhood where everybody seemed to know and help each other. Nevertheless, there was quite a bit of trouble in the families of both parents—some difficulties getting along with each other, but mostly alcohol. Father's father died early of liver cirrhosis; on mother's side there were several members who were alcoholics, and no one talked about grandmother's death. Did she commit suicide? Yet the families were close, accepted life as it came, and supported each other.

Tascha was the first child, and things were fine until Tom came along. Looking back to kindergarten and grammar school, Tascha remembers how she was not able to keep up with other kids. Everything was so difficult and frightening. Her parents did their best to help her, encouraging her to do things that others seemed to do and enjoy without hesitation. Even going alone to the deli around the corner to buy milk was scary somehow. When she succeeded after much coaxing and coaching, dad would make a big thing about it.

All those "firsts"—first time sleeping over with friends, first time riding a bicycle, first time at the ballfield, swimming, participating in school plays, cheerleading—Tascha would dread her parents mentioning any of these things, even though others her age had done them long ago. Never mind the other kids—what upset her the most was that Tom, a year and a half younger, was able to do all those things easily. And her parents, especially mom, were so proud of Tom. How Tascha wished that there was one thing she could do better than Tom.

Tascha was good at some things—keeping her room clean and orderly, never fighting with Tom, setting the dinner table, cleaning up after dinner, doing all her chores perfectly well. In fact, Tascha would often make up for Tom's laziness and selfishness. Tom would upset mother by wiggling out of chores, disappearing unnoticed to see friends, spending hours on the phone chatting about "urgent" matters. To keep the peace in the family, Tascha would do Tom's chores. It was not difficult for Tascha, nor did she resent it. Keeping tensions low was a top priority, because whenever someone was unhappy or angry, Tascha would feel this bad feeling inside her body. She would feel butterflies in her stomach, or her arms and legs would tingle, or she could not catch enough air, and she would feel dizzy in her head.

Because of these bodily sensations, she never said "no" to anyone if she could help it. Friends often made her do things, because she was unable to speak up for herself. As a result, Tascha had no enemies, and that's the way she wanted it to be. Tom was especially forceful and insistent in making requests and, as if paralyzed, Tascha was unable to get the word "no" over her lips in Tom's presence. Asking for a favor or demanding fairness was out of question.

Then there was this thing that she had with receiving things, not only gifts but also such essentials such as clothing. It was difficult for her to accept gifts from anyone—her parents and other family members as well as friends. Somehow she felt indebted to them, even guilty, as if she did not deserve it and was unworthy of the special attention. Also, often she felt that the gifts were so special, so fashionable, and she did not feel fashionable or one of the crowd. She felt best when she was able to buy her own clothes from money she earned herself. Starting at age 11 she asked around for jobs, impressing her family and neighbors with her eagerness and diligence.

Tascha remembers how she hated it when at age 12 or 13 she became chubby. Mom did not like it at all, since she wanted everybody in the family to look great, as the family of a successful man should look. But her dad did not seem to mind her gaining weight—or did he? He was a very busy man and did not really show his feelings. At least he did not withhold food from her as her mother did. Mom was very upset when dad took the children to the ice cream parlor after dinner, just to have fun.

Her chubbiness was another reason to feel inferior. Her mother had been a little overweight at some point but had gone on stringent diets; she still eats hardly anything and is very thin. Nothing could be worse than disappointing her in matters of looks and weight. Mom is a perfectionist.

Her family was well liked in the community, where dad was successful and made a lot of money. Dad did not like to show his wealth but mom started to live it up. Tascha did not like any of this. She actually thought they all were a nicer family before dad became successful. Now the family competed with other families, as if life were a popularity contest. Tascha remembers how hard she tried to be accepted by the most popular group of kids. They were bright, basically good students, but they also did bad things, such as taking street drugs or getting wasted on alcohol at every party, of which there were many.

Tascha thought she was lucky when Jack became her boyfriend in 11th grade. A leader of this group, he always came up with new ways to party harder and wilder. He was a bully, though, who manipulated everybody into doing things he wanted. Tascha became his devoted servant—maybe slave is a better word. She wonders if he really liked her as much as he always said. He would order her around, making her drive him all over the place at his whim, especially when he was drunk or stoned. She would have to give him money for his drugs, and he would call the shots every minute they spent together. Even sex became something he demanded frequently without thinking of her. If she ever resisted, he would scream and yell at her, verbally abusing her so much that she was afraid that he would attack her physically. He struck out at her on several occasions and hurt her badly, but none of her friends and family noticed.

Tascha cannot understand why she kept going out with Jack. Was it to be accepted in that group, as a way of telling everybody that she had finally made it, that she was no longer shy, clumsy, and fearful Tascha that she used to be. Or, was she afraid of Jack and his power over the group? If she broke off she would have to explain to everybody why she would not see Jack anymore. Everybody would hear how badly Jack had treated her, but people would not even believe her because Jack had a spell on everybody.

How could such a great guy act like that without anybody knowing about it? And then Jack—he would not sit back and feel bad; he might seek revenge. Tascha shudders and gets nervous thinking how violent he might have become.

Things came to an end with Jack the night of the senior prom, when Jack, quite drunk, cornered Tascha in one of the bedrooms and demanded sex from her. When she refused because she had no protection and could become pregnant, Jack became angry and abusive. Talking to him did not help, crying did not help either. Jack blocked the door. She ran to the window, below which her friends, including her brother, were partying, and screamed for help. But nobody seemed to hear her calls. Jack grabbed her, threw her onto the bed and raped her. Tascha ended that party the way she always did—she drove everybody home because she was the only one who had remained sober.

Tascha did not tell anyone about the rape. Her parents had been so happy that finally she was popular, a "normal adolescent." Her father was very religious and would not understand. Her mother would have been fed up with yet another problem they were forced to deal with. Tascha remembers how, afterwards, she was obsessed with one thought—to get away from home, from her friends, from her town. This seemed the only safe way out of her situation. The last month until graduation passed too slowly; she could not wait to leave for college.

COLLEGE

The first two years of college went well, Tascha thought, and this was not surprising. Wasn't college supposed to be her answer to her difficulties at home? She had chosen a college that permitted a flexible course schedule so that, at least for a while, she could avoid the real difficult courses, subjects that had made her feel constantly nervous in high school.

In addition, she had done something about her weight. After graduation she decided to trim down from 170 lbs., the most she had ever weighed and overweight for her height of 5'5". She had heard that in the first year of college one would gain weight, and she wanted to be prepared for that. She worked hard at it during the summer before college and managed to lose 15 lbs. As a freshman and sophomore she had lost another 10 lbs. and kept her weight down. She felt much better about herself.

She had made many friends. But more importantly, she was going out again, with a guy she studied with in a group project. Jack came to her mind only when the new guy was too quick in hugging or kissing her after they got together. Then some of the panic feelings returned, reminding her of the rape.

But now things have caught up with her and she "cannot stand it." She has been working obsessively working day and night, but feels nervous most of the day. Her mind simply will not give her any rest. Sometimes she feels she could explode; unbearably restless, she cannot stand to be in her apartment for long. When she studies she reads without understanding what she has read. And all those tests! She is afraid of the teachers, feels she cannot please them, that she is viewed again as a troubled person. A loser again!

And she has started overeating again. Her weight is going up and up, no way of holding it down. She does not eat because she is hungry. No, food has become something else. It has become a substance to make her better, to control her nervousness, one of the few things—maybe the only thing at this point—that gives her a feeling of calm. Her weight is up to 155 lbs., which to her feels like 300 lbs. For months now she has tried to resist weight gain by not having breakfast before class and by skipping lunch as much as possible. But in the evenings, when she virtually locks herself in her apartment, she cannot resist. After shopping on her way home, buying all kinds of snacks, cookies, and finger food, she just eats and eats while sitting at her desk. She has carefully limited her time with her boyfriend to a one or two evenings on weekends, saying that she needs the other evenings to study. And he understands—he is the kind of guy who always understands. Tascha sometimes wishes that he wouldn't, but then, as long as she gets away with it she can do her own thing and eat.

DIET

But today Tascha really has had it. Did her mother not make it very clear that being overweight would make her a social outcast? That being slim is the best formula for success? How could Tascha allow herself to add insult to injury by getting fat in addition to all her academic difficulties? Losing weight could be her way of being special. Her parents would be proud of her again after having been critical of her recent weight gain. And her female friends—how they would envy her slim figure! And then the guys, in school and back home—once she is slim they might actually feel sorry that they did not pursue her. Even Jack might have second thoughts about the way he treated her.

Tascha thinks about ways of losing weight. One of those diets that are advertised all over? Or signing up at a commercial weight reduction center? Maybe if she just managed not to eat at all in the evenings after having skipped breakfast and lunch and having some fruit to squelch hunger pangs—the so-called zero diet—that would do the trick. After all, one thing she always was able to rely on was her willpower and determination when the going got rough.

To Tascha's surprise, using the zero diet method is not as difficult as she thought, after the first few days. Those are tough, indeed. But on the third or fourth day she suddenly feels that she might succeed. As the days go by, the hunger pangs somehow lessen, or become less compelling; stuffing herself in the evenings has become less attractive. She actually walks by the deli every night on her way home with a grin on her face. Somehow eating has lost its grip on her.

More surprising than that, Tascha notices that she feels more energetic. What used to be a frantic mode of taking care of everything, always being on the verge of exhaustion, and often finding it difficult to start a task, or even the whole day, somehow has become easier and more routine. And as the weeks go by she generally seems to be less worried and nervous, not only about school, assignments, tests, teachers, but also about other people— her boyfriend, friends in general, her parents, even Tom.

The diet is very effective. Tascha never thought that one could lose weight this quickly. After the first week she has lost about 4 lbs., then she loses about 1 or 2 lbs. a week, sometimes more, and is still able to eat here and there a little bit, especially when going out with friends who would become suspicious if she ate nothing at all.

While initially she thought that she would be happy if she lost about 10 lbs., several weeks into the dieting she raises her hopes and thinks it would be great if she could lose 20 lbs., bringing her weight down to 135 lbs., although, to be honest, she feels that her ideal weight really is 125 lbs.—no more, no less.

After she has lost 10 lbs. almost everybody notices. How great she looks! How they admire her for having so much willpower! Even the guys pay more attention to her. Or does it only seem that way because she feels better about herself and it feels more natural to her to receive attention? Maybe both. Tascha certainly thinks it is all solely because of her weight loss.

Tascha notices something else. Her body wants to move more. In fact, while in the past she had to force herself to exercise and as a result did it only sporadically, she now wants to work out daily and does so with greater intensity than ever before. Somehow it seems so much easier and afterwards the feeling of physical exhaustion feels good and wholesome. She dreams of getting better at working out. Her body slimming down and her muscles gaining tonus and strength—what could look better!

She eats very little. But food itself is more on her mind as she works on losing the second 10 lbs. Looking through magazines, her eyes rest on every item related to food; recipes became obligatory reading. Walking through town, she can barely stop herself from studying restaurant menus. When there is a party with friends Tascha volunteers to go shopping and prepares elaborate dishes; when dinner is served she helps everybody to hefty portions, urging her friends to take seconds and warning them that she as the cook would otherwise feel offended. As long as she does not have to eat anything herself!

As the Christmas holidays near, Tascha anticipates her return home with a sense of victory. Her parents, especially her mother, will be very happy that Tascha is a "winner" again. But there are challenges in going home as well. There is all that food, and the family will watch her carefully. How will she be able to continue her zero diet and not start to worry her parents?

To Tascha's surprise, everything at home goes well. Yes, there are some worried looks, but everybody wants to be upbeat and refrains from saying anything. Not having to study for a few days actually allows her to be more at ease. If it weren't for this thinking about food that persists at home and intensifies as she starts class again, she would be fine.

Tascha thinks this preoccupation with food is strange, since her interest with food should have gotten less now that she has stopped overeating. Actually, thinking of food is getting in the way of studying and of falling asleep. She lies in bed and thinks of what not to eat the next day, how she will manage to eat the absolute minimum without raising her friends' suspicions. She spends hours rethinking various food combinations and, like a computer, automatically adding up the total calories of each combination. Sometimes Tascha thinks that part of her mind must like to think of food every night, even though it is a nuisance that is getting worse every day, especially now that she is working on reducing her weight to 125 lbs., a weight that she thought she would never be able to reach and which, at the same time, would be perfect for her in every way.

Like the finale of a great symphony, when Tascha reaches 125 lbs. everything seems to going superbly, at least on the outside. Almost everyone thinks of her as a winner, someone who has done the impossible task of getting her weight under control. A few doubters wonder about Tascha's overly busy life, her restlessness, the hardening of her smiles, and the intensity of her reactions. But Tascha feels that their concerns have been eased somewhat by her assurance that she is aware of anorexia nervosa and its dangers. She will start eating normally again now and concentrate on keeping that weight. Has she not reached her goal? She likes herself and everybody likes her for it.

Up to this point her daily food intake consists of orange juice for breakfast and a cup of herb tea later in the morning, some fruit for lunch, and cooked vegetables for dinner, as well as a few tiny pretzels in the course of the day washed down with plenty of diet Pepsi. On rare occasions she opens a can of tuna for protein. She has found that the caffeine in sodas is very effective in suppressing occasional hunger pangs that interfere with her excellent sense of well-being. By now she evades dinners in restaurants with friends, claiming that she is too busy with school work.

Because she has become quite constipated in the course of her weight loss, she also uses laxatives regularly, and recently she has used more of them, at times four or five Exlax a day. She hates not being able to move her bowels no matter how little is there to move. Sometimes she thinks to herself that the laxatives will move the food faster through her bowels, thereby preventing her body from getting fat. Whatever it is, she knows that she feels better after her bowel movements, no matter how many laxatives it takes.

Now that she has reached 125 lbs., her goal weight, Tascha starts to eat a little bit more. With a sense of victory she says to herself, she always knew that she would be able to stop dieting. But she also thinks that maybe she should use this lucky streak to drop her weight a little bit more, just to lock in a lower weight and protect herself from suddenly gaining, should it prove difficult to keep her low weight once she starts eating again. Somehow, this is too good to give up just like that.

Nevertheless, Tascha adds a pretzel here or there and for dinner a slice of bread, the taste of which she has been greatly missing. (The smell of fresh bread was one of the secret indulgences whenever she passed by a bakery.) She even adds a soup when she has lunch with friends in the cafeteria.

However, she notices that some bad feelings begin to creep in again, some apprehension when getting ready for everyday tasks, less energy and pep in general, feeling a little blue, not finding things as exciting as they were when she was dieting.

Especially in the evenings after dinner, when she has forced herself to eat a little more if only for her boyfriend's sake, she is

suddenly gripped by many of these bad, nervous feelings, something she has not really felt for some time. On those nights she
also feels more bothered by everything, even little things. Once
these worries start they will not go away quickly; actually, they
get worse and every worry gets magnified.

Two weeks later Tascha weighs 123 lbs. but actually does not
mind it so much. Wasn't there this thought before, the one that
she did not quite wish to admit, asking why she should give up
dieting? Anyhow, some of these bad feelings have recently dissi-
pated and that is more important to her than keeping her weight
at 125 lbs. as originally planned.

After another month or so, during which she really tries hard
to eat more, she steps on her bathroom scale again, convinced
that she has actually gained since some bad feelings had returned
again. To her surprise the scale shows 120 lbs., 5 lbs. less than six
weeks earlier. This really worries Tascha. More than once she
wonders if her diet has gone out of control. And each time this
thought brings about a stronger feeling of nervousness, almost a
rush of anxiety; yet, there is this other thought—that she actually
looks better than ever before. Now she feels so firmly in control
of her eating that she is not worried about getting fat again. Tascha
decides that weighing herself is what causes her worries and confused thoughts, and she resolves that from now on she will no
longer step on the scale but eat as much as she can.

Nevertheless, things really are getting tough. Her friends in
school have become alarmed over her weight loss and no longer
shy away from confronting her whenever they can. They have
even started calling her anorectic and saying that they were mis-
taken, if not foolish, to believe that she had found a way of dieting
safely. Besides, they tell her, she no longer looks good, thin as
she is, with her bones sticking out all over her body and her face
gaunt and narrow and pale. But Tascha thinks to herself that her
friends' protest is only a sign of envy. They are the ones who
don't have control—control over their eating, that is.

But then, she also thinks that they may be right. Certainly the
guys have not paid as much attention to her lately; the "wow"

looks are no longer forthcoming. She also worries about what her parents will say when she goes home for the summer. So far she has been able to stave off their attempts to get her to come home, claiming that she is too busy and things are really great. And her parents, happy that things are finally going right for Tascha, want to believe her, even though Tom has warned them that Tascha looks anorectic.

Also, Tascha has not had her period when she was supposed to have it. A month ago the flow was much less than usual, and this time it seems to have stopped altogether. She knows she is not pregnant, since she has not had sex during the past month. Her boyfriend went on strike, saying that he did not find her bony body sexy anymore. Tascha had been complaining of discomfort during intercourse and did not mind her boyfriend's lack of interest.

In addition, Tascha is getting physically weak. She is not able to exercise as much because dizzy spells make her unstable. Her muscles, although very tight and firm, seem to have gotten lazy. They just don't do the work the way they used to do. Cramps in her legs when jogging and shortness of breath much earlier on the run signal weakening of her body. However, Tascha can do without exercising, she thinks—just eat fewer calories to make up for the calories that she is not burning off.

But she had sworn to herself that she would not lose any more weight, hadn't she? What has happened to that decision? Well, Tascha cannot remember anymore that she was really serious about eating more when she had reached 125 lbs. That was only to prove her friends wrong. What she really thinks is that she is a better, purer, more special person than any other person she knows. They are undisciplined, indulging, uncontrolled, lazy, depraved beings—in one word, pigs. Only she is capable of virtually floating with her light, weightless body through the day, unencumbered by human needs and worry.

But there are things she does not like these days. Although food is no longer constantly on her mind, she cannot concentrate on school work. Her thoughts are racing so fast and come out so jumbled that she cannot grasp information, not even a paragraph in her textbook or a few sentences of an English essay.

The other problem these days is sleep. When she was well into her weight loss program she had trouble falling asleep because her mind was busy thinking about food. Recently, she has started to wake up at 5 or even 4 a.m., even though she has not fallen asleep until 1:30 or 2 a.m. And how awake she is! Her body is restless, demands to get out of bed and do exercises: stretching, sit-ups, anything to move her muscles. Otherwise her body might explode, a terribly unpleasant, almost painful feeling.

Tascha does not want to see this as a sign of trouble. She simply makes getting up at 4 a.m. her new routine. She reasons that she will get done more during the day that way. If only she weren't so exhausted! A few hours into the morning she feels weak; yet her mind, incapable of settling down, demands constant activity. The results are catastrophic. Her grades have dropped by the end of the spring semester, even though she has spent day and night over the books.

The big countdown has started for the day when she will have to go home. Whenever this thought comes up she panics until she cannot feel her body anymore and her mind goes blank. Soon her parents will see her; she knows that they will be shocked about her weight. What if her parents will immediately take charge, insist on her eating more, and seek professional help?

Reflecting on that, Tascha, for the first time since she started dieting, feels hopeless and despairing. She panics at the thought of getting fat again.

HOME

Although her parents have been prepared by her brother, seeing Tascha with their own eyes is still a shock. Her mother is able to hold back her tears only for a brief moment. Her father looks very sad; he says nothing but tries to give her a hug, only to be turned away. Tascha knows how much she has disappointed her parents. She feels that she is back to where she was many years ago, being the troubled child again who has let her parents down.

Surprisingly, her world did not collapse entirely. Soon there is this other thought. Let them worry, she thinks. This is her way of asserting herself. Her mother, especially, put her through a lot in the past; now it is Tascha's turn to feel strong. Emotionally she feels stronger, less affected by tension and ill feelings, and she likes it this way. As long as she does not cave in and let others take control.

Being out of school and free of the pressure to study, Tascha thinks, may allow her to devote all her energy to eating enough to stop her weight loss. Her parents want to believe in her ability to recover on her own; however, to their dismay Tascha looks as if she is losing more weight. Tascha has been eating more; however, her body seems to burn the food faster, even though she has not been exercising much. She often feels dizzy, and a short walk exhausts her as much as a five-mile run had in the past.

At this point Tascha no longer resists her parents' urging to see the pediatrician who has taken care of her for many years. He takes a careful history, gives her a physical examination, takes blood for tests and weighs her. The diagnosis is clear. Tascha has anorexia nervosa. With her weight of 108 lbs. her condition is serious, and he recommends seeing a psychiatric help immediately. He promises that he will continue to see her regularly for medical checkups.

Tascha agrees to see a psychiatrist with great reluctance; she is not allowed any way out. She finally joins her parents for the first visit. Tascha is ready to get help—or is she?

2

The Clinical Phases of Anorexia Nervosa and Their Relevance to Endorphin Addiction

THE TERM "ADDICTION" usually refers to a process in which the use of certain substances leads to a compelling habit of increasing use, resulting in successive changes in mind and body. The progression of these changes follows an orderly and predictable path from health to mental and physical devastation.

In this chapter we will examine the clinical evidence for the notion that the self-starvation process in anorexia nervosa is identical to the behavior and psychology of drug addiction. This implies, of course, that there is a substance to which a person with anorexia nervosa becomes addicted. It further implies that this substance plays an essential role in causing the behavioral and mental changes characteristic of this condition. Third, it implies that this substance is singularly responsible for perpetuating and maintaining anorectic behavior throughout all stages of the addictive process.

We are not talking about a substance that the anorectic is taking into her body. The substance I am referring to is secreted by the body as a result of starvation. In this chapter I am inviting the reader to just imagine that there is such a substance or physiological mechanism to which the anorectic has become addicted by simply going on a diet and starving herself. Would such a mechanism explain many of the behavioral features and changes that have been widely described in the literature and that have remained an enigma? I am appealing especially to clinicians who have watched the progression of this condition and have been frustrated in their treatment efforts. Identifying these features as the orderly manifestations of an addictive process may answer some of the questions that have continued to puzzle them, as well as anorectics and their families.

This substance is actually a group of substances, called endorphins. Their biochemical nature and the evidence for their role in anorexia nervosa will be extensively addressed in Chapter 3. For our discussion here it is sufficient to know that endorphins are a group of highly addictive substances which play an important role in the regulation of many functions of the body. These substances have much in common with opiates, drugs that have been used against pain since antiquity. Therefore, they are called endogenous opioids, a name indicating that these substances produce opiate-like effects (opioids) and are generated within the body (endogenous). Similarly, the name ''endorphin'' stands for ''endomorphine'' or internal morphine, a term usually used in the plural to reflect the inclusion of many structurally related molecules in this family of compounds with opiate-like activity. In accordance with this general concept of endogenous opioids, I will refer to the substance that underlies the self-starvation addiction of anorexia nervosa simply as ''endorphins.''

Central to the addiction concept of anorexia nervosa are two principles that merit special emphasis because they diverge from established approaches to the understanding of this condition.

One is the principle that much, if not all, behavior and thinking in anorexia nervosa are governed by the mechanism of reward (and nonreward). Also called reinforcement, this mechanism refers to the unique property of all addictive substances: that is, humans (as well as animals) will engage in behavior or actions to self-administer these substances once they have been exposed to them. In contrast, a non-addictive substance will not cause a person to automatically continue self-administration. In short, humans will not stop wanting addictive substances, whereas they may lose interest in non-addictive substances. The reason for this is that addictive substances affect certain brain centers in ways that are pleasing or rewarding to the individual, so much so that the individual wants more of this effect. What is experienced as rewarding need not be always euphoria, an elevation of one's mood, or a "high"; it can be simply a reduction of anxiety or improvement of a depressed mood.

The second principle is that there is a direct causative relationship between the state of eating (or non-eating), on the one hand, and the state of mood and feelings, on the other. The endorphins form the physiological link in this interaction. Non-eating and weight loss promote a sense of well-being or improvement of depressed mood via release of endorphins. Eating and weight gain lead to a reduction of endorphins, resulting in increased anxiety and/or depression.

This acute and immediate interaction between the state of food intake and mood has been neglected by most research in the field, which has focused primarily on advanced weight loss states. One reason may be the wide use of Feighner et al.'s (1972) diagnostic criteria for anorexia nervosa, which specify a weight loss of at least 25% from ideal body weight, thus taking a rather static view and missing out on the dynamic relationship between acute eating state and mood. As a consequence, to this day research is mostly conducted on emaciated patients and their course of recovery. In my opinion, more important information can be gained from studies that investigate the progression of symptoms and biochemical abnormalities from the onset of this condition to emaciation, as we will do here.

We can extend this study even further back, to the years preceding anorexia nervosa, and look closely at the early developmental stages and the personality structure of the anorectic, as well as the family dynamics she grew up with, as has been done by many researchers. Then, if we integrate findings from the anorectic's early life and family setting with the events taking place during her progressive weight loss, many of the bewildering features of anorexia nervosa become comprehensible and even logical.

As a reference for the clinical features of drug addictions I will use a review article by Jaffe and Clouet (1981), which summarizes some 130 research papers in the field of opiate addiction. This paper was helpful to me at the time it was published and, I am certain, it still is valid as far as general concepts of addiction are concerned. Jaffe and Clouet describe as central clinical features of the addictive process the phenomena of reinforcement and reward, tolerance, dependence, as well as withdrawal and abstinence, and craving associated with withdrawal. The authors also discuss two factors that are important precursors of addiction: (1) the mood state of depression and demoralization that precedes the use of drugs and makes an individual vulnerable to addiction, and (2) the social acceptability of the use of a particular addictive substance. In examining the addictive features of anorexia nervosa let us start with these latter features.

VULNERABILITY

Addicts do not become addicted for fun. Depression, social and personal demoralization, low self-esteem, as well as biological sensitivities existing since birth, are typical precursors of drug addiction. Similarly, depression and distress have been widely recognized as precipitating states of anorexia nervosa. For example, Warren (1968) found depression in 85% of his sample of 20 anorectics, and Cantwell, Sturzenberger, et al. (1977) found a high percentage of affective disorder upon long-term follow-up of anorectics and a high incidence of depression in their families, thus establishing an associational link between depression and anorexia nervosa. Using larger samples, Eckert, Goldberg, et al. (1982) and Hendren (1983) confirmed and elaborated on this link, as did many studies thereafter.

Similarly, if one takes a careful history, one always finds states of serious depression and distress in anorectics prior to dieting. Often going on for years and associated with anxiety, worry, and low self-esteem, depression and distress are states of nonreward that cause the pre-anorectic to cry out for something that will make her feel less depressed and balance her mood. In other words, she reaches out for a compensatory reward. For the pre-anorectic this compensatory reward is food, and eating becomes an irresistible preoccupation not only for its gustatory pleasures but also in response to a biological signal to eat given by the distressed brain.

The widely discussed "addictive personality" is nothing but the outcome of this chronically depressed mood and the constitutional inability to maintain an internal equilibrium. While most people might reach out for ways of reducing distress and anxiety without going to extremes, people with addictive personalities tend to seek more rewards and become addicted to whatever rewards they pursue.

Going back to Tascha, we are able to identify factors that would make any person in her situation insecure and depressed. She was a very sensitive child who had difficulties keeping up with her peers and her brothers. This feeling of being different from others was made worse by her parents' attempts to help her, no matter how good their intentions were. Somehow she got the message that her slowness was not acceptable. When she became chubby in early adolescence, like many teenagers, or because she overate to compensate for her unhappiness, her mother's overt disapproval made her feel truly ostracized. Her acceptance of the abusive and self-destructive relationship with Jack reveals how desperately she wished to be accepted by her peers.

In view of these background experiences and her personality marked by sensitivity and low self-esteem, it is not difficult to imagine that a major setback or distress would make her highly vulnerable to developing anorexia nervosa should she decide to go on a diet.

FIRST EXPOSURE: LOSING WEIGHT AS A SOCIALLY
ACCEPTABLE WAY OF FEELING BETTER

In order to become addicted to a drug an individual has to be exposed to it. While the avenues of initial exposure may be multiple, the social and cultural availability and acceptability of a particular addictive substance is an important factor in this process.

In this regard there is a parallel to anorexia nervosa as well. Without dieting in pursuit of slimness for social reward or for other reasons, the addictive cycle leading eventually to anorexia nervosa is not initiated. Slimness is highly rewarded in our culture, and even more so in families of anorectics. The extraordinary value placed on a slim and trim body sets the stage for the anorectic-to-be when she finds herself overeating and gaining weight. Instead of a socially available drug she chooses dieting because of its social acceptability. Thus, dieting as an avenue to a positive feeling state constitutes the first motive for the decision to diet, and a very powerful motive in families where slimness is highly valued.

For the same reasons, the incidence of anorexia nervosa varies greatly in different societies, and in our society within different sociocultural groups. I have had the opportunity to treat women with anorexia nervosa from other countries that are known to have attitudes towards slimness very different from ours, countries in which being fat is considered a sign of wealth and sex appeal. Without fail, it has turned out that these women have lived their lives outside of the prevailing social attitudes and standards of their country. Some have frequently traveled to Western countries or adopted Western middle- and upper-class standards from exposure to Western magazines and movies.

The Decision to Diet

Tascha's decision to diet in her junior year was made under quite dramatic circumstances that eventually led her to succumb to anorexia nervosa. After having had two reasonably happy years,

Tascha's world seemed to cave in when she had to meet an academically demanding schedule. Furthermore, her brother's arrival on campus brought the troubling family dynamics of her childhood right into the college, which she had thought of as *her* territory. In her distress she started to overeat again to give herself some form of reward, and this time found herself getting totally out of control. It is no surprise that she decided to go on a diet again, as she had done successfully earlier. Only this time the decision was reached while being desperately depressed and dissatisfied with herself and feeling agitated, nervous, and confused.

The decision to diet is not always made under circumstances as dramatic as Tascha's. Especially in younger girls a seemingly unremarkable event often leads to the decision to diet. Sometimes a pediatrician has told the anorectic-to-be to lose a few pounds, or a certain special dress does not fit anymore, or a boyfriend, a parent, or a sibling has made offhand remarks about her weight. Sometimes, reasonably slim adolescents find themselves suddenly gaining weight during a time of loneliness, separation, or distress due to altered life circumstances.

Even the natural change of figure that occurs with sexual development during puberty poses a threat to some girls that they feel must be counteracted. In some of these cases, the girl's body develops sexually before those of her peers, or she has a petite body that suddenly becomes quite rounded. Sometimes a viral illness or other discomfort leads to a loss of appetite, allowing the potential anorectic to experience what it is like to weigh a few pounds less and giving her hope that she can realize her long-held, often secret dream of being slimmer.

It is easy to underestimate the power of this wish to be slim, especially when the precipitating event for the decision to diet seems relatively unremarkable. Similarly, it is easy to underestimate the severity and duration of the underlying distress and depression that resulted in the decision to diet. In cases in which the distress appears to be of short duration, closer analysis often reveals that long-lasting but very tenuous patterns of coping have suddenly failed as the individual has been confronted with a new situation or has entered a new phase of life, like college. Actually, since the premorbid distress determines the need for social reward by dieting, we can estimate the degree of pre-anorectic distress and depression from the intensity of anorectic's dieting efforts.

PHASE I, THE EARLY WEIGHT LOSS PHASE

Adaptation to Starvation

The early weight loss phase is marked by a series of physical and mental changes that together constitute the body's adaptational changes to promote survival. Mediated by endorphins, these adaptive responses of the organism are universally found in starvation states of any cause. They are triggered within a few days of serious dieting and continue to be active as long as the body is deprived of food.

Anorectics-to-be adapt to a reduced diet during this phase like everybody else. However, anorectics respond to and experience these natural changes in a unique way, so that they are powerfully influenced by these changes and eventually controlled by them. For the discussion of the addictive process here, we will confine ourselves to the mental features of adaptation to starvation.

Reinforcement and Reward

Of the mental changes, the most important phenomena are reinforcement and reward, two terms that are sometimes used interchangeably and constitute the core of the addictive process. Humans, once exposed to addictive substances, will not stop wanting them and will keep doing things to get them (*reinforcement*). This is so because these substances give a pleasing feeling to the person (*reward*); this can be elation or a "high" but is often just a reduction of depressed feelings or anxiety.

Reinforcement and reward—and for that matter nonreward—come into play during this phase in several ways. First, there is the experience of nonreward caused by giving up the rewarding substance *food*. This is a form of withdrawal, since forgoing food is experienced in many ways like the withdrawal from an addictive drug. Anorectics find the initial dieting just as difficult and unrewarding as anyone who is on a stringent diet, whether the deprivation is voluntary ("the woman next door" or the wrestler who "sucks" weight to have a competitive advantage in a lower weight class), or involuntary (the prisoner of war or the inhabitant of a famine-stricken country). The first hurdle to overcome is the feeling of deprivation from the universally rewarding substance, food, that will cause cravings and hunger pangs.

If anything, the anorectic-to-be might find resisting food more difficult, since she opposes a stronger command, the impulse to eat excessively prior to her decision to diet. This phenomenon constitutes the key element in the differential diagnosis of weight loss in anorexia nervosa and severe clinical depression. Individuals suffering from depressive illness lose weight because of a true loss of appetite and interest in eating and food. Anorectics, on the other hand, resist with great effort a heightened appetite and interest in food. This resistance to a powerful wish to eat constitutes the essence of anorexia nervosa, which to this day some researchers in the field seem to disregard when they are searching for a biochemical mechanism for the "loss of appetite."

Second, soon the anorectic-to-be will, like any other person on a stringent diet, experience the reward she consciously has been aiming for, the societal reward. In Tascha's case friends and relatives commented that she looked more attractive and happier, and classmates who had never paid attention to her—even strangers—suddenly noticed her.

The response to this societal reward, however, distinguishes the non-anorectic dieter from the anorectic. The non-anorectic dieter will stop dieting at a reasonable goal weight; she will, if anything, be happy to increase her calories from a reduction level to a weight maintenance level. In contrast, the anorectic is not capable of reverting to a maintenance diet at the goal weight and will continue to diet long after the societal reward for slimness has ceased because of her gaunt and emaciated look.

Nevertheless, the anorectic continues to be aware only of this pursuit of societal reward as reason for starving herself. It will haunt the anorectic throughout her illness, sometimes throughout life, and is typically expressed in her fear of getting fat whenever she eats. However, the societal reward of slimness is not the true motivator, but constitutes the proverbial red herring of anorexia nervosa. What the anorectic does not know is that her behavior is governed by a true and much more powerful motivator.

This brings us to the third reward phenomenon, the key to the development of addiction. This is the reward provided by endorphins, a reward so powerful that the pursuit of it can carry the anorectic to extreme emaciation and even to death.

The daily reduction of food intake below maintenance requirements causes the body to switch to starvation mode by stimulating endorphin secretion. The physical condition under which this mechanism is triggered appears to be a switch by the body from burning carbohydrates to the use of fat stored in fat cells and does not depend on the person's weight. Someone weighing 300 lbs., let's say, and losing weight rapidly, will experience this mechanism as readily as a normal-weight or below-normal-weight person.

As designed by nature, endorphin stimulation seems to serve as a master switch, causing most, if not all adaptational changes of the body and mind. Most important among the mental changes is the protection of the starving organism from the effects of starvation by providing heightened coping power and a reduction of suffering. Therefore, strictly speaking, endorphins were not designed to be a reward—a substance that simply gives pleasing feelings. However, since it is rewarding to the mind to feel less anxiety and depression, the term reward is used appropriately. Endorphins benefit the voluntary and involuntary starver equally. However, the beneficial effects of endorphin reward are *experienced* differently, thus affecting the outcome in very different ways.

The "woman next door" goes on a diet purely for the sake of social reward and does not suffer from depression or anxiety prior to going on a diet. In other words, she is not vulnerable to addiction. She finds that the price, i.e., food deprivation and a restricted life-style, is not compensated by endorphin reward. She had been coping well enough anyway and, if anything, she feels miserable while dieting. Therefore, she soon finds herself returning to normal food intake, often before she has reached her goal weight. She may even wish that she could ''have a little bit of anorexia nervosa.''

Tascha's story illustrates this point very well. Her first two years in college were clearly quite happy and rewarding, and in many ways her dieting experience was similar to that of ''the woman next door.'' She was thriving in her new environment, with new friends, including a caring boyfriend, and classes that were academically not demanding. During her freshman year she was able to lose 25 lbs.; she then kept her weight down, without becoming anorectic. This is not surprising. She was happy in her life and enjoyed the social reward of being more attractive as a result of weight loss. But more importantly, she was happy enough that she was not vulnerable to the addictive cycle to which she later succumbed.

Similarly, the wrestler usually will return to a normal diet after the match. Sometimes he will eat even more to compensate for the ''borrowed'' energy expended during the match. However, I have treated young men who were unable to resume eating again. They developed anorexia nervosa because they suffered from anxiety and depression prior to losing weight and thus were vulnerable to the reinforcing effects of dieting.

Prisoners of war or famine-stricken people are not vulnerable to the rewarding effects of endorphins either. They most likely were better off prior to being deprived of food. They simply benefit from endorphin reward by coping more effectively with their circumstances. Thus they are less likely to give up and greatly improve their chances for freedom and/or survival. However, once their misfortune is reversed and sufficient food becomes available, their need for endorphins ends, and they return quickly to normal food intake. If anything, they are likely to be voracious eaters for a while.

The situation is very different for the anorectic-to-be. She benefits greatly from the rewarding effects of endorphins, but not just by suffering less while she starves. Her sense of well-being has much improved over the time she was depressed or anxious; she feels happier, more vigorous, and energetic. Actually, the anorectic-to-be only *feels* less troubled; because she is coping better, her perception of her life situation has improved—no actual change in her life circumstances has occurred. Feighner et al.'s (1972) description of "apparent enjoyment in losing weight" and "manifestations, that food refusal is a pleasurable indulgence" aptly characterizes the reward experienced in this phase.

During this stage Tascha noticed that the lethargy of her depression gave way to energy and initiative. Her exhaustion in meeting the demands of each day gave way to a sense of control and calm. Even her many worries and nervous feelings about not meeting the expectations of her teachers and friends subsided. Her low self-esteem, once an insurmountable burden that influenced everything she tried, turned into a sense of being alright, if not great. Tascha liked herself again.

The improved sense of well-being is so beneficial to the anorectic-to-be that the price she is paying for it, i.e., being deprived of food and leading a restricted life-style, does not outweigh the benefits. Thus, endorphin reward becomes a more powerful reinforcer for the anorectic than for "the woman next door." Reinforcement takes place when the anorectic-to-be learns unconsciously that she has to eat fewer calories than her body burns in order to experience less depression, to have a more positive attitude towards life, and to keep her newfound energy level.

During this early phase of self-starvation the anorectic-to-be does not show distortion of her body image. Accordingly, she plans to reach a weight well within the range of her "ideal body weight," which is a weight considered healthy for a given height and age based on statistical analysis of the overall population.

Preoccupation with Food

Preoccupation with food is another universal mental adaptation to starvation mediated by endorphins. It increases in intensity from day one of dieting and takes on obsessive proportions. Dieters do not like it at all.

Tascha noticed that anything related to food became of ever greater interest. As if by magic, no food-related story, recipe, or advertisement would escape her eyes as she thumbed through magazines. During the day, but especially at night when her mind was not totally occupied by an intense task, she would obsess about food for hours.

Often this preoccupation is expressed in compulsive behavior related to the handling and preparation of food, called *vicarious eating*. Equally bewildering to herself and her parents, the anorectic suddenly becomes interested in shopping, cooking elaborate meals, and urging—even forcing—others to eat what she had cooked. The mother is virtually thrown out of the kitchen. The anorectic will satisfy her mind's insistent attention to food as long as she does not have to eat anything herself.

What is this strange phenomenon? It is a powerful brain mechanism to promote survival by increasing the drive to eat. If we consider famine conditions, we realize the adaptive advantage of being forced by our mind to make food a priority. As a result of this mechanism, the starving person will not only seek food constantly but also accept as nourishment totally unfamiliar and sometimes disgusting organic matter. As long as it can be swallowed, it may have some nutritional value and make the difference between death and survival.

The anorectic feels quite bewildered and threatened by her preoccupation with food. As she is making every effort to lock in a state of body and mind in which she no longer feels hunger pangs, she is experiencing ever more powerful obsessions with food. The anorectic interprets these obsessions as validation of her fear of getting fat and feels driven even further into the state of self-starvation. Thus, preoccupation with food contributes to the addictive process; at the same time, it can become so disruptive and intrusive that in my experience it is the most frequent complaint among anorectics seeking treatment.

Exercising

Another important clinical feature of this early weight loss phase of anorexia nervosa is the tendency to exercise excessively. Exercising as such is a health-promoting activity, the importance of which has been recognized for many years, especially since life in our society has become virtually free of the need for physical exertion. However, exercising plays an interesting role in the experience of the anorectic-to-be during this early phase of starvation.

Accelerated motor activity is one of the universal effects of starvation, especially in advanced stages of weight loss. Starved people, as long as they are physically able to do so, seem to want to move their bodies more. The early signs of this phenomenon, of course, come as a welcome experience to many dieters, who always wanted to exercise but were unable to make themselves do so. Similarly, anorectics-to-be will welcome this brain command to move their body faster and harder. In fact, most of them will do so in excess.

Tascha responded to this need of her body to move by accelerating the intensity of her workouts. However, in contrast to the pace of previous exercising, she found herself stretching the limits of exertion further and further. Working out no longer was a matter of pleasure but became a compulsion. In other words, Tascha converted the brain command to move faster into a rigorous self-imposed exercise schedule aimed at physical exhaustion.

This shift is a uniquely anorectic feature not found in other forms of starvation. Since physical exertion is known to be a powerful endorphin trigger, the shift signals the addition of another method of achieving endorphin reward, a method used by all serious exercisers and harboring the potential for addictive excess.

The role of increased physical activity in starvation states is not clear. A case could be made for the adaptive function of increased body movements as a means of generating heat to keep the body temperature from falling or as a means of mobilizing the body to search for food. However, muscle activity burns valuable energy as well and thus contributes to the acceleration of weight loss. In any case, this phenomenon is a destabilizing factor pushing the anorectic further along the addictive process. Certainly, the anorectic's deliberate shift to intensified pursuit of exercising by sheer willpower will haunt her when she is in the throes of advanced starvation.

Summary

The early weight loss phase is the reward phase par excellence, since the anorectic's behavior is not associated with any harm. While she enjoys the social reward for slimming down, the anorectic-to-be benefits greatly from the endorphin stimulation brought about by self-starvation and exercising. She feels more positive about life, her improved coping power gives her emotional strength, she feels vigorous and energetic. In short, the anorectic-to-be would like to stay in this phase forever, if she could. However, her distress, depression, and anxiety prior to dieting make her vulnerable to becoming addicted to these rewards.

Jaffe and Clouet (1981) make it clear that there is no sharp line separating a casual opiate user from a compulsive user. We know from other forms of addiction that a substance known to be associated with addictions is in itself not biochemically addictive, in the sense that any consumption of it will inevitably lead to addiction. Many people drink and enjoy alcohol, for instance, but the consumption of alcohol in itself does not make everyone an alcoholic. Those people, however, who suffer anxiety and depression will excessively pursue the calming and relaxing effects of alcohol and become addicted. We speak of addiction to alcohol only when the person has lost the ability to choose between drinking and not drinking and ultimately will give up physical health and previous values for the sake of pursuing alcohol.

Similarly, the endorphin effects of starvation per se will not necessarily cause the addiction of anorexia nervosa. The eventual outcome—whether the dieter stabilizes her weight and returns to life as usual or becomes addicted—greatly depends on the emotional and cognitive strength of the person and the degree to which the addictive mechanism has taken hold by the time she decides to return to normal food intake. Unfortunately, the dieter does not know when it is too late to turn around.

PHASE II, ADVANCED WEIGHT LOSS PHASE

The advanced weight loss phase begins when the anorectic has reached her goal weight and decides to stop dieting, only to find that she cannot maintain her weight. To her surprise, she finds herself losing more weight, even though she is trying to increase her daily food intake. What has happened?

Overcoming Tolerance

The anorectic experiences for the first time the power of addiction. She encounters the effect of tolerance, the need for increasing amounts of the addictive substance to maintain the "reward" effect generated at first by smaller amounts. If she had known about tolerance and were to look for its signs, she might have noticed a brief spell of irritability and dysphoria, an unpleasant feeling bordering on anxiety and depression, whenever she ate a little more. However, her brain notices tolerance instantly and, in order to overcome it, gives her the command to lower her weight further. The anorectic, in turn, carries out this command, unaware of its addictive origin and purpose.

In biochemical terms, tolerance occurs when the brain's addictive centers have become used to the effects of a certain level of endorphins and demand more. In a way, these centers have become hungry for endorphins and are never satisfied. Thus, a vicious cycle of ever increasing demand for endorphins is initiated, which the anorectic is compelled to fulfill by progressively losing more weight.

The anorectic's experience is identical to that of the heroin addict. When he experiences tolerance to the brain reward of heroin, he automatically seeks to increase the drug dose or the frequency of use. Without the phenomenon of tolerance there is no addiction. It is the prevention of the unpleasant effects of tolerance, which are similar to but less intense than those experienced later during withdrawal, that is the driving force of the addictive process.

The danger for the anorectic-to-be of becoming trapped by addiction is especially great because of two circumstances that not even the heroin addict has to contend with. One is the "normal" and health-promoting aspect of dieting. The anorectic-to-be is under the impression that she is making herself "a better person," while the heroin addict knows that drugs are dangerous. Second, whereas the heroin addict knows that he is becoming addicted as soon as he needs more heroin to keep experiencing a "high," the anorectic-to-be finds out when it is too late, usually when she has reached her goal weight and tries to resume eating.

As we see in Tascha's story, most anorectics lower their goal weight as they keep dieting and wind up close to the weight at which their menstrual period ceases. As a result, the anorectic finds herself in a situation similar to that of a heroin addict who decides that a habit of three bags a day is safe, only to discover that he has overcome tolerance many times and addiction has set in. Although it is unlikely that a heroin user might think that way, this is exactly the situation of the anorectic. She is likely to have been subject to the tolerance effect throughout the early weight loss phase. However, she has unknowingly overcome tolerance by progressively losing pound by pound. By the time she decides to stop losing weight it is too late. Her body and mind are powerfully controlled by endorphins.

The anorectic's recognition that she is unable to stop losing weight as she has reached her goal is a landmark in the course of this condition; clinicians can elicit this landmark from patients and their parents or friends no matter how far the addictive process has gone. If not confronted or criticized for their "irrational" behavior, most anorectics will admit that there was a point at which they felt thin enough. From this point on one can observe the devastating power of addiction in its effects on physical and mental functioning.

The major physical change around this point is the cessation of the menstrual period, due to the effects of increased endorphin secretion. Anorectics may react to this event with a variety of feelings; however, it is not nearly as critical a feature as some classical, mostly psychoanalytic literature suggests.

Dependence

The mental changes during this phase are striking. The anorectic initially responds to these changes with bewilderment. On the one hand, she feels emotionally strong and copes well as long as she continues to lose weight; on the other, she inexplicably has lost control over whether or not she diets.

Her bewilderment is accentuated by the perplexity of parents, siblings, and friends. She is aware of a major divergence between her own inner experience and the feedback from others. The social reward of slimness has run its course; it is no longer forthcoming. Family and friends who previously had admired the anorectic for her weight loss and appearance begin expressing their disapproval with warnings about further weight loss and often outright criticism for this "stupid behavior."

Most disturbing to the anorectic at this point, however, is that in addition to having lost control of her dieting, she realizes now that her thinking, too, is changing. As her mind comes under the influence of the addiction, a characteristic change in the anorectic's "personality" becomes evident. A split occurs in her subjective experience and attitude: As the addiction increasingly takes control of her thinking and behavior, the healthy part of her mind loses ground. Dependency has set in. The reward centers of the anorectic's brain have succeeded in subjugating the anorectic. Because she has become dependent on the "benefits" of endorphin reward, her actions and thinking are being forced into compliance with the pursuit of one principal aim: securing and maintaining a constant flow of endorphins to the reward centers of her brain.

Parents often describe their daughter's change of attitude at this stage as the worst experience they have had in their lives. It is very moving to hear them recount how they helplessly watched their daughter, unable to reach her or to relate to her on some common ground. As one parent put it: "It was as if a huge wave grabbed her and carried her away, out to the sea."

Nevertheless, no matter how much the addictive process has changed the anorectic's thinking, she is able to differentiate between the new emerging set of values, governed by the addiction, and the former values, no matter how faint, representing health. If not driven into a defensive mode of reasoning, the anorectic is quite willing to identify these two opposing ways of judging her situation: a healthy, objective view that something has gone wrong, and an addictive view, which regards her experience as good and healthy and denies that anything is awry. Feighner et al. (1972) characterize the clinical features of this phase very well when they speak of "denial of illness, failure to recognize nutritional needs, a distorted, implacable attitude towards eating that overrides hunger, admonitions, reassurance and threats."

The mechanism of dependence in anorexia nervosa is identical to the phenomenon of dependence in heroin addiction. Addicts continue to use opiates mostly in order to avoid symptoms of tolerance and withdrawal, and not any more to experience a "high" that has become increasingly elusive because of tolerance. They literally depend on the drug to save them from the severe physical and psychological symptoms of withdrawal. These are so unpleasant and sometimes frightening that their mind adapts to their need for the drug by changing their social values and attitudes. As a result, previously held values are abandoned and replaced by a set of views of oneself and the world that justifies the continued use of the drug and ways of securing a constant supply. Since the nonmedical use of opiates is outlawed in our society, the new value system of the heroin-dependent addict will inevitably include the justification of antisocial and criminal means of maintaining drug supply.

Fortunately, the anorectic does not have to resort to criminal behavior to secure a constant supply of her drug, the endorphins. Her mind has learned that all she has to do is to eat just a little bit less than her body needs. While that involves incredible self-deprivation and leaves her open to severe criticism, the anorectic knows that no one will call her a morally bad person. She is not using a street drug or alcohol to feel better.

However, her dependent mind comes to her rescue. It will help her deal with the criticism and her own confusion by changing in very specific ways. These include the mental defense mechanisms of denial, self-idealization and martyrdom, body-image distortion, and the "funnel effect."

DENIAL

The first feature of dependence is denial. The anorectic simply does not know about the dangers of her situation anymore. Her judgment has become less perceptive and objective. She has been, in the true meaning of the word, "brainwashed" by endorphins: She no longer recognizes how greatly her attitudes toward food have changed. She has acquired new values that are real and convincing to her. Her initial doubt and worry about the loss of control over her ability to keep a healthy weight have given way to denying that she has any reason to worry. Whatever happened is good for her, and she is willing to defend her behavior and attitudes against anyone challenging it. The defense mechanism of denial is not always solid, though, and requires the help of other defenses.

SELF-IDEALIZATION AND MARTYRDOM

When denial breaks down, the anorectic is faced with a dilemma. On the one hand, she cannot help giving in to her anorectic behavior and worrying herself and everybody around her; on the other, she feels and copes much better than before. Her mind does not wish to do without this new sense of emotional strength. Her addicted reward centers come to her aid by cognitively correcting this discrepancy of opposing feelings. Frequently found in other contexts, this phenomenon is called correction of cognitive dissonance, a form of defense to establish mental equilibrium. As is to be expected, this correction occurs by suppressing the mental representation of healthy forces and devising elaborate ideational support for the addiction.

Whatever the content of the ideational constructs in support of the addiction, they amount to making the anorectic feel morally good, if not superior. Typically, the anorectic feels above other human beings who still give in to the need to eat, ''to pig out,'' as she would call it. She feels a sense of lightness as she frees herself of the heavy physical mass that comes with normal body weight. Throwing off this burdening weight brings with it relief from the burdening feelings of ordinary human existence. She perceives herself as superhuman, ethereal and pure, no longer guided by the low, instinctual needs of the flesh. It is quite impressive to observe how the dependent mind creates a new self-idealizing value system that is radically different from existing norms—if not the opposite—undisturbed by the reality of the anorectic's situation. The danger to physical and emotional growth, even the danger of death, is suppressed under the dominance of endorphin reward.

In addition to idealizing herself, the anorectic sometimes develops a sense of martyrdom, a defiant rejection of the standards and values of the people around her, standards by which she is judged and rejected for her way of being. As if there were a higher cause, spiritual or moral, for which she would be willing to suffer and accept the role of an outcast, she quietly gains strength in her belief that she is right and others are wrong. Whatever higher cause the anorectic consciously subscribes to in her newfound identity, it is endorphins of which she has become a captive worshipper. She is serving a new master.

The anorectic's identity as a martyr is reinforced by the feeling of being under siege by the world around her. This leads to a third secret thought in support of the addiction: how much easier life would be if the whole world were anorectic. Certainly, if that were so, the anorectic would not have to deal with her own conflicting feelings, nor would she be exposed to confrontations by others. With this fantasy she simply reverses the reality; she "knows" she has found the secret of mental well-being, others have not. Sometimes she feels so convinced of having found the answer to her problems that she wants to go out to teach others, she wants to make believers out of nonbelievers. If only the odds of persuading others were not stacked so highly against her.

These fantasies impose themselves on the anorectic's mind with the power of a strong subjective reality. Therefore, it is not surprising that she resorts to lying, cheating, or secretly pursuing her anorectic activities despite strict prohibitions. The anorectic might not even realize the devious nature of her acts. Aren't they all in the service of her new master? Sometimes this behavior is wrongly considered evidence of a character flaw or a form of manipulation. Without question, the anorectic's behavior affects her parents, sometimes hurting them deeply, and causes a crisis from which no family member or friend can escape. Nevertheless, the way to recovery is not through counteracting these "manipulations," controlling her behavior, for example, or not caring anymore. Recovery is possible only by accepting these behaviors as signs of dependence and by changing the conditions underlying the anorectic's addiction.

BODY-IMAGE DISTORTION

A third clinical feature of dependence is the development of a distorted perception of body weight and appearance, i.e., body-image. Parents and friends of anorectics, and certainly clinicians, notice without fail this most puzzling phenomenon: The anorectic continues to lose weight and is close to emaciation. She looks gaunt and pale and clearly appears underweight by anyone's standards. Nevertheless, she insists that her body looks normal to her; if anything, she is a little "too fat." She might even insist that she looks good, if not great; she does not even notice how others are taken aback by her frightening appearance. Here again we observe how, under the influence of dependence, the anorectic's mind departs from society's norms. In an idiosyncratic fashion her mind simply adopts new standards of what constitutes a healthy weight and a good-looking body.

Strictly speaking, this phenomenon also falls under the category of correction of cognitive dissonance. The anorectic might not continue her addictive behavior if she were aware of how far she has strayed from society's and her own former standards. Therefore, the addiction causes the anorectic to develop new norms. These are perfectly logical if viewed from the perspective of the addictive reward centers, which seek to maintain the addiction at all cost. As is typical in any addictive process, these norms actually undergo constant changes. A weight, substantially below her current weight, that the anorectic herself might regard as low and unappealing, becomes acceptable the moment she has reached it.

Body-image has been one of the most researched features of anorexia nervosa (Slade and Russell, 1973; Strober, Goldenberg, et al., 1979). Most researchers have focused on this remarkable feature in the hope of identifying a cause of self-starvation. For example, Slade (1985) suggested that body-image distortion may act as negative reinforcer for weight-loss control. As we see here, however, it is not a cause but the result of starvation and the subsequent addictive dependence on starvation. Truly recovered anorectics are equally baffled by their distorted body-image and the subjective power of their distortions while they were emaciated. Some anorectics have compared this experience to "a bad dream."

THE FUNNEL EFFECT

Dependence on endorphins leads to another powerful feature that becomes apparent at this stage and persists until recovery. It is what I call the "funnel effect." I use the metaphor of a funnel to describe the tendency of anorectics to abandon a wide range of pursuits that heretofore constituted life's pleasures. Whatever used to make them feel good—gifts, hobbies, or spending money for clothes, personal items, decoration, or attention and special favors from friends, parents or siblings, or love and sex, whatever it was—becomes progressively less acceptable.

Very much like the attitude towards eating, the change in the attitude towards pleasure is different in depression and anorexia nervosa. In depression these forms of pleasure become objects of disinterest or appear undeserved. The anorectic, in contrast, has a heightened interest in these forms of reward and feels deserving of them but deliberately abstains from them. She spends a good part of her waking life thinking about nice things and how to get them or do them. In fact, she feels hurt when others do not urge her to buy something nice or do not try to do favors for her. Nevertheless, she will not permit herself to indulge in rewards. It is as if denying herself the pleasure of food has spread like cancer to other areas of pleasure in her life.

The progression of this cancer-like spread of self-deprivation follows a certain pattern. After food, the anorectic first gives up the pleasure of being with friends. Seemingly small failures in attention from friends become an excuse to avoid them, ostensibly feeling unworthy of their company but, more importantly, feeling less encumbered in her addictive pursuit without them. Once the anorectic becomes virtually friendless, she starts depriving herself of material things. Although she may long to buy and own things, she finds it increasingly difficult to buy anything that is not absolutely necessary; even the purchase of necessary items causes her to torture herself with guilt feelings.

An example is Heather, who has not bought herself a pair of winter boots for the last three years, even though she has enough money to do so. First, virtually every pair of boots in New York City is scrutinized to find a match for her stringent criteria: The boots must be widely useful boots, but pretty nevertheless, and they must be the best pair of boots for the money, preferably bought during a sale. Heather's mind is torn and tormented by two opposing wishes; deep down she is obsessed with the wish to have new boots, but at the same time she must not loosen her grip on self-deprivation. In order to overcome her fear of indulging herself, the boots must be all-purpose and inexpensive. Any real or imagined objections others, including her parents, may have to the purchase must be overcome. For example, unfriendly salespeople or disparaging remarks of friends cause her great irritation, since they represent the disapproving part of her mind.

If, after much looking and pondering, Heather were finally to buy her boots, her problems would not be over. Rather than enjoying her purchase, Heather would keep checking to make sure that another pair of boots might not have been a better buy. If she were to find a small fault or scratch on the boots, she would be deeply disappointed at the thought of having made a mistake. Perhaps she would return the boots. And yet, through all this Heather deeply desires a beautiful pair of boots, which she denies herself through these rituals.

The term "funnel effect" connotes that the range of pleasures represented by the width of the funnel at the rim is narrowed down to a small opening through which pleasure and reward continue to flow. However, often only one reward continues to flow, that is, the endorphin reward. In fact, the emotional and physical energy that prior to the addiction was consumed by a diversified range of pursuits is now concentrated on this one reward.

Actually, the widening of the range of pleasures as the anorectic overcomes her addiction is an important goal of recovery and an excellent measure of progress.

THE REVERSE FUNNEL EFFECT

In the context of the "funnel effect," we observe a countervailing phenomenon. In a way it is a "reverse funnel effect" that applies to all activities that involve hardship, self-discipline, work, self-denigration, and deprivation—in short, activities that oppose the simple pursuit of pleasure.

These unpleasurable but virtuous pursuits have a place in life, perhaps proportionally a larger one than represented in the narrow opening of a funnel. However, the anorectic cannot get enough of them and pursues them to the point of exhaustion and collapse. The funnel is reversed. The anorectic's pursuit of an ever widening range of these activities, comparable to an ever growing rim diameter of a funnel, points to the incredible imbalance in the anorectic's system regulating pleasure and displeasure.

Here again we observe the mind-corrupting effects of addictive dependence. As if it were not enough to eliminate competing pleasures, endorphin addiction locks itself into the mind of the anorectic by creating a need for endorphins. It does so by forcing her to exhaust herself in overwork and self-deprivation so that the endorphin reward becomes so much more necessary and justified. The degree to which this phenomenon is part of dependence becomes apparent when the anorectic tries—and initially fails—to give up some of these pursuits of displeasure.

Some people might say that this self-punitive stance is evidence of the anorectic's wish to suffer, a form of masochism. I don't agree. It is the powerful reward of endorphins that benefits the anorectic and causes the anorectic mind to engage her in this behavior. I am not convinced that psychoanalytic theory is correct in positing a wish to suffer in the repertoire of the human mind. Behind every behavior or thought that appears masochistic, one must assume—and one is often able to identify—a reward or "benefit" that is the true driving force behind the behavior. The anorectic's pursuit of displeasure can be understood only in the context of this interplay of reward and nonreward.

PHASE III, BURN-OUT OR DEPLETION PHASE

Transition from the Advanced Weight Loss Phase to the Burn-out Phase

There is no clear-cut event that marks the transition from the advanced weight loss phase to the "burn-out phase," which should more appropriately be called the "depletion phase." Essentially, the difference between the advanced weight loss phase and the depletion phase is that tolerance can no longer be overcome. The overcoming of tolerance is conditional on a number of factors, in the absence of which the advanced weight loss phase comes to an end and the burn-out phase begins.

One factor is the progressive lowering of weight. It requires that the anorectic still has enough weight she can afford to lose, and if so, that she is allowed to lose that weight. The heightened awareness of anorexia nervosa in the general public, due to the efforts of support organizations and the media, has brought greater pressure on the anorectic to fight this condition. As a result, anorectics find themselves forced to stabilize their weight much earlier than in the past.

Even if the anorectic is permitted to go on dieting, there is a second factor essential for the overcoming of tolerance. This is the functional capacity of the endorphin system to deliver ever increasing amounts of endorphins. This capacity is not limitless. The endorphin system—or, for that matter, any mechanism in the chain of events mediating endorphin reward—can be depleted. Thus the term ''depletion phase.'' The endorphin system is known to be primarily responsive to short-term or acute stimulation. In contrast, the anorectic employs this system on a long-term, chronic basis, eventually reaching a depletion of endorphins that no further weight loss can overcome.

In this regard the anorectic addiction is different from heroin addiction. In the latter the addictive substance is supplied to the body from the outside. Its supply is challenged in many ways but not by the limitations of the body's manufacturing capacity. Interestingly, however, even the heroin addict arrives at a stage of burn-out, when the heroin-dependent systems no longer respond in their usual ways to the heroin supplied from the outside.

We would assume that until the time depletion occurs the anorectic benefits from an ever rising level of endorphins. This may not be so at all. The anorectic may suffer from a general weakness of the endorphin system before starvation, or there may be a progressive reduction of endorphins as a result of nutritional deficits. If this is so, the stimulation of endorphin secretion by self-starvation may be a form of self-medication against endorphin deficiency. Or, the starving anorectic might stimulate the endorphin system in a desperate attempt to stem the ebbtide of ever lowering endorphin levels. In any case, the efficiency of endorphin stimulation comes to an end in the burn-out or depletion phase, resulting in a drastic change in the anorectic's sense of well-being.

The Clinical Features of the Burn-out Phase

The burn-out phase can last months, sometimes years, during which the anorectic has usually stabilized her weight, but has not yet gained weight. Usually it requires very intensive therapy to help the anorectic start gaining weight again. Unfortunately, many anorectics hold out as long as possible, even in therapy. Some become chronic because no one cares enough to initiate therapy. The burn-out phase presents with characteristic mental and behavioral features that become more apparent the longer this phase lasts.

EXPERIENCING TOLERANCE

First, there is the phenomenon of dysphoria as a result of tolerance to endorphins. The anorectic feels the return of some anxiety and depression, enough to make her nervous and ill at ease. Most pronounced are signs that she does not cope as well as she did in the previous phase. She is highly sensitive to what she perceives as lack of caring and concern by people around her. Events that do not go her way, no matter how minor, are overly stressful. Major events, over which she has no control, sometimes trigger outright anxiety attacks. In short, some of the anorectic's earlier difficulties resurface.

INTENSIFICATION OF DEPENDENCE

Second, despite the onset of tolerance there is no reduction in the signs of dependence. Quite the opposite is true. Because she feels worse, the addicted side of the anorectic's mind makes every effort to lock in a view of herself that is decidedly in favor of self-starvation. Whether she is forced into living with tolerance by the outside, let's say her parents, or by the depletion of her endorphins, all she knows is that her worst enemies, nervousness and depression, are regaining ground. Here we are able to observe the interplay between anxiety/depression and addictive behavior in its typical form. We are getting a glimpse of what withdrawal is like.

Whenever the addiction is threatened in its dominance, we observe a powerful reactive reassertion of the addiction, automatic and unbeknown to the anorectic. As is the nature of the addictive reward centers of the brain, they guard the continuation of the addiction as if their life and the life of the body depended on it. While this metaphor may sound overly dramatic, it is not at all farfetched. These reward centers were designed by nature for the principal purpose of guarding those functions of the organism that are most essential for the survival of the individual and for the species in general, such as food intake and reproduction, among others. By linking these control mechanisms to reward and reinforcement, nature built into the organism a mechanism that makes the continuation of life more likely.

The problem arises only when the reward function of these centers is exploited, either by drugs or by self-manipulation, for purposes not provided for by nature, such as in anorexia nervosa. Then these centers serve another master, lose sight of the interests of the whole organism, and actually become selfish and destructive to life. It is as if a guard dog becomes confused and protects an intruding burglar with the same determination and vengeance as he commonly protects his master.

Therefore, we observe the powerful response of the addicted reward centers to any challenge to their continued stimulation by endorphins. The onset of tolerance is one of these challenges, the first sign of nonreward. As a result, all features of dependence are intensified.

If the anorectic is interfered with by others in her wish to continue dieting, she will fight back and insist on having her way. She may become more secretive, lying and cheating with great ingenuity, and she will not feel above manipulating her opponents in every way possible in her attempt to overcoming tolerance by losing further weight. She will forcefully deny any problem, she will skillfully argue her case that she is better than others and a martyr of her beliefs, she will insist that she looks just fine, and she will deny herself more pleasures.

If others do not interfere with the anorectic's self-starvation, she will experience tolerance when chronicity has depleted her capacity to secrete endorphins. We see the same intensification of the signs of dependence, only she is less verbal in accusing others of interfering with her self-starvation and usually appears more desperate and pained. No matter what she tries, she does not succeed in overcoming tolerance.

Typically, the anorectic may make a last-ditch attempt at this phase to stimulate endorphins by increasing exercising. But her muscles have wasted, and her body has resorted to extracting energy out of muscle tissue in order to keep important cells functioning. She finds that her body simply resists her efforts to control it the way she did when she began to lose weight.

DISAPPEARANCE OF PREOCCUPATION WITH FOOD

The disappearance of the anorectic's preoccupation with food, as well as of the vicarious eating behavior associated with it, is a telltale clinical sign for endorphin depletion. This fading of obsessive thoughts and compulsive behavior related to food is very much welcomed by the anorectic, since this particular endorphin effect has been enemy number one ever since she started dieting. In fact, it was present even before she started dieting in the form of an impulse to overeat, when she felt a need to calm her upset feelings with food.

CENTRAL NERVOUS SYSTEM AROUSAL

The burn-out phase is marked by fourth set of symptoms, caused by a central nervous system more active and excited than usual. This is the result of heightened activity of the stress response system, the so-called "fight or flight" system. It is not clear whether the apparent hyperactivity of this system is due to increased activation by factors specific to this phase or whether this arousal state has been always present and now exerts its influence because of a lack of downward modulation by the now inefficient and depleted endorphin system.

Although the anorectic is troubled by these symptoms, the arousal may not be unwelcome. In the absence of the coping power derived from endorphins, the stimulating and energizing effects of the arousal system may be experienced by her as preferable to gaining weight and feeling depressed. Thus, as the anorectic is deserted by the endorphin system, she is influenced by a second motivational system that, although weaker because of many unwanted effects, still might result in reluctance to resume eating.

Clinically we observe that the anorectic's nervous system is "jumpy" and hypervigilant, very different from the previous phase, during which there was some sense of purpose and calm. The anorectic constantly has to move her body; she cannot sit still without wiggling her legs and feet; she rarely, if ever, sits back in a chair and relaxes. She keeps up this pace even though her weight loss and lack of proper nutrition have so weakened her physically that she is quickly exhausted.

Another sign of central nervous system arousal is the anorectic's sleep pattern. During the previous phase she had been staying up longer, kept awake by her restless mind. To add insult to injury, now she keeps waking up earlier, 3 or 4 a.m. Going back to sleep is impossible. She is wide awake, and she has to get up because her body wants to move. Perhaps she will exercise; at the least she will do some muscle stretching to calm her body. Getting at best three to four hours of sleep is devastating to her daily functioning. Worse yet, her lack of sleep in itself contributes to central nervous system arousal. In other words, another vicious cycle is activated within the vicious cycle of the addictive process of self-starvation. The anorectic is fighting a desperate battle to stem the rising tide of dysfunctions in her body and mind.

The inability to concentrate is another sign of a hyperactive state of brain functions. It is similar to her heightened motor activity, only here the control is lost in the realm of thinking. The brain is no longer able to organize the flow of thoughts so that the anorectic is unable to focus on reading, listening attentively, or doing any one thing at a time. As a result, the anorectic has difficulties keeping her grades up in school, something that has always been a source of pride. All the reading she may have done in the past is reduced to thumbing through a few magazines, mostly just looking at pictures. Her mind cannot follow through on understanding even a single paragraph of a story.

The concentration problems now, in the burn-out-phase, are different from those during earlier phases. Earlier, concentration suffered because of preoccupation with food, the intrusion of food-related obsessive thoughts and behavior; now concentration suffers in the absence of food-related thoughts as a result of a mind in turmoil.

Conclusion of the Burn-out or Depletion Phase

It may come as a surprise to some readers when I maintain that even during burn-out the anorectic is going through a growth process, despite her suffering. Just like other addicts, the anorectic has to hit the proverbial bottom before change is truly possible and has a reasonable chance to last. The anorectic has to experience the power of her addiction, even if she does not know that she is addicted. No reasoning or threatening has anywhere near as much effect on the anorectic's attitude as her painful experience of being consumed by the addiction, only to find out in the end that she has been wrecked by it and has received nothing in return.

The anorectic continues to grow emotionally because the learning process continues. Just as she had "learned" to pursue endorphin reward in earlier phases by starving herself, she "learns" with some disillusionment now that self-starvation is not working for her anymore.

On balance the anorectic still has to overcome considerable motivational forces in favor of dieting. She is still obsessed with the desire to lose weight and panic-stricken at the idea of having to gain. She continues to struggle between the wish to deny the seriousness of her condition and to justify further weight loss, on the one hand, and the realization that she no longer can fight whatever is going on inside her, on the other. As her denial is losing power, a window is opened, albeit small, through which she can see her hopeless situation. At this point, most anorectics will give in to the urging of their parents or friends and agree to seek professional help.

The anorectic has to reach this point of surrender to the futility of her self-starvation even if she has entered therapy at an earlier phase. She has to arrive at some degree of inner conviction that there must be a better way. Just showing up at the therapist's office for appointments after she has been railroaded into therapy does not constitute enough desire for recovery to carry her through the difficult times ahead when she will go through the withdrawal process, to be discussed in Chapter 4.

3

Biochemical Evidence for Endorphin Mediation of Anorexia Nervosa

A NOREXIA NERVOSA RESEARCH over the past several decades essentially has followed two approaches. With very few exceptions psychiatrists and psychologists have made every effort to understand the illness on strictly psychological grounds, without consideration of the possibility that biological abnormalities could contribute to it. Meanwhile, medical researchers (like internists and endocrinologists) have focused exclusively on the physiological abnormalities of anorexia, ignoring its psychological features. The result has been a vast body of findings in both fields; only recently have a few investigators begun to integrate these findings.

THE PATH TO DISCOVERY OF ENDORPHIN MEDIATION OF ANOREXIA NERVOSA

First Steps

My research on anorexia nervosa began in 1977 when I was offered the unique opportunity to work as a psychiatrist in the Pediatric Clinical Research Center of the New York Hospital-

Cornell University Medical Center, at the time under the direction of Dr. Maria New.

One day I was asked to participate in the study of a patient with anorexia nervosa. The understanding was clear: My contribution would be to study her condition from a psychiatric and psychological point of view, while the medical staff would study the biological abnormalities of this condition. I relished the chance to observe an anorectic patient without implementing therapy immediately, and to conduct the study under highly controlled circumstances with the help of an excellent staff.

After observing this patient for many days I formulated an idea quite uncharacteristic of my role as a psychiatrist, very much to my own surprise and that of the medical staff. I felt that the persistent self-starvation of our patient could not be properly explained by the psychological theories then available about anorexia nervosa. Perhaps some of these psychological theories explained the patient's precursor personalities and family situation. But, I suggested, possibly a change in the biochemistry of the starved anorectic, perhaps a hormone, either facilitates or perpetuates the self-starvation behavior that we observed. I proposed that we not only explore what was known at the time about the biological abnormalities but also study the behavioral effects of these abnormal hormones and other biochemical substances, an entirely new but vague concept.

This thinking was unconventional, of course, since the psychiatric profession at the time seemed quite comfortable with the psychological theories of anorexia nervosa. Similarly, my pediatric colleagues shared this generally accepted view of anorexia nervosa as a psychological illness associated with starvation-induced biological abnormalities. Understandably, they were skeptical.

It should be mentioned that at that time psychiatry did concern itself very much with some biological aspects of psychiatric disease. Such study, however, was confined to biochemical substances of the brain, i.e., neurotransmitters, that were abnormal in certain psychiatric disorders, and to research into the use of drugs to treat psychiatric illness. Research on the behavioral effects of hormones had been done only in animals; in fact, this field, still very much in its infancy, was considered somewhat heretical.

Behavioral Effects of Hormones Abnormal in Anorexia Nervosa

Our first task was to review the existing literature on the biochemistry of anorexia nervosa to see which hormones were considered abnormal and how consistent these abnormalities were. We were especially interested in reviewing what was known at the time about the effects of these hormone abnormalities on behavior, specifically human behavior.

Let's take, for example, amenorrhea, one of the first symptoms of anorexia nervosa to appear and one of the last to disappear once weight is regained. Principally, two hormones regulate the monthly menstrual cycle, the follicle-stimulating hormone (FSH) and luteinizing hormone (LH). These hormones are secreted by the pituitary, a brain gland located below the brain stem that carries the brain's signals to the body's organs in the form of hormone secretions. FSH and LH trigger the release of so-called sex hormones in the ovaries. We know that in anorexia nervosa FSH and LH are diminished; they return to normal levels when weight is regained. My question was: Do we have evidence that these hormones directly affect eating behavior or actually permit self-starvation? The answer is not clear, although some evidence does exist as to the eating-inducing effects of sex hormones. For example, women who take contraceptives based on the hormone estrogen have a tendency to eat more.

Actually, the cessation of the menstrual period or the lack of its onset in puberty is a major sign of anorexia, causing many patients to consult a gynecologist first. In the gynecological literature anorexia nervosa is not only sometimes referred to by another name, hypothalamic hypogonadotropic amenorrhea, but often also treated by supplementing the lack of natural hormones with artificial ones. This is an example of the exclusive vantage points from

which various medical disciplines approach the problem of anorexia nervosa. Only a composite picture of the knowledge and
views of different disciplines will allow us truly to understand this
illness.

Another abnormality in anorexia nervosa is the lowering of thyroid hormone. We know that abnormalities in the levels of thyroid
hormones produce behavioral changes. Too much hormone will
produce a hyperactive, hypervigilant, restless state; too little will
result in a lethargic, sometimes depressed state and slowing down
of mental functions. For these reasons, some internists or endocrinologists have given anorectics supplemental thyroid hormone,
hoping that this treatment would increase their desire to reverse
weight loss and make them less depressed. The question has been
raised, though, whether this condition is merely a symptom of
advanced starvation or whether it represents the core of the illness
to be treated by hormone supplementation. The available evidence is suggestive of the former, i.e., that thyroid hormone is
diminished as a result of advanced starvation.

Abnormal cortisol regulation is another generally agreed upon
abnormality. Cortisol and several other related hormones are produced by the adrenal gland in response to adrenocorticotropin
(ACTH) secretion. ACTH is principally a pituitary hormone similar to FSH and LH, although recent evidence shows that it is also
produced by other parts of the body, including the brain itself.

Cortisol has been of major interest in psychiatric research because of two findings. First, cortisol and ACTH have been known
for a long time to be part of a stress and coping system triggered
principally by physical stress. The pioneering work was done by
Hans Selye (1936), although as late as the 1970s it was reexamined
in research on coping behavior of humans and animals.

Second, cortisol, the peripheral hormone, has been found to be
elevated in individuals with certain types of depressive illness.
This discovery resulted in a test that involves measuring cortisol
suppression after administration of the blocking agent dexamethasone. In those with major depression, dexamethasone does not
cause cortisol levels to drop as much as they do in nondepressed
individuals.

During my search I found some interesting studies describing the behavioral effects of ACTH on animals conducted by De Wied (1977) in the Netherlands and S. Levine (1976) in the United States. They found that administration of ACTH to laboratory animals changes their states of vigilance and habituation. (Habituation refers to the phenomenon that the brain responds to new events with special attention, which fades as the stimuli are repeated and appear less interesting or dangerous.) Under the influence of ACTH laboratory animals tend to increase their avoidance of noxious and painful stimuli; they remain more vigilant and do not habituate as quickly. These observations were of some relevance to anorexia nervosa, in that anorectics tend to be hypervigilant and do not easily habituate to new stimuli. But this notion would not explain their avoidance of food specifically.

It was this group of studies, however, that addressed the relationship of ACTH to endorphins and the body's pain mechanisms. Several papers had reported on the anatomical and functional closeness of the ACTH system and endorphins. Thus, since ACTH is elevated in anorexia nervosa, endorphin activity might be increased as well. Once this link was established, it opened the way towards exploring the role of endorphins as a pain-killing mechanism in anorexia nervosa. I naively reasoned that, if endorphins were involved, their pain-killing properties might facilitate and actually permit the anorectic to starve without feeling hunger pangs or perceiving hunger sensations.

How Endorphins Were Discovered

At this point little was known about the physiological effects of endorphins, especially their role in human behavior, if any. Scientists knew a great deal, however, about the effects on the body of related substances—morphine or other opiate-like substances—not just their pain-killing effects but also their unwanted side effects on hormones and other systems.

Pain is one of the worst miseries caused by illness or disease, although it is part of the body's protective systems. Since ancient times we have known that substances derived from poppy plants, called opiates, control pain very effectively. However, opiates have the disadvantage of being highly addictive, without which they would be the perfect answer to the problem of pain. Scientists have made every effort to modify basic opiate substances, hoping to retain their anesthetic properties while making them less addictive. To their dismay, they have found that the less addictive these substances become, the less effective they are as pain-killers.

However, they have found also that a specific chemical structure of opiate compounds is required to achieve pain control. For example, the morphine molecule in the so-called "right turning" structural version is an extremely powerful pain-killer, while the "left turning" molecule, its mirror structure, is anesthetically inactive. Since opiates have to be so specific in their chemical structure to have a pharmacological effect, scientists thought that perhaps opiates attach themselves to receptors on the surface of pain-conducting cells that normally receive a pain-killing substance produced by the body. Thus, if the body produced a substance similar to opiates, it was hoped, this substance could be used to control pain without producing addiction.

The first identification of such pain-killing substances called "endorphins" elated the scientific community. However, it soon was recognized that endorphins are just as addictive as opiates— or more so—since they attach themselves to the same receptors that biochemically mediate dependence and tolerance to morphine (Sharma, Klee, and Nirenberg, 1975). Nevertheless, while their discovery has not produced a natural nonaddictive pain-killer, the importance of endorphins for other systems of the body is momentous, given what we have learned about their role in illness and health of humans.

The Role of Endorphins in Anorexia Nervosa

Two lines of thought were the focus of our explorations into the role of endorphins in anorexia nervosa. If endorphins were involved in self-starvation, their elevation or depletion might be just another abnormality, like lower levels of sex hormones. Or they could play a central role and be responsible for at least some of the physical and/or behavioral changes occurring in anorexia nervosa. With regard to the role of endorphins in bringing about physical changes, a review of the literature produced some surprising and promising results, as shown in Table 1.

The first column lists major hormone systems abnormal in anorexia nervosa, some of which have been discussed above. The author names and publication years listed in the second column under the heading "Anorexia Nervosa" indicate whether these researchers thought the particular hormone was increased or decreased, indicated by plus or minus signs. Ambiguous results showing a trend are indicated by ($+$) or ($-$). The third column, under the heading "Morphine," shows what was known then about the effects of morphine on the same hormone systems. The pattern of plus and minus signs in that column shows that many researchers found that these hormone systems are influenced by morphine in the same direction as in anorexia nervosa. The fourth column, under the heading "Endorphins," lists the scarce evidence at the time of the effects of endorphins on these hormone systems, as shown by experiments with laboratory animals. Since this table was compiled in 1978, in the early days of endorphin research, data on humans were not yet available. Nevertheless, this column shows a trend similar to the patterns seen for morphine and anorexia nervosa. The fifth column offers additional evidence by showing the effects of an endorphin-blocking agent, naloxone, on these same hormones. In all instances naloxone seems to reverse the hormonal effects of morphine or endorphin administration.

In a similar way, data were emerging at the time suggesting that the endorphin system might affect vital functions, such as heart rate, respiratory rate, body temperature, blood pressure, in the same direction as these functions change in anorexia nervosa; that is, they are down regulated.

These findings were quite remarkable and extremely interesting. Did they mean that perhaps endorphins were a sort of master

TABLE 1

Endocrine and Hypothalamic Abnormalities in Anorexia Nervosa Compared to the Effects
of Morphine, Endorphins and Naloxone on These Systems (Research as of 1978)

	ANOREXIA NERVOSA	MORPHINE	ENDORPHINS	NALOXONE
LPH	no data	no data	no data	no data
ACTH	+	George, 1971 + Munson, 1973 (+) Selye, 1936 +	no data	no data
cortisol	Katz et al., 1976 + Brown et al., 1977 + Vigersky & Loriaux, 1977 + Mecklenburg et al., 1974 + Boyar et al., 1974 + Warren & Van de Wiele, 1973 + Danowski, 1972 +	+		
GH	Brown et al., 1977 + Vigersky & Loriaux, 1977 + Mecklenburg et al., 1974 + Danowski, 1972 +	Bruni et al., 1977 rat + Shaar et al., 1977 rat + Cocchi et al., 1977 rat + George & Kokka, 1976 + Martin et al., 1975 rat + Kokka & George, 1974 rat = Tolis et al., 1975 man Goldstein, 1978 review +	Bruni et al., 1977 rat Enk (+) Shaar et al., 1977 rat Enk + Cocchi et al., 1977 rat Enk + Rivier et al., 1977 rat Enk + End + Cusan et al., 1977 Enk. anal + Goldstein, 1978 review +	Bruni et al., 1977 rat — Shaar et al., 1977 rat — Goldstein, 1978 review —

PRL	Brown et al., 1977 (−) Vigersky & Loriaux, 1977 n(+) Mecklenburg et al., 1974 n(+)	Gold et al., 1978 primate + Bruni et al., 1977 rat + Shaar et al., 1977 rat + Cocchi et al., 1977 rat + Rivier et al., 1977 rat + Kokka & George, 1974 rat + Tolis et al., 1975 man + Goldstein, 1978 review +	Bruni et al., 1977, rat Enk + Shaar et al., 1977 rat Enk + Cocchi et al., 1977 rat L-Enk + Rivier et al., 1977 rat Enk End + Cusan et al., 1977 rat Enk. analog + Goldstein, 1978 review +	Gold et al., 1978 primate − Bruni et al., 1977 rat − Shaar et al., 1977 rat − Goldstein, 1978 review −
LH	Katz et al., 1976 − Brown et al., 1977 − Vigersky & Loriaux, 1977 − Mecklenburg et al., 1974 − Boyar et al., 1974 − Warren & Van de Wiele, 1973 − Danowski, 1972 −	Bruni et al., 1977 rat − George, 1971 rat − Mirin et al., 1976 man − Goldstein, 1978 review −	Goldstein, 1978 review −	Mirin et al., 1976 man + Goldstein, 1978 review +
FSH	Vigersky & Loriaux, 1977 − Mecklenburg et al., 1974 − Warren & Van de Wiele, 1973 −	Bruni et al., 1977 rat = Mirin et al., 1976 man − Goldstein, 1978 review −	Goldstein, 1978 review −	Bruni et al., 1977 rat + Mirin et al., 1976 man = Goldstein, 1978 review +

(continued)

TABLE 1 (continued)

	ANOREXIA NERVOSA		MORPHINE		ENDORPHINS		NALOXONE	
TSH	Brown et al., 1977	=	Bruni et al., 1977 rat	−	Bruni et al., 1977 rat Enk	−	Bruni et al., 1977 rat	=
	Vigersky & Loriaux, 1977	−	George & Kokka, 1976 rat	−				
	Croxson & Ibbertson, 1977	−	Bakke et al., 1974 rat	−				
ADH	Vigersky & Loriaux, 1977	−	Philbin et al., 1976 man	−				
	Mecklenburg et al., 1974	−						
Thermo-regulation	Vigersky & Loriaux, 1977	−	Goldstein, 1978 review	−	Guillemin et al., 1977	−	Goldstein & Lowery, 1975	=
	heatstress	++			Goldstein & Lowery, 1975 rat	+		
	coldstress	− −	Lomax, 1974 man	−				
	no shivering	−		−				
	Mecklenburg et al., 1974	−						
	heatstress	++						
	coldstress	− −						
	no shivering	−						

LEGEND: +—increase, −—decrease, n—normal, =—no change, (+) or (−)—ambiguous results showing a trend, LPH—beta-lipotropin, ACTH—adrenocorticotropin, GH—growth hormone, PRL—prolactin, LH—luteinizing hormone, FSH—follicle stimulating hormone, TSH—thyroid stimulating hormone, ADH—antidiuretic hormone

hormone triggered in anorexia nervosa that caused the biochemical abnormalities observed in the state of starvation? As pain-killing substances, endorphins certainly could facilitate self-starvation by reducing hunger pangs and other discomfort usually associated with starvation. The widespread use of the opiate blocker, naloxone, as a research tool for the study of endorphins suggested an experimental design to explore the role of endorphins in the biochemistry of anorexia nervosa.

Thus, I formulated the hypothesis that if endorphins caused the hormone abnormalities listed in Table 1 during the starvation state, the blockade of endorphin activity should reverse these hormone changes. We tested my hypothesis in a simple experimental design in which the blocking agent, naloxone, was administered to anorectics, and hormone levels were measured before, during, and after administration of naloxone.

Hormonal Effects of Naloxone Infusion

Naloxone was administered to seven female adolescents who fulfilled the Research Diagnostic Criteria for anorexia nervosa (Feighner et al., 1972), weighed less than 75% of ideal body weight, and volunteered to participate in this study. Additionally, one obese subject, weighing 136 kg (approx. 299 lbs.), and one bulimic patient, weighing close to ideal body weight, were studied.

The study procedures evolved slowly for precautionary reasons, and the doses were increased from one patient to the next, so that many but not all subjects received the following treatment. Naloxone* was administered in four different dosages (0.2 mg/kg; 0.4 mg/kg; 0.8 mg/kg; 1.2 mg/kg), dissolved in sufficient normal saline solution to be infused by intravenous drip over a four-hour period. Each of these administrations was matched in a

---

*Naloxone was and still is widely used to treat heroin overdose but had not been given to anorectics before. Therefore, this study was approved and supervised by the U.S. Food and Drug Administration under a Notice of Claimed Investigational Exemption for a New Drug.

double-blind arrangement by a four-hour intravenous infusion of a placebo, consisting of the inactive ingredients of naloxone, dissolved in normal saline solution. That way a comparison was possible between the hormone levels measured during active drug administration with those measured during inactive drug administration. Neither patient nor staff knew until after the study whether the active or inactive drug was given.

Blood samples for hormone measurements were taken just before the infusion, and one, two, four, and six hours after the infusion began. The hormones measured were luteinizing hormone, follicle stimulating hormone, ACTH, cortisol, growth hormone, prolactin, and thyroid-stimulating hormone. Thanks to the collaboration of Dr. Charles Inturrisi of the department of pharmacology at the New York Hospital-Cornell University Medical Center, we were able to obtain blood levels of naloxone for each point of hormone measurement. In addition, various behavioral measurements were taken at same intervals.

The results were quite encouraging, although not conclusive, since we were unable to study normal control subjects to serve as comparisons. Certainly, the findings were highly suggestive of an involvement of endorphins in anorexia nervosa.

The LH response to naloxone infusion will serve as example to illustrate the findings of this study in principle. In six patients naloxone infusion at 0.2 mg/kg and 0.4 mg/kg over four hours failed to produce a rise in serum LH levels. There was no significant difference between placebo and naloxone infusions. Even infusions of 0.8 mg/kg and 1.2 mg/kg naloxone in one anorectic patient did not result in increased LH release. Table 2 shows this patient's maximum LH levels in comparison with the LH response of the obese patient. While the anorexia nervosa patient does not show any rise in response to naloxone, the obese patient shows a marked LH elevation. The higher placebo LH value of the second placebo trial measured in the obese patient is due to a normal increase of LH in the second half of the menstrual cycle. Even if one takes into account differences in the absolute dosage of naloxone given these patients because of their weight differences,

TABLE 2

Highest LH Levels (mU/ml) After Naloxone Infusion in Relation to
Maximum Serum Naloxone Levels (ng/ml)

	Plac LH	nal 0.2 mg/kg		Plac LH	nal 0.4 mg/kg		Plac LH	nal 0.8 mg/kg		Plac LH	nal 1.2 mg/kg	
		LH	serum nal		LH	serum nal		LH	serum nal		LH	serum nal
Anorexia Nervosa Subject Weight 35kg	11.5	10.1	34	11.5	10.0	74	13.5	10.0	275	10.4	10.3	875
Obese Subject Weight 136kg	14.7	50.2	93	40.7	105.0	117						

they do not explain the marked difference between the anorexia nervosa patient and the obese patient of the LH response to naloxone.

We compared our results with those of a study of healthy women by Lightman et al. (1981), which showed that the normal suppression of LH secretion by endorphins can be reversed by endorphin receptor blockade with naloxone at dosages comparable to ours.

Our findings suggested that the lack of LH response in our anorexia nervosa group might be due to very high endorphin activity, which was not sufficiently blocked by naloxone given at dosages that produced a blockade in normal subjects. We also realized at the time that other, as yet unknown factors could be responsible for our results. On the other hand, overresponsiveness of LH in the obese patient may be due to decreased endorphin activity that is easily blocked by naloxone.

Behavioral Effects of Naloxone Infusion

The biochemical part of this study gave some support, albeit incomplete, to the hypothesis that endorphin activity is elevated in anorectics with advanced weight loss. However, we observed a totally unexpected behavioral effect of naloxone infusion; initially, this was cause for concern that the subjects may be harmed by the study—until the significance of this behavioral observation became apparent.

The subjects changed markedly in their overall behavior and attitudes after infusion of naloxone but not after placebo infusion: The well-known hypervigilant, irritable, restless, reticent, sometimes manipulative, sometimes distancing behavior changed into a state of quietly sad, soft, but almost peaceful demeanor. The subjects would find themselves tearful and weeping "for no reason," sometimes for hours, seeking closeness with staff members for comfort to share worried feelings and thoughts. There was an apparent defenselessness that the subjects did not seem to dislike, although they expressed bewilderment about such a sudden and unexpected change of their "personality." These changes occurred for about 12 hours after naloxone administration, only to give way to a return of their usual difficult self the next day. Furthermore, these changes were more apparent with increasing naloxone dosage and set in with such regularity that they gave away the "cover" of the double-blind design of the study protocol.

We observed also that the usual avoidance of food and fear of getting fat appeared to give way, to some degree, to a more accepting attitude. However, the drug administration was not sufficiently long to see a clear-cut effect.

Significance of Observations Made in the Naloxone Study

The observations made in the pilot study encouraged us to continue the search for a role of endorphins in anorexia nervosa.

First, our results produced suggestive evidence that endorphins may be elevated during the starvation state. Thus, we have some support for the notion that endorphins may facilitate the self-starvation process in anorexia nervosa by reducing the sensations and discomfort of hunger, a process consistent with the pain-killing function of endorphins.

Secondly, elevated endorphin activity seems to be the master mechanism of hormonal changes, as well as of changes of basic vital functions, such as body temperature, heart rate, respiratory rate, in anorexia nervosa. If this is so, endorphins may mediate the body's adaptation to starvation, such as suppression of reproductive capability and switching the body to a state of lower energy consumption. This function of endorphins may not be unique to anorexia nervosa but part of a universal survival principle of nature.

Third and most importantly, the behavioral observations of the naloxone study point towards an answer to the question of how anorectics benefit from this endorphin mechanism.

Anorectics somehow give the impression that they are tense,

nervous, and dysphoric, as if they were depressed, except that they don't seem to act depressed. Therefore, when one uses the usual psychiatric criteria for depression, anorexia nervosa does not seem related to depression. However, Warren (1968) and Cantwell, Sturzenberger, et al. (1977) identified a high percentage of affective disorders in anorectic patients after recovery and in their families, as did Eckert, Goldberg, et al. (1982) and Hendren (1983), using larger samples. However, none of these studies has answered the question: How is anorexia nervosa linked to depression? We see now that anorectics stimulate the endorphin mechanism by self-starvation and feel less depressed and vulnerable than prior to losing weight. For this reason anorectics do not feel or appear as depressed as they otherwise would; unknowingly, they have found an antidote for depression. The marked shift of the patients' behavior to sad defenselessness when endorphins were blocked by naloxone gives us a glimpse of the benefit anorectics derive from self-starvation. The quick behavioral response to naloxone at a dosage that did not produce a hormonal response is indicative of the sensitivity of this mechanism.

Our results to this point produced supporting evidence for a fairly complete and entirely new concept in the understanding of anorexia nervosa. This concept, in a nutshell, would read as follows:

> Among depressed and distressed people, those who greatly value slimness decide to reduce their weight to make themselves feel better. While starving they unknowingly trigger a universal survival mechanism mediated by endorphins. As a result they undergo adaptive changes of body and mind. The mental effect of this adaptive mechanism is improved coping and a lessening of depression and distress.

What this concept could not account for is the compelling power of the self-starvation process, the motivational forces underlying this relentless pursuit of thinness, the obsessional nature of the anorectic's body-image, and the enormous difficulties in reversing this process.

Could these features be explained by the fact that endorphins are addictive? As we have seen earlier, endorphins are highly addictive, indeed. In reviewing the literature on addictions, especially heroin addiction, we realized that every behavioral phenomenon of each phase of anorexia nervosa has an analogue among the clinical features of heroin addiction (Jaffe et al., 1981). We had listened to anorectics describe their experiences, but we had not heard that they were describing a life of addiction. It is a life so well captured by one of the patients of Hilde Bruch (1978), the pioneer of anorexia nervosa research, when she said: "It is as if you were slowly poisoned, something like being under the chronic influence of something like alcohol or dope." This patient described the life of endorphin addiction without knowing that the "alcohol or dope" was actually endorphins secreted by her body as a result of starving. Because these words capture the essence of anorexia nervosa so well, they serve as the motto for this book. Thus, the compelling power of self-starvation results from the addictive nature of endorphins. We can add another sentence to the concept summarized in a previous paragraph:

Because of the addictive properties of endorphins, anorectics unconsciously learn and are forced to lower their weight successively in order to maintain the anti-depressant and anti-distress effects of endorphins.

REVIEW OF RECENT EVIDENCE FOR ENDORPHIN
INVOLVEMENT IN ANOREXIA NERVOSA

The exploratory studies that led me to formulate the endorphin theory of anorexia nervosa were concluded about a decade ago. At the time, our results clearly pointed the way towards a large-scale inquiry into the biochemistry of endorphins in self-imposed starvation. Unfortunately, I was not able to continue the laboratory research for lack of federal grant support, although I continued to explore the clinical ramifications of this theory as I treated many patients with eating disorders.

However, other investigators had begun similar studies as well, and I was confident that soon the exact nature of endorphin involvement in these conditions would be clarified. Looking back now, I must conclude that my confidence was not justified; to this day, despite the accumulation of a substantial body of research, we have failed to identify the exact role played by endorphins in anorexia nervosa.

As the reader will see in the next two chapters, devoted to the treatment of anorexia nervosa, there is no real need to know the exact biochemical nature of the substance to which anorectics have become addicted. Treatment is based on reversing the self-starvation behavior that has brought about the addiction. It is a natural method of treatment in which the use of naloxone—or of any other drug—to counteract the endorphin effect is neither necessary nor desirable.

Nevertheless, some light has been shed on the role of endorphins in anorexia nervosa. Although not essential for the understanding of later chapters, the experimental evidence to date is reviewed here for the interested reader. Using different vantage points, these studies have clarified many issues and, on balance, have produced a body of evidence in support of the notion that endorphins are involved in the mediation of anorexia nervosa.

As we set out to review this research, let us briefly outline the chemical structure of endorphins, since it is relevant to the studies to be discussed. Endorphins share the peptide structure of chemical building blocks, and are cleaved out of long chains of peptide molecules, the so-called precursor molecules. For example, the important precursor molecule pro-opiomelanocortin (POMC) is cleaved into the N-terminal fragment (N-POMC), adrenocorticotropic hormone (ACTH), and beta-lipotropin, the C-terminal fragment. Beta-lipotropin in turn is divided into beta-melanocytestimulating hormone (beta-MSH) and beta-endorphin, which latter is the basic molecule from which alpha-endorphin and gamma-endorphin, as well as enkephalin, are cleaved (Figure 1).

As the review by Hedner and Cassuto (1987) shows, the family of endorphins includes many more substances with opiate-like activity, such as dynorphin, which have different molecular structures and attach to different receptors on the surface of cells. Endorphins can function as hormones, carrying messages over long distances within the body and affecting other hormones down the line of command. Or they can function as neurotransmitters, carrying signals from one cell to the next and interacting with numerous other neurotransmitters. Furthermore, they are found in different compartments of the body, in blood plasma and cerebrospinal fluid (CSF), in the cells of the bowels, the brain, glands, and in certain blood cells, just to name a few.

In view of this complexity of the endorphin system, it is not surprising that the answers as to its role in eating disorders is not forthcoming as quickly as one would wish. Our discussion will deal with only a minute aspect of this system in very general terms and will be confined mostly to human studies.

Direct Measurements

In exploring the role of the opioid system in anorexia nervosa, investigators have taken a variety of approaches. For example, some researchers have measured total endorphin activity, or levels of specific substances belonging to the endorphin family, in various compartments of the body during emaciation and upon recovery, and compared the results with normal subjects who served as controls.

Of special interest is Kaye, Pickar, et al.'s (1982) study, the first to assay endorphin activity in anorexia nervosa. The investigators found higher total opioid activity in the cerebrospinal fluid of anorectics who were severely underweight than in the same patients after weight restoration and in normal controls. Thus, the self-starvation state seems to raise endorphin levels. Furthermore,

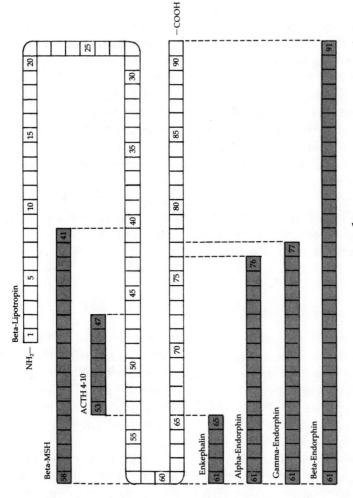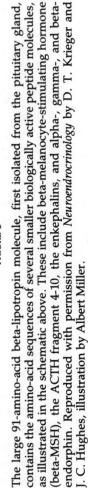

FIGURE 1

The large 91-amino-acid beta-lipotropin molecule, first isolated from the pituitary gland, contains the amino-acid sequences of several smaller biologically active peptide molecules, as illustrated in the schematic above. These include beta-melanocyte-stimulating hormone (beta-MSH), the ACTH fragment 4-10, the enkephalins, and alpha-, gamma-, and beta-endorphin. Reproduced with permission from *Neuroendocrinology* by D. T. Krieger and J. C. Hughes, illustration by Albert Miller.

opioid activity in these anorectics after weight restoration was still lower than in non-anorectic control subjects. While this finding could be the result of the preceding state of emaciation, it also might be due to some kind of pre-anorectic endorphin deficiency, the cause of the anorectic's vulnerability to becoming addicted to self-starvation.

Similarly, Brambilla et al. (1985), a group of Italian researchers, measured elevated beta-endorphin levels in the plasma of 7 out of 14 anorectics. After treatment with the anti-depressant drug desimipramine, beta-endorphins levels returned to normal.

Melchior, Rigaud, et al. (1990) also found a highly significant elevation of basal plasma beta-endorphin levels in patients with anorexia nervosa compared to normal controls. Since these results contradicted their theory about appetitive behavior of anorectics, the authors concluded that the opiate system ''activity'' must be decreased, although they had actually measured elevated beta-endorphin levels.

However, Gerner and Sharp (1982) found no difference in the levels of beta-endorphin in the cerebrospinal fluid of anorectics, patients with other psychiatric disorders, and normal controls. Gerner's anorectic subjects included 7 out of 25 patients who had gained to greater than 80% of ideal body weight at the time of the study, thus were in a state of refeeding.

Finally, Kaye, Berrettini, Gwirtsman, et al. (1987) measured all peptides in the cerebrospinal fluid directly derived from the pro-opiomelanocortin (POMC) molecule, with the exception of beta-MSH but including beta-endorphin. They found that all peptides were significantly reduced in underweight anorectic women, increased soon after weight recovery, but not as much as the values obtained for long-term weight-restored anorectic patients and normal controls. Kaye infers that the precursor molecule, POMC, must be reduced as well, suggesting that it may be indicative of an abnormality in the POMC system.

In discussing the discrepancy between these results and those they had obtained earlier, Kaye et al. (1987) point out that beta-endorphin represents only a very small fraction of a large number of peptides with opioid activity in the brain that perhaps were captured in the earlier study.

While these results mostly suggest an elevation of endorphin levels in anorexia nervosa, they are ambiguous. The problem with these studies and most studies to date is their continued use of weight loss relative to ideal body weight as the principal dimension of severity of anorexia nervosa. The investigators seem to assume a tonic, steady-state influence of weight on the endorphin system.

The pitfalls of this approach are evident from a study by Pahl, Pirke, et al. (1985), who have shown that only half of the patients admitted to the hospital showed metabolic and endocrine signs of starvation, despite low body weight. The truly starving half of the study sample differed from the nonstarving group by presenting with elevated levels of beta-hydroxybutyric acid (BHBA) and a lower level of triiodothyronine (T3). BHBA is a metabolic indicator of lipolysis, the dissolving of fat from fat cells, and serves as a reliable measure of starvation. The investigators also found that only four weeks after admission to the hospital the metabolic signs of starvation disappeared in the starving group as well.

Therefore, the value of the information obtained in studies controlling for weight only is likely to be limited. Lipolysis seems essential for the stimulation of the endorphin system and occurs to a larger degree during the phases of acute weight loss early in the course of anorexia nervosa.

Effects of Naloxone and Naltrexone on Weight Loss

The study of the effects of endorphin receptor blockade with intravenous naloxone or naltrexone on the weight of anorectics is a more global approach. It is based on the assumption that whatever effect is measured after administration of the blocking agent is due to an interference with the action of endorphins.

Moore, Mills, and Forster (1981) administered naloxone to anorectics in continuous intravenous infusions for an average of about five weeks. Actually, these investigators did not set out to study the endorphin system but to take advantage of the anti-lipolytic action of naloxone. A significant weight gain and a reduction of activity were observed during naloxone infusion in comparison to before and after the experiment. Although the results are somewhat inconclusive because of simultaneous treatment with the anti-depressant amitriptyline, Moore et al.'s findings are suggestive of increased endorphin activity as evidenced by the significant weight gain during opiate receptor blockade.

Similarly, Marrazzi and Luby (1989) assessed the effects on weight gain of up to four weeks of opiate receptor blockade with naltrexone, a blocking agent like naloxone, but administered orally. The investigators observed a steady and significant weight gain in most anorectics during naltrexone administration. However, the significance of these results is diminished because of frequent changes of the study protocol between subjects, as is the nature of exploratory studies, and the simultaneous administration to some patients of total parenteral nutrition. Unfortunately, the investigators did not address the issue of depression and anxiety as precursors of anorexia nervosa and, therefore, did not provide psychological data on the influence of naltrexone on these symptoms.

Based on these studies, Marrazzi and Luby (1986) proposed an auto-addiction opioid model of anorexia nervosa. Their review of studies on the role of endorphins in anorexia nervosa is the most extensive discussion of this subject published so far and is highly recommended to the interested reader.

The Role of Endorphins in Hormone Systems Abnormal in Anorexia Nervosa

The study of the effects of endorphin receptor blockade on hormone systems abnormal in anorexia nervosa is another, albeit indirect, approach. The reader may recall that my initial exploratory study followed this design. We found that in anorectics the hormone systems measured were relatively resistant to modulation by naloxone, while they were highly responsive in one obese subject. These results were suggestive of elevated endorphin activity but lacked comparison with normal control subjects. Since then the results of studies of similar design make it clear that the exact role of endogenous opioids in the regulation of these hormone systems remains elusive.

Of special interest is the hypothalamic gonadotropic axis, which regulates the menstrual period, the absence of which is the most conspicuous symptom of anorexia nervosa.

Quigley, Sheehan, et al. (1980) were among the first to document a role of endorphins in the amenorrhea of anorectics by demonstrating an increase of luteinizing hormone (LH) after naloxone infusion, 1.6 mg/h for 4 hours. Baranowska, Rozbicka, et al. (1984) essentially replicated Quigley et al.'s results regarding LH with a single dose of naloxone of 0.2 mg/kg, amounting to 7 mg naloxone for a 35 kg patient. Interestingly, both groups found a response of LH increase in only approximately one-half of the patient population. The LH responders in Quigley's population averaged 78% of ideal body weight (IBW), whereas the nonresponders weighed 99% of IBW. The differentiating parameter in Baranowska et al.'s population for LH response was not weight (all averaged about 60% of ideal body weight) but a history of amenorrhea before weight loss—which was not further explained—whereas the nonresponders lost their period during weight loss.

Nevertheless, these and many other studies of the hypothalamic gonadotropic axis, such as Lightman, Jacobs et al. (1981), provide suggestive evidence that elevated endorphin activity in anorexia nervosa has an LH-suppressing effect that is partially reversible by naloxone administration.

The hypothalamic pituitary adrenal axis (HPAA) is another endocrine system that has been the focus of extensive studies ever since plasma cortisol was found to be increased early in anorexia nervosa research. Recently, studies of this axis were intensified to gain insight into the role of endorphins, in view of the fact that POMC is the common precorsor hormone of ACTH as well as opioid peptides. However, these studies seem to produce more conflicting results as they become more refined in design and technology.

Consistent with an elevation of plasma cortisol in anorexia nervosa, increased activity of all hormones higher up in this axis of cortisol regulation has been documented as well—with the exception of ACTH. For example, Kaye, Gwirtsman, et al. (1987) measured elevated cerebrospinal fluid levels of corticotropin-releasing hormone (CRH), the highest level of the HPAA. This CRH elevation normalized with weight gain, except in some more seriously depressed patients. However, Gwirtsman, Kaye, et al. (1989) documented low cerebrospinal fluid ACTH and normal plasma ACTH levels in the presence of elevated cortisol levels in spinal fluid and plasma of underweight anorectics and a return to normal following weight recovery. Thus, while the releasing hormone at the highest level of the HPAA is increased, the second tier hormone, ACTH, is decreased, which, nevertheless, is associated with an increase of the third level peripheral hormone, cortisol. This constellation is perfectly inconsistent with conventional concepts of the regulation of endocrine systems.

The situation becomes even more contradictory if we add the results of studies related to the endorphin system. Conceptually, this is of interest in view of shared molecular origin and central regulation, as well as perhaps a mutually modulating function of the endorphin and ACTH related systems. As mentioned earlier, Kaye, Berrettini, Gwirtsman, et al. (1987) found decreased CSF concentrations of beta-endorphin and other opioid peptides derived from pro-opiomelanocortin (POMC) in anorectics compared to healthy controls. To explain these contradictory findings, the authors speculate about a dissociation of central and peripheral ACTH and opioid related systems.

However, no discussion here of the greatly conflicting findings in these studies can do justice to the intense efforts to investigate these endocrine parameters and the debate evolving from it. The interested reader might wish to read the discussions of the Kaye, Berrettini, Gwirtsman, et al. (1987) and the Gwirtsman, Kaye, et al. (1989) study results. One gets a flavor of the painstaking attempts of these investigators to reconcile their contradictory laboratory findings and to relate them in a meaningful way to the clinical features of anorexia nervosa. It simply may be too early to establish corroborative evidence on a molecular biological level for the clinical role of endorphins in the addictive process of anorexia nervosa.

The Role of Endorphins in Food Intake and Weight Regulation

Early endorphin researchers focused on the elucidation of a physiological role of endorphins in the regulation of food/water intake and weight regulation. Margules, Moisset, et al. (1978) were among the first to note that elevated endorphin levels are associated with overeating in strains of genetically obese mice and rats. Meanwhile, Holtzman (1979) observed that endorphin receptor blockade by naloxone produced a dose-related suppression of food and water intake in rats. The same results were obtained in obese humans who responded to naloxone with a decrease in food intake (Atkinson, 1982). These findings and similar observations by others, made in a variety of experimental designs, suggest that endorphins have a role in the regulation of food/water consumption and weight. Specifically, endorphins seem to stimulate appetitive behavior, and blockade of endorphin receptors by naloxone decreases food and water intake.

Thus, there is a growing body of evidence of the stimulatory effects of endorphins on eating behavior that seems incompatible with the notion that endorphin stimulation is the result of weight loss, as in anorexia nervosa, for example. However, this may not be as much of a contradiction as it seems. Endorphins may very well stimulate food and water intake and, at the same time, their activity may be increased by starvation.

First, let us take a look at the role of endorphins in hibernation, a special situation of food/water intake in animals. Hibernation is a seasonal adaptation of some animals that is characterized by two extreme states affecting food and water intake: overeating to build up fat storage in preparation for winter, and a shutdown of food and water intake during the state of hibernation. The role of endorphins in hibernating animals seems an especially suitable model, since hibernation is in many ways analogous to the extremes of human eating behavior, feast and famine.

Margules, Goldman, and Finck (1979) studied the effects of naloxone on the lowered heart and respiratory rate, body temperature, and arousal level of hibernating Turkish hamsters. The researchers observed an increase in these parameters after naloxone injection during hibernation, an effect that was not observed in nonhibernating hamsters whose body temperature had been lowered artificially. Since endorphins are known to contribute to the down regulation of these vital functions of the body, these observations suggest that endorphins induce the adaptive physiological changes of hibernation.

How can we reconcile these observations with the evidence mentioned above that endorphins also stimulate food intake in animals and humans? One possibility is that endorphins have a biphasic effect on the regulation of food intake and weight. Many hormones are known to have biphasic effects on body functions, meaning that lower hormone activity sometimes produces effects opposite to those of higher levels.

As the days become shorter and winter approaches, the hamster's brain, by stimulating endorphin secretion, gives the signal to increase feeding and to hoard food. At some point the fat storage has been built up and the feeding behavior stops, as the hamster falls into the torporous state of hibernation, mediated by still higher levels of endorphins. The shift to the hibernation state is apparently not triggered by starvation due to lack of food, since the torporous state is interrupted by spontaneous arousals during which the animal feeds from hoarded food supplies and eliminates wastes. Margules et al. postulate that these spontaneous bouts of arousal are mediated by a naloxone-like regulatory mechanism that counteracts the endorphin mechanism of hibernation torpor.

Animal hibernation can serve as a model of human eating disorders in several ways. Characteristic of the overeating in obesity and bingeing/hoarding in bulimia is a voracious attitude towards food, as if all supermarket shelves might be wiped clean of food tomorrow. Even anorectics have a strong tendency to eat in excess of their caloric requirements before they decide to diet. During self-starvation this drive to eat does not disappear until the burn-out/depletion phase. On the other hand, many adaptive changes of vital functions during hibernation are similarly found in anorectics during severe weight loss, such as lowered heart rate, respiratory rate, and body temperature, among others.

But at this point the similarities end because of a major distinction between humans and animals. This distinction relates to the immediacy with which biochemically mediated behaviors are implemented. We call animal behavior instinctual since it is rigidly executed, as if preprogrammed and mediated by a complex array of neurotransmitters or hormones. In contrast, we tend to believe that humans have a wide variety of options in their thoughts and actions, even though much human behavior is likewise mediated by these substances.

It is debatable, however, how much of a range of options over hormone mediated behavior humans have. For example, overeating and bingeing associated with stress-induced endorphin stimulation seem as irresistible for many humans as the signal to feed in preparation for hibernation for the hamster. But the difference between the hamster and the anorectic-to-be is obvious; she resists the endorphin-mediated command to eat more. Every dieter takes advantage of this uniquely human capacity to resist this command to eat, although there are limits of the extent to which humans can permanently oppose these commands.

What happens, then, when a biologically mediated mechanism like the command to eat is resisted, and not only that, but the person decides to eat even less than the usual amount of food? Like many biological feedback mechanisms, endorphins, the substance mediating food intake, will rise even further to force a correction. As a result of increased endorphin activity, the anorectic experiences an even stronger command to eat, as evident from her preoccupation with food and vicarious eating behavior. If the anorectic continues to resist this command, preoccupation with food becomes part of the endorphin-mediated survival mechanism for starvation, which produces physical adaptive changes similar to those found in the hibernating hamster. Of the many features of this survival mechanism the anorectic seeks only one effect, the psychological reward of improved coping and reduced anxiety/depression. It is as if the anorectic wished to partake in some of the blissful, worry-free torporous state of mind of the hibernating hamster. It may seem ironic, but the anorectic, by refusing to eat, triggers a similar adaptive mechanism as the Turkish hamster, who gives in to the endorphin driven command of preparing for the altered state of hibernation.

Although the studies discussed provide evidence for a role of endorphins in the regulation of food intake and weight, Levine and Billington (1989) warn in their review that endorphins may not be very important physiological regulators, nor is endorphin receptor blockade with naloxone or naltrexone an effective means of long-term weight management. It is quite possible, though, that endorphins play a greater role than can now be confirmed in abnormal physiological states and constitute an acute, reactive phenomenon related to the immediate metabolic stress of starvation. Recently, much more potent stimulants of feeding not belonging to the family of endorphins have been discovered, which are the structurally related peptides, neuropeptide Y and peptide YY. They may play a role in anorexia nervosa as well. For example, Kaye, Berrettini, et al. (1990) found elevated levels of neuropeptide Y in the cerebrospinal fluid of underweight anorectics, which normalized after long-term weight restoration.

4

Treatment of the Anorectic State: Withdrawal and Craving

THE IDENTIFICATION OF the process of endorphin addiction as the underlying mechanism of self-starvation in anorexia nervosa offers an entirely new perspective on the treatment of this condition. It gives insight into the most bewildering and enigmatic aspect of anorexia nervosa, which is the self-starvation process itself.

As we have seen in Chapter 2, self-starvation is a form of self-medication against unbearable anxiety and depression. The endorphins triggered by progressive starvation mitigate, if not temporarily relieve, those aversive feelings. Therefore, to recover the anorectic inevitably will have to go through a period of time during which she will feel more depression and anxiety as she gives up the beneficial effects of endorphins by gaining weight. For these reasons the anorectic and everybody around her have to know that they are in for a rough time.

In addition, the going will be rough because the underlying anxiety and depression do not come out of nowhere. As pointed out earlier, the distress usually has its roots in the interaction of family members within the family system. Family issues will have to be addressed right from the beginning of therapy if the anorectic is to see some way out of her untenable situation and give up her addiction. As we will see later, however, any form of disturbing the established balance of the family is upsetting for every member involved and contributes to the rough going of the early treatment phase.

In the treatment of anorexia nervosa it is important to keep the addiction separate from the underlying conditions of depression and anxiety, to differentiate between the anorectic *state* and *trait*. The acute process of successive steps of weight loss, together with the physical, behavioral, and mental changes, is called the anorectic state. In contrast, the background against which the addiction took place—the constitutional sensitivities of the anorectic, her personality development, and the psychodynamics of her family—are referred to as trait. This distinction between state and trait has been found to be very useful in psychiatric research and clinical work. Only by making such a distinction can one clarify which part of a patient's behavior and thinking is the result of mental mechanisms during the acute disease process, and which part is the result of long-term patterns of personality development, inborn vulnerabilities, and chronic symptoms of dysfunction.

It is especially important for the treatment of addictive conditions to differentiate a person's experience during the state of addiction from the antecedent trait of vulnerability. Knowledge about the endorphin addiction mechanism underlying the anorectic state adds greatly to the understanding of the self-starvation process and points the way to a consistent, logical therapeutic approach. It does not add to the understanding of the anorectic trait. But, as most readers are aware, there is an extensive body of knowledge about the family dynamics and personality traits of anorectics, which has found its way into a variety of treatment modalities.

The treatment of anorexia nervosa entails three major tasks, all of which are equally important. They constitute the therapeutic triad, a treatment approach that requires three legs to stand on, just as a three-legged stool cannot stand without all three legs in place. The first task is a cognitive one, the understanding of the addictive process as it manifests itself in the self-starvation state of the anorectic. The second is the reversal of the addictive state by gaining weight, a behavioral approach to guide the patient through withdrawal to recovery. These two tasks deal with the overcoming of the anorectic state and are discussed in this chapter.

The third task entails the treatment of the anorectic trait, to be discussed in the next chapter. The focus is here on psychotherapeutic work with the patient and her family to alleviate the underlying causes of the anorectic's vulnerability. While the emphasis on one or the other feature of this triad may vary at any given time, progress is possible only if all three aspects of the treatment move together, in synchrony.

THE NEED TO ACTIVELY INTERVENE IN
THE PROCESS OF SELF-STARVATION

Before discussing the actual steps of treatment, let us review the anorectic's position when she enters treatment to show why intervention is necessary to reverse the anorectic state.

As we have seen, the endorphin addiction takes hold of the anorectic and changes both her physical and mental functioning. We have also noted that the addictive nature of this process, leading to dependence, precludes a reversal to health without assistance. Unless it is reversed, the endorphin addiction of anorexia nervosa can be fatal.

Therefore, no one—neither the anorectic nor her family and friends—should expect her to start gaining weight some day on her own. Someone thinking more clearly than the anorectic has to step in and insist that she confront her situation and end her denial with the help of therapy. This does not mean, however, that the anorectic should be force-fed. The anorectic has a right to learn about the full extent of the addictive process, even if that learning process causes her to lose more weight.

To conceptualize what the anorectic is up against, we can say that she is under the control of a very selfish center, or centers, of the brain. This brain center, as yet not exactly localized, takes control of the endorphin addict's thoughts and actions. It is selfish in that it demands increasing levels of endorphins at the expense of the victim's other pursuits and gratifications and eventually health; if unchecked, this center will kill her.

It may appear puzzling that a function of the body that appears designed by nature to increase the chance for survival and to reduce the suffering under famine conditions will actually kill the anorectic, if it goes unchecked. The answer to this puzzle is quite clear, albeit a teleological one. This universal mechanism must not be self-limiting in order to protect the famine-starved individual from the agony of death if food remains unavailable. Although this teleological approach to science, which aims to understand natural functions in terms of their usefulness to the organism, is questionable, it makes some sense in this context.

We can observe this principle at work in natural states of starvation. It is evident in famine-stricken countries where citizens do not stand up and kill each other but rather starve to death passively. We can also observe it in the behavior of political prisoners on hunger strikes. When permitted by authorities to continue starving, these people slip into coma and die. The most recent and widely publicized examples are those of IRA prisoners, notably Bobby Sands.

PART ONE OF THE THERAPEUTIC TRIAD:
LEARNING ABOUT THE ADDICTIVE PROCESS

Learning about the addictive process is the first element of the therapeutic triad. It is necessary because the anorectic does not understand how the addiction has taken control of her. All she knows is that she has not taken street drugs. She went on a diet to ''better'' herself because she was unhappy with herself. She also knows that, when she reached a weight somewhere around her ideal weight and felt satisfied with the result, she was unable to stop dieting. Then her family and friends said that she was thinking and acting differently and demanded explanations for her behavior. Not only is she confused and bewildered by her mental changes, but she is also forced to justify her altered state of mind and body.

If at this point the patient learns of the addictive mechanism as the cause for her mental and physical changes, she feels a great deal of relief. Not only does it explain every facet of her experience, but it also enables her parents or friends to understand the compelling nature of this destructive condition.

The relief, however, is short-lived, since this new information immediately creates a conflict. On the one hand, she welcomes being offered an understanding of the forces at work inside her; on the other, she feels the resistance of the part of her mind that is dependent on the addiction. She seems divided in two: One part of her personality appreciates the new insight offered and hopes to return to normal life; the other part is intent on pursuing the addiction.

This constellation represents the essential struggle that pervades therapy from the first consultation to a point long past termination of treatment. Knowing about this conflict helps the patient to understand what has happened during weight loss and to anticipate her experiences on her way to recovery. The patient has to understand that this conflict and any behavioral expressions of it are not bad. If the patient acts on her dependence, for example, and defends her low weight as normal, or loses further weight, she is neither a bad patient nor a morally bad person. Only if she is encouraged to express both sides of her thinking—the addicted side and the healthy side—can she learn about the addictive process and how to fight it.

Against the background of this ambivalence the task of learning about the addictive process of self-starvation is two-dimensional. The first dimension is a retrospective, historical one. The anorectic needs to learn about her own individual experience of succumbing to the addictive process, beginning with the day she decided to go on a diet. In fact, the patient needs to trace her history back further and explore her specific distressing life circumstances that made her vulnerable to addiction. Similarly, the evolution of her idealization of slimness and its roots within the context of her family and social environment have to be explored as well.

The therapist needs to elicit carefully every aspect of the patient's intrapsychic and behavioral experiences in the course of the self-starvation process. Of special cognitive value are the land-marks that distinguish the three clinical phases of anorexia nervosa as they were outlined in Chapter 2. Particular emphasis must be placed on the elucidation of signs of dependence, especially those that are in the realm of the patient's ideational life, such as self-idealization, body-image distortion, and martyrdom. These signs are not as easily identified as those of behavioral nature, such as the funnel effect and the reverse funnel effect. The anorectic deserves to understand the evolution of these experiences as the expression of one unifying principle operative in her, the principle of endorphin addiction. In short, the patient will learn to put the many puzzling pieces of her past together the way Tascha eventually was able to understand her own story.

The second dimension of learning takes place in the here and now of daily life with anorexia nervosa. Mostly observational in nature, this task serves to establish a baseline of anorectic behavior. However, it also deals with taking stock of daily actions, thoughts and feelings as they change in response to food intake, no matter how small. Essentially, the patient learns about the interaction of eating state and feeling state, at this point without any attempt to increase food intake. Nor is she expected to change any other patterns of her daily life. However reluctantly, the patient will realize how distressing situations or verbal exchanges with people around her cause her to eat still less. On the other hand, if things go well and tension in the family gives way to light moment, she might notice a slight easing of her fear of eating. Thus, the anorectic learns about the reinforcing effects of starvation when she needs to cope the most. Once she has accepted that endorphins mediate this mechanism she has laid the ground work for overcoming her sense of being a victim of anorexia nervosa and her healthy mind gains in strength.

The anorectic's healthy mind needs all the support it can get, cognitively and emotionally. It needs to understand and experience how the addiction is at work, every day, every hour and minute—a very, very difficult learning process. Anyone not anorectic can conceive the difficulty of this process to some degree by imagining having to live counter to one's most important and cherished principles and beliefs.

There is a well-established principle in psychotherapy that problems and difficulties may not be overcome entirely, but they become more manageable once one understands when and how they occur. Fortunately, learning about the addictive process and applying one's knowledge will lead to recovery, especially when every thought and action can be fully understood and even predicted as part of a consistent, logical system of interactive brain functions.

Learning about the addiction is a cognitive process that is closely associated with the behavioral work of kicking the habit, the second part of the triad. Only by trying to give up addictive behavior does a person fully experience and understand the interplay between this behavior and its reinforcement/reward function. It is a basic rule of behavioral addictions, as is the case in drug addictions, that there is nothing more convincing in understanding the essence of addictive behavior than to experience anxiety or depression as this behavior is relinquished.

Part Two of the Therapeutic Triad: Behavioral Aspects of Giving Up the Addiction of Self-starvation

The principal treatment goal is to help the patient give up the addiction by reversing the way she brought it about. She must learn and accept that there is no magical drug or magical therapist; the only way to achieve abstinence is to resist her craving for a return to self-starvation as she gains weight. This principal mode of treatment of anorexia nervosa—that is, reversing the addiction by gaining weight—is the reason why it is not necessary to know which particular substance in the family of endorphins is responsible for the addictive process. Since weight loss triggered stimulation of this substance, weight gain will reduce it and with it the addiction.

Learning to Live with Tolerance

If the anorectic has not yet reached the stage of tolerance, the stage during which she eats enough to stabilize her weight, she has to master living with tolerance as the first step of recovery. She has to tolerate feelings of irritability and some anxiety without promptly lowering her weight again.

For a typical anorectic who has reduced or stopped exercising, we propose a diet starting at 600–700 kilo calories, with the goal of soon reaching 900–1100 kilo calories per day (kilo calories are often simply called "calories"). Most patients are at first panic-stricken at the thought of eating 700 kilo calories and find this amount of calorie intake totally unacceptable.

Why would the anorectic feel panic just discussing the diet, one might ask. She has not yet started eating. Yes, even at the *thought* of stabilizing weight the addictive part of the anorectic's mind panics and warns, "You're in for deep trouble." This anxiety increases further when the patient meets with the dietitian to specify which foods of her choice add up to 700 kilo calories. Suddenly, the task of recovery becomes very real. She will have to eat again, and it comes as a shock. We must understand that even 700 kilo calories appear overwhelming to someone whose addiction has prevented her from eating virtually anything. Nevertheless, most patients agree to work towards eating this amount of food, usually with considerable reluctance.

Indeed, most patients soon manage to eat almost all the food prescribed and usually return for their session with some sense of accomplishment. While many patients believe that they must have already gained weight, they often find to their surprise that they have lost more. They have lost weight because at this point anorectics require many more calories than they did when normal weight or slightly overweight. In order to survive with little or no food, their bodies have switched to a mode of mobilizing calories from fat tissue. This is nature's last resort for maintaining life in body cells when carbohydrates, the usual energy source, are not available.

An interesting, not entirely understood observation about endorphins ties in with this phenomenon. A precursor hormone of endorphins is beta-lipotropin, a larger hormone from which endorphins are split off. This hormone was discovered in 1965 by C.H. Li, Chretien, and Chung, before the discovery of endorphins, and its only known function was the mobilization of fat from fat tissue. We can now surmise that increased endorphin activity may be related to elevated beta-lipotropin activity, i.e., fat-dissolving activity. Because of this, some patients may have to work their way up to daily diets of 2500 kilo calories and more in order to gain weight. This depends on how much weight the patient has lost by the time she begins to stabilize.

Very soon some patients will return to their session with a feeling of apprehension. The anxiety changes to panic when the scale confirms their suspicions: They have already gained, perhaps as much as four pounds. Here the patient needs prompt assurance that these pounds are not "true weight gain." Rather, these pounds are the result of replenishment of intracellular and extracellular water. One can observe this initial water retention in patients who prior to treatment had abstained from protein almost entirely and therefore lack protein as a water-binding substance. In some cases, anorectics "gain weight" from water retention because they had been treating fluids like food and had become dehydrated from not drinking. Or they may retain water because of changes in body electrolytes, certain salts that play a role in the regulation of body fluids. In any of these situations the patient has to understand that the increased weight is not "real" in the sense that they have gained fat or muscle tissue.

One of the principal tasks during this early phase of therapy is to help the anorectic understand the many distortions of her addicted mind, which become more evident as the addiction is being challenged. These thoughts and behaviors in defense of the addiction are by no means easily identified as such. Since they essentially serve the purpose of denial they do not easily reveal their addictive origin. Therefore, I call these defensive maneuvers "mental tricks" that the addicted mind plays on the anorectic to maintain the addiction. We have to remember that the addictive part of the mind is as much a part of the anorectic as the healthy mind. Because the addicted mind constantly competes with, and usually wins over, the healthy mind, the patient must learn to identify these tricks as they occur. After discussing various incidents in which the patient has been tricked by her addiction, I give her a rule of thumb, the so-called bottom line rule: any thought and subsequent action that could cause her to lose weight, burn up calories, or render taken-in calories useless by purging is caused by her addicted mind. In other words, no matter what the conscious intent of the anorectic's thought or behavior, when the end result does not favor weight gain, the bottom line is that it was caused by her addicted mind.

Because of these mental tricks I make a contract with the patient encouraging open and honest rapport between us. Anorectics are notorious for their "dishonest character" and for lying, cheating, and misleading others. The truth is that people who become anorectic are actually subject to very high moral standards and seriously motivated to be good. However, the power of their endorphin dependence often is beyond their control, resulting in dishonesty and devious behavior.

Therefore, patients have to know that, although they have agreed to treatment and are making every effort to comply with it, they are prone to misrepresent their experiences or to cheat on their diets. Once this tendency to cheat is understood as an effect of dependence, the anorectic's healthy mind and the therapist join in watching out so that her addicted side does not gain the upper hand. In fact, the anorectic must be told that during her recovery she is expected to go through many experiences of trial and error, just like anyone else withdrawing from an addictive substance. That way the patient is likely to cheat less and to report faithfully any difficulties in abiding by the prescribed rules.

The attainment of a perfect record of abstinence—in the case of anorexia nervosa eating the prescribed diet—is not as important a goal as the quick recovery from inevitable relapses into addictive behavior. A phenomenon most frequently seen in people with bulimia and obesity is also quite typical for anorectics: Whenever there is a relapse into addictive behavior, i.e., not eating enough in the case of anorectics, the patient will feel "bad" and discouraged, and quickly conclude that, since she has now broken her record of eating her diet, she may as well continue eating less than required. This is a trick that her addicted mind plays on her. On the surface there is guilt and upset over having failed; underneath is the addiction asserting itself. Progress in recovery is not measured by the achievement of a perfect record but by the speed of recovery from a relapse.

In order to overcome the forces of denial it is essential that the patient keep a daily log in which she records the nature of food eaten, the amounts, and time of intake. The log also serves to record feeling states (depressed, anxious, etc.) and how much physical activity, including exercises, she engages in. The log reduces distortions in reporting; more importantly, however, it permits the anorectic to confront the reality of reduced intake, a sign of addictive behavior. This principle of overcoming denial by keeping records has been found critical in the treatment of addictions of all kinds. It is so important that the patient's readiness and ability to keep a log is a condition on which much of the progress in treatment depends.

After several more visits the patient will usually return looking quite apprehensive and anxious; if asked, she will readily admit feeling nervous and worried, if not panic-stricken. The patient is experiencing tolerance and she hates this state of mind. In fact, she will express thoughts and behavior that indicate craving for the resumption of weight loss, the return to the addictive state.

When the anorectic craves to resume weight loss again at this stage, she is most prone to resist eating with every fiber of her body. I have treated many patients in the hospital or in my office who have sworn to start eating again and wanted to be helped. But at this stage they are ready to give up. If in the hospital they demand immediate discharge. If ambulatory they show boundless creativity in fighting weight gain, often subtle, sometimes not so subtle. Here the therapist finds his/her greatest challenge—to help the patient through an endless variety of avoidance techniques.

As most evident during this phase, treatment of anorexia nervosa has been described as an ongoing battle between patient and therapist. This aspect of treatment causes many therapists inside and outside of hospitals to dislike anorectics and to avoid treating them. However, if one recognizes the addictive mechanisms at work, the anorectic's behavior becomes subject to a new understanding between patient and therapist.

Therefore, patients find it most helpful when they are told about the addictive thoughts, feelings, and behavior they will encounter on their way towards recovery. Informing patients in advance about ways of resisting treatment will not cause them to intensify their resistance, as one might fear. It helps them become more predictable to themselves, form a therapeutic alliance, and master their task more successfully. Therapeutic work is removed from a level of arguing about the irrationality of the anorectic's behavior to perfectly rational cognitive concepts of addiction. Furthermore, if the therapist assumes a nurturant-authoritative role (Levenkron, 1982) in dealing with these issues, the difficulties of this phase of treatment are overcome most effectively.

Over the next few sessions, the patient begins to understand about her addiction and she is able to anticipate her behavior patterns and to explain herself to others. Her diet is slowly increased by 100–200 kilo calories per day either once a week or once every other week, depending on how well she adheres to her prescribed diet.

It is helpful to the patient to reverse the mental tricks game in which the patient's healthy mind will learn to play tricks on the addicted mind. For example, many patients find it easier to eat if they do not finish all food on their plates. As long as they maintain this element of dieting their addictive mind does not become as alarmed, even though they are eating more and more as their prescribed diet increases in calories. For the same reasons restaurants are the recovering anorectic's favorite environment for

eating. A room packed with people who all are helping themselves to hefty portions seems to calm the anorectic's worries. By
observing how much more everybody else is eating she keeps her
addiction at bay and reassures herself that, relatively speaking,
she is still dieting.

Vice versa, never expect an anorectic to eat while you keep
her company without eating anything yourself. This situation will
trigger a deep sense of unfairness and upset. Just as the anorectic
envies other women who are slimmer, she envies people who
don't have to eat while she does. We have to remember here that
for the anorectic abstaining from food is associated with good
feelings and better coping power. Having to eat means feeling
anxious and depressed, as if being punished. Therefore, she will
jealously guard against being the one person having to eat alone.

This is true for a patient in the hospital, where nurses are sometimes assigned to sit with the patient during meals, or at the dinner
table at home. Don't expect an anorectic to eat while other family
members don't eat. No matter how much food parents plan to pack
in later that evening at a dinner party with friends, the anorectic's
mind in this regard is outright dumb and will experience her meal
alone with a deep sense of hurt. No matter how sophisticated the
use of disguise by the addicted mind is, when it comes to these kind
of situations, there is no perspective, only the simple-minded envy
of those who do not have to eat.

Parents

The early phase of treatment is a very trying time for parents,
other family members, and friends. During this time I see the parents regularly, either separately or jointly, if the patient is willing
to discuss matters in their presence. Parents need to learn what
the patient learns.

In particular, they must adopt a very specific attitude towards
their daughter's eating and handling of food. Having an anorectic
in the family tends to cause a chaotic, distressing situation at the

dinner table if the anorectic joins the family for dinner at all. Especially when the family constantly observes the anorectic and urges her to eat, she will sense disapproval. The focus on her eating prevents her from playing tricks on her addicted mind; she becomes anxious and resentful and simply eats less or leaves the table.

The anorectic must take charge of her eating as much as possible. *She* must be responsible for eating the diet prescribed. If the anorectic does not succeed on her own, one parent may have to check the daughter's preparation of meals. Often, her addiction may cause her to misread the scale and eat less with an apparently clear conscience, another trick of her addicted mind. This role of parents can be compared to that of the hospital nurse, who helps the patient adhere to her diet without being punitive or critical. Like the nurse, parents must simply do their job without being entangled in their narcissistic wishes and hurt feelings.

Understandably, parents are very worried and distressed about their child's condition; nevertheless, they can be helpful only if they fully understand what their daughter is going through as she learns to live with tolerance. Otherwise, the daughter will experience only a continuation of what made her anorectic to begin with, that is, a sense of herself as having let her parents down and having caused them to worry and be unhappy.

The Nutritionist

The nutritionist is an integral part of the treatment team. Her task is to design diets individually, according to each patient's food preferences. Initially the nutritionist prepares fixed menus containing the prescribed calories for three or four different days. This approach makes it easier for the patient to adhere to the diet, since there is less guesswork and, therefore, less addictive distortion. Soon, however, the nutritionist teaches the patient a system of determining proper caloric intake by establishing five lists of different food categories. A properly balanced diet consists of certain amounts of food from each list, which can vary in kind and be determined from day to day at the patient's choice. While this approach leaves more room for noncompliance, it ultimately gives the patient greater flexibility in eating foods available at the dinner table or in restaurants.

Learning to Live with Withdrawal

Sooner or later the patient will return to the office and show a true weight gain on the scale. Her agreement to stop losing weight will now become an agreement, however reluctant, to work on gaining weight. The anorectic has entered the withdrawal phase.

As noted previously, withdrawal is a term used in drug addiction. As the addict abstains from the drug he/she loses whatever "benefit" or reward he/she experienced under the influence of this drug. The resulting mental and physical changes often are so painful and frightening that the addict continues drug use for fear of this state of withdrawal, even though the euphoria-producing effects of the drug have long vanished. Closely linked to withdrawal is craving, an automatic response of the mind to the reduced stimulation of drug-dependent reward centers of the brain. The mind is yearning for the drug and is preoccupied to the point of obsession with finding means of obtaining the drug.

Fortunately, anorectics do not suffer any physical discomfort during withdrawal. Although endorphins are extremely powerful reinforcers of the brain, like heroin, they are nature's own choice drug, so to speak. As a result, withdrawal from endorphins does not result in the devastating physical symptoms known in other drug addictions.

Similarly, the mental changes of endorphin withdrawal are subtle, although equally powerful and a match for any street drug, when it comes to craving for them. Withdrawal sets in when the anorectic becomes increasingly irritable and nervous, beyond the level of the tolerance phase, over frustrations that even she herself recognizes as being small. This reaction causes her surprise and dismay and constitutes a breakdown in the patient's defenses and coping power. The anorectic must be forewarned about this phenomenon so that she can prepare for it.

A true telltale sign of withdrawal is an episode or several episodes of weeping ''for no apparent reason.'' These weeping states can last minutes to hours, during which anorectics feel emotionally very soft and in need of support. In contrast to the anorectic's usual attitude of keeping emotionally and physically distant from others, she wants to be close to someone and just cry quietly. There is a radical change from the anorectic's stubborn, harsh, vigilant, angry attitude during the height of the addictive process to this state of being deprived of all defenses during withdrawal.

This quietly weeping ''for no reason'' is identical to what I observed during the study, reported in Chapter 3, in some patients who had received higher doses of naloxone. And I have observed it regularly since then in anorectics during withdrawal when there is a true weight gain of 1–2 lbs. per week. In order for the patient to admit these weeping states to her parents, there must be an environment of caring and understanding in the home. In an environment of antagonism and anger the patient will do her very best to conceal her vulnerable state. One can imagine how frightening it is for an anorectic to lose her composure and control, attitudes she had relied on and taken pride in previously, when the home resembles an emotional battlefront.

During these episodes of weeping the anorectic will let the person comforting her know what she needs and what feels right to her. Maybe she needs a little bit of talking, but no big explanations and discussions, maybe holding a hand, or touching, but usually no big hugs. What is required most to be helpful is a caring receptivity for the anorectic's needs.

During this phase of recovery the anorectic brings up her fear of getting fat with great urgency and conviction. Although her preoccupation with food has decreased a bit, as she had hoped, the patient fears that she may lose control over her wish to eat. At this point the patient needs to understand that her fear of getting fat is a mental expression of her craving for endorphins. What better way could the addictive mind employ in its determination to fight withdrawal than to paint a vivid, frightening picture of getting fat with all its consequences? This enormously troubling fear of getting fat is the mind's expression of the deeper, unconscious fear of losing the endorphin effect; making this equation, that fear of getting fat is actually the fear of losing endorphin reward, addresses the essence of the anorectic's way of thinking, something she has to be taught over and over again. This equation is very difficult for the anorectic to accept.

Patients do not find it easy to talk about their loss of emotional strength during the withdrawal phase; therefore, these feelings and experiences must be elicited by the therapist. Generally, anorectics respond to their weight gain with very mixed feelings, the components of which must be carefully distinguished. The patient reports an overall sense of physical well-being as she eats more and gains weight, and she feels pride in this accomplishment. But one must not overlook the fact that she is also overwhelmed by the emotional turmoil and struggle of giving up her endorphin habit. Contrary to what many professionals in the field maintain, anorectics do not simply feel better because they are gaining weight as they are replenishing the nutritional needs of their body.

At a more advanced stage of recovery the anorectic may feel deeply disturbed by a powerful impulse to overeat that was not present while she starved. Having resumed eating, the anorectic has learned to appreciate food again, but she feels quite helplessly exposed to its seductiveness. Patients who give in to this impulse call it bingeing, although only a fraction of the binges reported by bulimics is usually consumed.

The patient has to understand that her experience is caused by the lowering of endorphin levels during withdrawal. The higher level of endorphins achieved during starvation had protected her from feeling hunger pains. Now she feels again hunger, but is not yet experiencing the satiety signal, the shut-off mechanism to terminate food intake that is normally available to the nourished body. The satiety signal returns slowly with weight gain but becomes fully operative only when the body has reached its normal weight.

Sometimes, therapists cannot resist the temptation of achieving "fast results" by taking advantage of this event and permitting the patient to overeat. Similarly, many parents would like to exploit their daughter's hunger by tempting her with favorite foods. The anorectic understandably resents this approach; she wants to be protected from her wish to overeat. Rapid weight gain would cause her overwhelming anxiety and depression and compound her biggest fear, the fear of getting fat.

It is imperative, then, to keep asking the patient whether these urges to binge occur and to help her resist them. This can be achieved best by using the prescribed diet not only as a minimum requirement of food intake but also as the absolute maximum. As a result, anorectics frequently ask for more food and might even complain about the restrictions of their diet. However, explaining that this rule helps to protect her from the consequences of gaining weight too rapidly reassures the patient and helps her abide by it. Eventually, the anorectic must learn to control this urge herself, so that a major danger of anorexia nervosa is averted— that is, the danger of becoming a binge eater or bulimic.

Exercising

Most patients tend to increase their exercise schedule along with their food intake. As discussed earlier, exercising to the point of exhaustion is a powerful endorphin trigger and popular alternative to self-starvation for many anorectics. Like the drug addict in withdrawal who switches to another drug, the anorectic tends to switch unconsciously to endorphin release by exercising when starvation ceases.

Usually, only the most emaciated patients have to stop exercising completely. Anorectics need some endorphins to help them cope. We have to remember that endorphins are not unhealthy; only the mode of stimulating endorphins by starvation is unhealthy. Therefore, patients who show a slow, steady weight gain should be permitted to exercise. However, they have to agree to eat more than they otherwise would without exercising. And these exercises must be carefully controlled to prevent the patient from becoming addicted to exercising.

5

Treatment of the Anorectic Trait: Part Three of the Therapeutic Triad

THE THIRD MAJOR element in the treatment of anorexia nervosa pertains to work on the underlying causes of the anorectic's vulnerability to the addiction of self-starvation. Anorectics are usually ready to talk about their depression and fears; nevertheless, with very few exceptions, they initially are at a loss to explain the causes of their difficulties. First of all, like other persons entering therapy, they are unaware of the ways their constitutional sensitivities and life experiences made them depressed and anxiety-ridden prior to starting the diet. Second, if they are aware of any difficulties with their parents or other members of the family, they are understandably very hesitant to talk about these troubled relationships.

Generally, the two elements of trait therapy for anorexia nervosa—family therapy and individual work with the anorectic—are no different from generally established therapeutic approaches. Therefore, this section will be brief and the interested reader is referred to the extensive literature. This is not to suggest in any way that family and individual therapy play a secondary role in the treatment of anorexia nervosa. Quite the opposite is true. Without trait therapy there is no lasting recovery for the anorectic, no matter how quickly she regains weight.

FAMILY THERAPY

Family therapy in conjunction with individual therapy is a must in the treatment of anorexia nervosa for two reasons. One is that, by the time the anorectic and her family seek professional help, the interactional pattern of the family unit has reached a crisis after months, sometimes years, of buildup. Every member of the family is suffering from anger and frustration about the intractability of the anorectic's condition. Second, the individual personality traits of the anorectic daughter are the result of growing up with a particular constitutional makeup in the context of a particular family. Therefore, family therapy is an essential condition for a true resolution of the anorectic's difficulties. Looking at the situation in another way, the daughter's illness is a symptom that something has been wrong in the family for quite some time. Therefore, the therapist's first task is to help the family muster the courage to seize upon the signal given by the anorectic daughter and engage in a therapeutic process from which every member of the family will benefit, no matter how difficult the process may be.

Some of the crisis feeling in the family will be reduced early on by the cognitive process of learning about the addiction and the behavioral approach to giving up the addiction. However, as therapy develops with a clear focus on the psychological dynamics among family members, therapy is experienced as more difficult. The family again develops a sense of crisis, albeit a more tenacious and protracted one. It is the crisis of rocking the boat of family equilibrium that is sometimes so difficult to bear that the parents have to abandon therapy for themselves and their daughter.

One has to remember that the symptom of anorexia nervosa, while causing a major disequilibrium, also serves as a desperate measure to keep the lid on deeper problems in the interactional dynamics of the family. In that sense the anorectic continues to maintain an equilibrium, albeit a tenuous one, within the family. The anorectic's newfound coping power, brought about by her addiction, is welcomed by the anorectic as a means to maintain self-control in matters where she really hurts, the troubled relationship with both or one of her parents. It is understandable, then, that the family seeks to stop only the noisy and upsetting symptoms produced by their daughter's self-starvation. Otherwise the family has a vested interest in maintaining the status quo. The biggest challenge for the therapist is to help the family overcome this need to maintain the status quo, a challenge sometimes so difficult that he/she will not always succeed, as every therapist knows.

Theories of Family Therapy

During the past two decades, family therapists have provided a major new perspective on the development of anorexia nervosa. Prior theories in the 1950s were based primarily on psychoanalytic theory, which focused on individual psychological issues such as female sexuality and identity, as well as the use of fantasies and the symbolic meaning of eating, as explanatory principles. Mara Selvini Palazzoli, a foremost Italian researcher and author of the book *Self-Starvation* (1978), pioneered the transition from psychoanalytic concepts to family systems analysis. About the same time, Minuchin, Rosman, and Baker described, in *Psychosomatic Families: Anorexia Nervosa in Context* (1978), new and valid methods of treating dysfunctional families.

Yager (1982) has correctly expressed caution about the all-inclusiveness of family theories and their tendency to generalize. He views anorexia nervosa as a symptom complex that results as the final common pathway for several different pathogenetic processes, including but not limited to the dysfunctional family. Consistent with Yager's view, I suggest that family approaches are valid and useful to the degree that they give insight into the anorectic *trait*, but they do not explain the anorectic *state*. Modification of the theory is necessary to take into account the endorphin addiction mechanism as the pathogenetic process of the anorectic state, the anorectic's persistent self-starvation.

For example, Minuchin and his group found characteristic patterns of interaction in families of anorectics. These include enmeshment, overprotectiveness, lack of conflict resolution, and unresolved marital and family conflicts. Any family living with these kinds of handicaps will experience heightened distress and tension, triggered not only by ordinary parental disagreements but also by the usual needs of adolescents. According to Minuchin, the anorectic symptoms serve as a focus—even preoccupation—deflecting the family from other more devastating issues such as divorce or the father's vocational setback. Thus, according to family theory, the anorectic is locked into her symptoms to save the family from coming apart.

Although these issues often trouble anorectics and their families, they definitely are not motivations strong enough to explain the excessive pursuit of slimness. On the other hand, the motivation of experiencing an endorphin-mediated reduction of anxiety and depression in these circumstances *is* strong enough to maintain self-starvation behavior. Therefore, the motives invoked by family therapists are, at best, a secondary by-product of self-starvation, a form of secondary gain, to use an old but useful psychoanalytic concept, referring to the protective benefits afforded a sick person.

Taking an Inventory of Family Dynamics

The therapist's task is to develop an understanding of the family dynamics by testing a variety of hypotheses. The information obtained and the observations of family interaction add up to a mosaic of data that highlights the many interdependent roles of its members. As the therapist develops an understanding of these dynamics, he/she can help family members recognize the patterns contributing to their daughter's anorexia nervosa and find alternative, more adaptive modes of interaction.

It is important to keep in mind that this inventory addresses the traditional family in which the mother and father are still in place, i.e., the family is not broken up by divorce, death of a parent, or for other reasons. Nevertheless, this inventory applies equally to truncated family constellations, since there is always a "virtual family," an imaginary family, in the mental lives of its members. This applies also to situations where the child was born out of wedlock, was adopted, born to a single mother, or where two truncated families joined to form a more traditional setting. If anything, these constellations add to the complexity of the anorectic's environment and require great caution in the task of exploring the family dynamics.

Following are just a few questions the therapist might keep in mind while working with the anorectic and her family. Although the issues outlined in this inventory will emerge at different times, this discussion will have a general point of departure, i.e., the constitutional makeup of the family, and proceed to a more specific focus on the anorectic's special role in the family.

THE EXTENDED FAMILY

1. What is the constitutional makeup of the family?

In many families with an anorectic child one finds members who have a biological tendency to addictions, both drug addictions and addictive behavior. This tendency is genetically transmitted and manifests itself in the form of a greater difficulty in maintaining equilibrium, an internal balance of the mind and sometimes body, when faced with everyday stresses.

Many families are aware of this legacy from several instances of anxiety disorder or depression in the extended family, or from drug and alcohol abuse, sometimes extending over generations. Understandably, parents with such a history have a strong desire to break this spell as they go about raising their own children. Especially when parents have overcome their own constitutional handicaps, perhaps a tendency to nervousness or social shyness, they tend to be alarmed, sometimes blatantly intolerant, when they discover in their child the same kind of sensitivities with which they themselves have suffered.

PARENTS (QUESTIONS 2-9)

2. How have the parents fared with their biological makeup?

Are there signs of special sensitivities in mother and father? Have they developed symptoms of psychological dysfunction, such as an anxiety disorder or depression? If they were vulnerable in their youth, have they learned to live with themselves and to accept their limits? Or is there evidence that the mother and/or father are overcompensating for their difficulties, for example by being overly ambitious, aggressive, controlling? Overcompensating is a form of defense that differs from nondefensive behavior by virtue of its rigidity, excessive quality, and intolerance to being challenged.

3. *What are the dreams and ambitions of the parents?*

Are they content with their life situation aside from their difficulties with their anorectic daughter? Are the parents dependent on acceptance by relatives, friends, neighbors? Or did they develop a sense of autonomy, their own set of principles and lifestyle without being guided excessively by status and social acceptability?

What about narcissism? Are the parents accepting and realistic as to what life has brought them or will likely bring in the future? Are they comfortable with themselves, or are they driven by a never satisfied desire for social status and success, for which the success of their children is a prerequisite? If the latter is the case, there is usually little room and tolerance for any difficulties of an anorectic daughter.

4. *Was there any tragedy, a serious or chronic illness, injury or death in the immediate family?*

Prolonged or unresolved grief reactions often constitute a trigger for a child in the family to become "too good." Serious or chronic illness of a parent tends to shift the role of being protected from the child to the sick parent.

5. *What are the marital stresses in the family?*

Is there open or covert discord between the parents regarding work, social life, hobbies, intimacy and sex? At any time was there marital tension suggestive of separation and divorce or actual discussion to that effect?

How compatible are the parents? Are there deeply rooted frustrations over unfulfilled needs, such as dependency, caretaking, etc.?

6. What kind of pleasures do the parents pursue?

What rewards are important to them and obtained on a regular basis? Are these rewards handled in a flexible manner or are their pursuits rigid and obsessive in nature?

7. What caused the family to value "thinness" so highly?

Without dieting for one reason or another, anorexia nervosa does not occur. Therefore, starvation-mediated endorphin addictions are most likely to happen in a society or family in which thinness is highly valued as an expression of health and social acceptability. Often these standards are set within the family, but not exclusively so. Sometimes anorectics have adopted the standards of their peers with very little or no reinforcement from their family. Nevertheless, it is useful to keep in mind some typical constellations of family influence on the formation of the anorectic's view that denying oneself food is a virtue and overindulgence shows weakness of character.

A typical constellation is the family in which food is overvalued. Children are expected to finish everything on their plates to show their appreciation for mother's cooking. And withholding food is a form of serious punishment. This pattern places unhealthy importance on food as a rewarding substance. Other families lack appreciation for the emotional nurturance purveyed by a family meal or cause their children to be orally deprived, thus setting the child up to overindulge in food during adolescence and later in life.

The imposition of a low-weight diet by the mother for the sake of priding herself on raising a child of perfect beauty is another constellation. This can be observed in children as young as four or five, whose mothers are often actual or frustrated anorectics themselves. This sometimes is the case regardless of the child's constitutional body build, for example, when a girl has a larger, heavier built body, more closely resembling her father than her mother. Tragically, some of these girls actually stop growing and develop weight problems later on in life because of their short stature.

Similarly, some fathers do not accept their daughters' natural tendency to develop the voluptuousness, chubbiness, or other physical disposition of their mothers and do not hesitate to reprimand their daughters for gaining weight.

In most cases, what the parents perceive as a desire to serve the daughters' best interests turns out to be primarily a self-serving and narcissistic desire to bring up a perfectly built child, regardless of the child's constitution and needs.

8. *How do parents communicate with each other?*

Are differences communicated directly or covertly? Are there any distortions and detours of communication, such as triangulation, where one parent expresses his/her misgivings through the child? For example: ''You are too demanding of Johnny,'' said by the mother, when she really wants to express her dismay that her husband has too many expectations of her.

9. *How do parents solve real conflicts between them?*

Are conflicts openly discussed until an acceptable solution has been found, no matter how noisy and painful the issue may be? Or do disagreements linger covertly, never resolved, causing an atmosphere of chronic tension and distress in the family?

THE ROLE OF CHILDREN IN THE FAMILY (QUESTIONS 10–12)

10. *How much importance is placed on parenting?*

Is there room for the children's needs corresponding to their age and developmental needs? For example, was Johnny signed up for nursery school because he was ready or because mother went back to work so that the family could afford to acquire another status symbol?

11. *If the anorectic child has siblings, how have they fared?*

How have these siblings developed in the same family environment, each with his/her particular biological makeup and personality structure?

12. *Are there special alliances between a child and a parent?*

Are there similarities or differences of personality styles and emotional response patterns that fostered special closeness or antagonism between family members?

THE ROLE OF THE ANORECTIC CHILD IN THE FAMILY
(QUESTIONS 13–16)

13. *What special constitutional and experiential factors caused the anorectic child to become vulnerable to anorexia nervosa?*

How is she different from her siblings, if there are any?

14. *What circumstances caused the anorectic to become the "too good child"?*

Children, by virtue of their emotional and material dependence on their parents, learn from early life on that their sense of comfort and internal balance largely depends on the comfort and stability of the family, specifically of their parents. In short, children are good team players. Not only are children highly reactive to tension and difficulties in the family, but they will also do their very best to alleviate tension by being good, often to a fault. In particular, a sensitive child who has more difficulties than others in maintaining an internal equilibrium in the presence of external tension will do whatever he or she can to alleviate upset in the family, often blaming him/herself for having caused the situation.

This personality feature can be adaptive in essentially healthy families but can lead to untold suffering in children growing up in families suffering from intractable tension and turmoil. If the focus and dependence on the social environment for the maintenance of an internal sense of balance and worth are excessive, the child may develop a narcissistic personality. Instead of establishing an internal capacity to maintain equilibrium and a sense of independence and autonomy, narcissistic individuals continue to depend excessively on others for their emotional stability and self-esteem. In the process they become highly vulnerable to feelings of rejection and distress once they are exposed to the harshness of adult life, where "mental stroking" is not so easy to find.

> 15. *Has either parent formed an unusually close relationship with the anorectic daughter, to the exclusion of the other parent?*

If so, is the relationship symbiotic, is there an unhealthy mutual dependence and closeness that interferes with the child's ability to develop independence and autonomy?

> 16. *Is there a reversal of parent and child roles?*

Are the parents capable of providing support and comfort when the anorectic is in emotional turmoil? Or does the child have to feel and do better before the parents' worries and despair subside? In the latter situation the child virtually takes on the role of a parent to her parents. She has to use her own resources to overcome her upset so that her parents calm down.

When this situation occurs, many parents refuse to accept the problematic nature of their attitude. Sometimes they insist on their right to be upset, almost self-righteously so. "How can I go happily about my life when my daughter is sick?" they might say, indicating that their depression over their daughter's illness is a sign of caring. This parental attitude places enormous burden on the child and often is a factor in intractable anorexia nervosa.

The Role of Parents in Family Therapy

Many parents of anorectics hold the view that only their daughter needs therapy since she is the one who has symptoms of illness. They hope that once she has gained weight she can go her own way into adult life without much delving into the past. Unfortunately, if treatment is confined to weight gain only, the anorectic will at best be left with poorly healed scars that will not only burst open whenever she relates to her parents but also affect other important relationships in her life. The task for the family is to face difficulties of the past so that every family member can overcome his/her feelings of hurt and anger. It is not enough for the anorectic to change; her parents must also change.

This point of view is reflected in the concept of the "identified patient." It connotes that the anorectic is identified as the patient by virtue of her symptoms of illness, which are most apparent and troubling. However, this concept implies that there are patients who are not identified. These are the other members of the family and the family as a whole. They are not identified because their symptoms may be less noisy and apparent, but they are patients nevertheless, since they are part of a dysfunctional family.

However, aside from the tendency to isolate the anorectic as the identified patient, there are differences in the way mothers and fathers generally involve themselves in therapy and accept or object to their role. These differences are largely determined by societal standards defining gender role behavior as well as maternal and paternal role behavior.

The assignment of blame for the daughter's difficulties—blame by others or self—is strongly influenced by societal norms. Mothers have been identified most often as the cause of their daughter's anorexia nervosa, presumably because of issues of nurturance and mother-daughter identification. In my view there is no evidence for it. Mother-bashing is out. Attitudes and problems of fathers are the principal cause of the daughter's illness as often as those of mothers. As a rule of thumb, the parent who has greater difficulty with the therapeutic process and clings more tenaciously to the maintenance of the status quo is the parent with greater psychological difficulties; these difficulties, in turn, contributed significantly to the daughter's pre-anorectic distress.

A closer look at families of anorectics shows that there is considerable fluidity as to the actual role a mother or father assumes, regardless of societal norms, which these families usually submit to diligently. The fluidity in the roles parents assume does not in itself pose a problem, as many healthy families indicate. As discussed earlier, the family dysfunction has deeper roots than parental role behavior as assigned by our society. Accordingly, the involvement of parents in family therapy can vary greatly, depending on the roles the mother and father have assumed in the family context.

Fathers who assume the more traditional gender and parental role generally find it difficult to engage in family therapy. In particular, the regressive elements of feelings, introspection, and easing of defenses are experienced as tantamount to giving up maleness. If these fathers do not attempt to leave therapy to the daughter and mother altogether, they lack understanding and show intolerance for their daughter's difficulties. They tend to apply to their daughter's illness the same approach they have used for all problems they have encountered in their often successful lives—that is, problems exist to be solved and eliminated. Often, this attitude has been adopted by the daughter and caused her to fault herself for not being able to cope with her distressful life.

It is imperative to convey to this kind of father that this attitude perpetuates and intensifies his daughter's anxiety and distress, if they have not actually contributed to her vulnerability and depression. It is crucial that he understands that his daughter cannot recover fully unless he makes his involvement in therapy a top priority and patiently explores his role in the family and relationship with her.

It must be emphasized that the rational, business-like father is by no means the rule in families of anorectics. There are many fathers, even highly successful ones, who have assumed the nurturing and supportive role traditionally assigned to the mother. On the other hand, there are mothers who are the driving force in the family, assuming the role traditionally assigned to the father. In those cases, the mother has to be helped to accept the therapeutic process with the same considerations as for the traditional father.

Generally, mothers find it easier to accept the therapeutic process and are capable of empathizing with their daughter's difficulties. However, when mothers feel intensely guilty, viewing their daughter's condition as a sign of their failure, no matter how irrational that sometimes seems, they find the therapeutic process unbearable. If this problem cannot be resolved, their boycott of treatment can lead to a premature withdrawal of the family from therapy.

Many patients seek therapy again at a later age, having continued to suffer badly from their unresolved difficulties with their parents. In my view, every effort should be made to treat the parents along with the anorectic, even when the daughter is an adult. Especially when she is financially and emotionally heavily dependent on her parents and, at best, leads a pseudo adult life, family therapy is the treatment of choice. Of course, this is not always possible. If the daughter has grown apart from her parents, and rigid, bitter attitudes on both sides preclude reconciliation, then individual therapy for the anorectic is preferable.

INDIVIDUAL THERAPY

Beginning with the initial consultation, individual therapy becomes established as the patient learns about the addictive mechanism and experiences tolerance and withdrawal. In this process the anorectic's ambivalent feelings present a constant challenge to the therapeutic alliance, as the therapist maintains a clear position against the addiction and for the recovery of the healthy side of the anorectic's personality.

The therapeutic focus shifts for a considerable time to the family

dynamics operative during her illness and prior to becoming anorectic. Nevertheless, there are many issues that require work in
the one-to-one setting of individual therapy. Although they are
outlined only briefly here because they follow principles of conventional therapy, these issues require a major effort in time, energy, and commitment.

To begin with, the anorectic has to come to terms with the
perhaps earliest element of the anorectic process, which is the
overidealization of slimness and the social reward that is derived
from it. Marlene Boskind-White and William White discussed the
societal factors leading to this attitude in their book, *Bulimarexia,
The Binge/Purge Cycle.* The authors describe how the desire for a
slim body is deeply rooted in traditional feminine values, to which
people with eating disorders are firmly committed. These values
become problematic when the degree to which a woman has attained a "perfect body," i.e., a slim body, becomes the principal
measure by which she is judged and esteemed. Overidealization
of body shape did not make sense in former times and certainly is
in conflict with the role of women today, especially in light of the
many contributions of women to our society, of which slimness is
the least.

In my view there is another, less obvious factor that contributes to the emphasis on slimness in our society. This factor stems
from the goal in any capitalistic economic system of keeping
consumption of goods as high as possible. What better method to
stimulate sales of goods than to create a population of needy and
eager women shoppers by promoting the idea of slimness as the
epitome of beauty? For every anorectic who abstains from any
reward other than endorphins, there are thousands of women
who have deprived themselves of food in their pursuit of slimness
without becoming anorectic. This is a huge population of deeply
dissatisfied and deprived people highly motivated to compensate
for their deprivation by buying anything in sight.

The anorectic has to reconsider her enslavement to the pursuit
of slimness and her identity as a woman in the light of our current

societal norms. Anorexia nervosa does not occur in societies in which slimness is not highly valued. It will remain to be seen if the incidence of anorexia nervosa decreases as societal standards deemphasize slimness as the principal virtue of women, a trend that already is on its way.

Other issues to be dealt with in individual therapy are related to the anorectic's constitutional sensitivities and how they have affected her personality development. In particular, she needs help in understanding how these sensitivities left her helplessly exposed to the rough give-and-take of her childhood environment and eventually brought about ineffective defensive structures. For example, a narcissistic personality structure evolves out of a heavy dependence on the environment for the maintenance of internal equilibrium. Eventually this constellation leads to a pattern of manipulating the social environment for the purposes of both protecting oneself from perceived emotional insults and dangers and boosting a fragile self-image. Similarly, perfectionism is not a virtue but an unhealthy personality trait. It evolves from the need to compensate for an impoverished self-esteem through the pursuit of excessive, unrealistic achievements.

Then there are experiences in the life of the anorectic—traumatic experiences, failures, and setbacks, as well as recent precipitating stresses and hurdles that acutely resulted in anxiety and depression. These experiences require extensive exploration, emotional and cognitive working-through, and/or help in finding alternative ways of mastery.

Closer to recovery, the anorectic needs to mourn for the time, often years, of "normal" life lost because of her addiction. If she does not go through this mourning process, there is an unhealthy tendency to make up for the time lost. Sometimes encouraged by their parents, anorectics seek out unrealistic goals in an attempt to redeem themselves in their own eyes and in the eyes of their families and friends. Unfortunately, if these goals are actively pursued, they will trigger another round of anxiety and distress.

Eventually, the anorectic will arrive at a sense of mastery over her experiences and take pride in her successful recovery. By applying what she has learned from her past she will be able to look more confidently towards her life ahead.

OTHER ASPECTS OF TREATMENT

Medication

The identification of an endorphin-mediated addictive process underlying anorexia nervosa raises the question: Might this condition be treated with medication that specifically affects the endorphin mechanism?

Certainly the opiate receptor blocking agent naloxone (Narcan) would interfere with the mechanism of reinforcement and interrupt the addictive cycle. It has been used for many years for the treatment of heroin and other narcotic overdoses. It has also been widely used in endorphin research and, as discussed in Chapter 3, was the principal drug used in studies investigating the role of endorphins in anorexia nervosa. More recently, naltrexone, a drug like naloxone but administered orally, has become available.

What, however, would be accomplished if we gave this drug to anorectic patients? Clearly, the endorphin system would be blocked, resulting in biochemical or mental reversal of the addictive state. However, is this desirable in the view of the function of endorphins as coping hormones? As noted earlier, the reinforcement effect of endorphins is based on their effects as an anti-anxiety and anti-depression agent; they increase the anorectic's coping power in a life situation that has so far precluded other acceptable solutions. Blocking the endorphin mechanism, therefore, would acutely deprive the anorectic of her ability to cope before she has found viable alternatives to her situation through therapy. Therefore, a slow but steady withdrawal through weight gain is preferable to the use of naloxone or naltrexone.

Another question is often asked. If endorphins are beneficial, but the method of raising them by starvation is harmful, what if anorectics were given endorphins directly in the form of injections (or pills)? This would certainly make starvation unnecessary, but the patient would become addicted to the endorphin injections. Even though the anorectic might start to eat again, she soon would require more injections or larger doses to alleviate her chronically depressed and anxious state of mind. This situation is similar to the tendency of chronic pain patients to become addicted to analgesics, while the giving of a narcotic for acute, self-limiting pain rarely, if ever, causes addiction.

A modified version of this idea is the use of enzyme inhibitors. Enzymes are substances that the body produces to break down naturally occurring or externally given substances so that they can be eliminated. An enzyme inhibitor raises the level of a substance by reducing the breakdown function of the enzyme affecting this substance. Thus, one could raise the level of naturally produced endorphins in anorectics. Even better, enzyme inhibitors may raise endorphin levels in people whose own endorphin supplies tend to be low and who, therefore, tend to become addicted.

This idea is intriguing; however, inhibiting enzyme action may not circumvent the addiction problem, since the level of endorphins is increased artificially. And even if such administration were practical, it would not address the core problem of the anorectic: the psychological dilemma of being locked into a difficult life situation with no apparent way out.

Less specifically related to the endorphin mechanism is the use of anti-depressant and anti-anxiety medication. Although there are reports about their effectiveness as a principal form of treatment, in my view they constitute an adjunct to other treatment modalities. Literature on other addictions shows that the general practice is first to induce withdrawal from the addictive substance, and then to control any major anxiety or depression that may come to the fore with the appropriate medication. Similarly, anorectics must initiate the withdrawal process first. If the anxiety or depression is so severe that the anorectic cannot continue to gain weight, or if she begins to lose weight again, the use of an anti-depressant or anti-anxiety drug can be very helpful.

It is important to keep in mind that there is no "magic pill" for the treatment of anorexia nervosa, neither a pill functionally related to the endorphin system nor any of the many psychoactive drugs; nor is there any experimental drug so far that would produce an instant "cure" the anorexia nervosa. There is no short cut for the difficult task of overcoming anorexia nervosa by sheer willpower and hard work in individual and family therapy. Nor should there be such a drug, in my opinion, in the interest of the anorectic and her family alike.

Hospitalization

Some patients are so overwhelmed by the addictive forces that their good judgment and will to recover are not strong enough to fight them. In those rare situations I see a need to hospitalize the patient. The other indication for in-hospital treatment is a situation in which the crisis in the family has become so severe that progress at home has stagnated or is absent because of unbearable tension and hostilities.

Generally, hospitalization should be considered a treatment modality of last resort. Anorexia nervosa stems from problems of coping with the stresses of "real" life, either within or outside the family or both. Thus, real life, not the hospital, is the setting within which the anorectic has to learn new perspectives and more adaptive ways of coping.

Moreover, admitting the anorectic to the hospital singles her out as the only one in the family requiring treatment, often connected with the implication that she is the troublemaker, the bad member of the family. As discussed above, this is not so. Generally, psychiatrists have been too quick to admit young people troubled by all kinds of psychological problems to the hospital, sometimes for many months, to take the child off the parents' hands, so to speak. Certainly, of least benefit to the anorectic and her family is a setting in which the patient is hospitalized far away from home and continuity of family and individual therapy in and outside the hospital is not possible.

Finally, the time lost from school or work and its implications, the meaning of hospitalization for the anorectic's identity and self-esteem, as well as dependence on hospitals and problems reentering real life, are issues that have to be taken into account in weighing the benefits of hospitalization.

Hyperalimentation and Nasogastric Tube Feeding

Severely ill anorectics treated in hospitals have been induced to gain weight by receiving highly nutritious fluids through an intravenous or nasogastric tube. In rare cases these procedures are indicated to save an anorectic's life. Unfortunately, however, this form of treatment has become commonplace, the treatment of choice in some centers.

These methods do not account for the underlying mechanism of the illness or the patient's psychological needs. Although the procedure forces patients to gain weight, many patients submit to it only to be released from the hospital. Once discharged, they quickly resume weight loss even if they have had additional individual or family psychotherapy. This treatment method also has the disadvantage of suggesting to the patient that she is truly incapable of providing for her own nutritional needs; in addition, she might perceive this treatment as punishment for being morally ''bad.''

Behavior Modification

Behavior modification or some aspects thereof have been the most widespread, effective form of treatment in the acute phase of starvation, both in inpatient and ambulatory settings. Behavior modification is based on the notion that living organisms, including humans, tend to act in ways that bring about rewards or pleasures and avoid behavior that causes them pain or punishment. Behavior modification has been effective because it is based on the principles of reward; by eating again the patient receives privileges that otherwise would be withheld.

For example, hospital staff treating anorectics usually design behavioral modification contracts around access to daily activities in the hospital. The patient understands that only if she is capable of providing for her own nourishment by eating the required diet will she be given those privileges. As the patient gains weight she is permitted to leave her room, to watch television, see her family, just to name a few early privileges. Later on she is permitted special privileges, such as leaving the hospital to visit her family, going to the movies and other treasured activities.

We know that the reward of receiving special privileges does serve as an incentive for the anorectic to give up endorphin reward by eating again. However, certain caveats must be observed. Often behavior modification is carried out in a moralistic and punitive way, the implication being that the patient is bad for not eating and is being punished by means of deprivation. If the role of endorphins in the patient's self-starvation behavior is taken into account, the patient understands why she needs an incentive to give up endorphin reward. Her healthy side, which wishes to get rid of the addiction, will cooperate rather than fight with the staff. This approach also lessens the likelihood that the patient will resume eating only to fall back into her self-starvation pattern once she has left the hospital.

Progress in Therapy and Prognosis

Progress in therapy is determined by the degree to which the patient can deal with her addiction cognitively and emotionally. Much depends on the patient's ability to separate the elements of her thinking controlled by her addicted mind from those influenced by her healthy mind. It also depends on the patient's ability to take necessary action, that is, to eat despite her fear of eating. These capacities are related to ego strength—the mind's ability to judge situations correctly, to implement necessary actions, and to tolerate discomfort and anxiety.

Treatment progress also depends heavily on the degree of distress from anxiety and depression the anorectic experiences as she goes through endorphin withdrawal. In very rare cases this distress may be unrelated to psychological dynamics in the family. Most often, however, lack of progress due to severe distress is the result of the parents' difficulties in accepting that they have to change also. The daughter wants to be a good team player and will do everything in her power to make things better, no matter how stubborn and noisy she sometimes may be.

As a rule, the anorectic returns to normal weight within six to twelve months if conditions are favorable. In more severe situations, the return of menstruation as a sign of physical recovery and suppression of excess endorphin levels does not occur for 12–18 months. In my experience, a relapse into a self-starvation pattern is very rare. Once an anorectic has understood the power of endorphin addiction and its control over her life, self-starvation loses its magical appeal.

6

The Addiction of Bulimia:
Clinical Features, Biochemistry,
and Treatment

BULIMIA, THE CONDITION of compulsive overeating and purging, is probably as old as the first times when humans no longer lived on a limited food supply but started to have surplus food and feasts. Certainly the ancient Romans were known to maximize their orgiastic feasts by tickling their palates with goose feathers so that they could vomit and help themselves to another round of delicacies.

Bulimia has many similarities with anorexia nervosa, despite some differences to be discussed below. Therefore, many references will be made to anorexia nervosa, and this chapter should be read in conjunction with the chapters on anorexia nervosa.

THE CASE OF JACQUELINE

Jacqueline, an attractive, blond-haired woman, 23 years of age, of small stature and slightly chubby figure, consulted me for bulimia. She had been bingeing and vomiting several times a day for many months and was so preoccupied with it that she feared she might lose her job. It was apparent that she was very depressed as she sat in her chair with tears rolling down her cheeks while she told her story. She had always been somewhat chubby, very much to her mother's dismay, but had been dieting seriously only since junior year of college, at one of the best schools in the country.

Always having been an insecure and shy person, Jacqueline nevertheless felt very good about herself as a senior, when she had become quite slim. Although she obsessed about dieting, she probably did not quite qualify for the diagnosis of anorexia nervosa. Her grades had always been very good, and basically she spent her college years in ways that would have made most parents quite happy. But she felt that she was never good enough in their eyes, judging from their constant urging and scolding; they reminded her "a thousand times" that life was work, work, work.

According to Jacqueline, her parents were almost paranoid about pleasure. She did not think it had to do with their Catholic religion, since they were not very religious. The father, an accomplished professional in a technical field, knew nothing but work and worry, even if by most people's standards there was little to worry about. He was a "depressed" man who had been told many times to seek professional help. Jacqueline's mother's formal education ended with high school, shortly after which she got married. Her life was devoted to her husband and two children, Jacqueline and her younger sister. The parents lived a very isolated life. They did not have friends or occasional company, nor did they have any hobbies or fun together. After both daughters had left the family to pursue their careers away from home, the parents' major preoccupation was to make sure by daily telephone calls that their children would not get into trouble or take life too easy.

While Jacqueline was looking for her first job after graduating from college, she found herself distressed and worried, afraid that she never would be able to make it in the "big city," away from home. This was just what her parents had predicted. Soon she started eating more again, but her eating was different from before. While wandering the streets alone or when in the apartment without her roommates, she would stuff herself with all kinds of cheap sweet pastry. And very soon she had regained the weight that she had lost in college.

She hated sending out resumes and interviewing for jobs that would permit her to work as editor and writer some day. How could she present herself as the right person for a job when she felt absolutely worthless and useless to everyone—including herself for that matter? Job hunting had become even more difficult since she had gained weight. But nevertheless, she found an entry level job with a small advertising agency.

New situations were never easy for Jacqueline. As if she was not entitled to be in the role of a beginner, someone who learns and makes mistakes in the process, she tried to be perfect on the job from day one. And she was almost perfect, driving herself harder every day, to the point of exhaustion. Certainly her boss was very happy with her and said so. But Jacqueline never felt it inside. She was unable to feel good enough for anything. Especially regarding her weight the feeling of contentment was out of reach, although no one else would have called her overweight. She thought anyone could see she was a slob, someone with no self-discipline or self-respect.

One day, when she complained to her roommate about her weight gain, the roommate suggested "the solution," that Jacqueline could get rid of the food by vomiting. Aren't all girls doing that to stay slim? Jacqueline had known about vomiting as a way of staying slim; she had even heard about the dangers of it. But, as if she needed permission from someone, her roommate's suggestion did the trick. Jacqueline started to vomit every time she binged, and it worked. Her weight loss was not that great, but she *felt* great. She felt more content generally, and every night after work she knew that her secret indulgence was waiting for her. Often she could not get home fast enough to "do her thing."

Actually, there was another good thing waiting for her after work. Her boyfriend was waiting as well. She had met him at college and they had become friends soon after she had moved to the big city, where he lived near his parents and had started his own business. Jacqueline's boyfriend also had his act together, always seemed to know what to do about a problem, like a nice, supportive father.

Jacqueline needed this kind of support and guidance, and she soon became very dependent on him. Her only worry was to make sure that she pleased him—otherwise he might leave her. Never mind that he was very possessive, that they would only see his friends, that he would tell her what to wear, what to say at parties, and how to smile. Also, never mind that she was not physically attracted to him and sex was not satisfying. He gave her a sense of belonging, he cared for her, and she felt safe with him.

The boyfriend had also become critical of her weight. She was not as perfect as he expected her to be. When she started to vomit after bingeing her weight loss made him happy. But she could not tell him about her secret. He certainly would disapprove of her and might even leave her. The solution was to carve out of each day about two hours in the evening before she would see him, during which she would binge and vomit. But that was not enough. Pressed for extra time of privacy, Jacqueline started to binge and purge on the job, during lunch hour, and sometimes during other times of the work day. Her work did not suffer from it, not at all. She worked for two during the time at her desk.

But one day she knew that a co-worker had heard her vomit in the bathroom. And that was it. The secret was out. Even though the co-worker did not say anything, this event gave Jacqueline reason to think. She was desperately afraid of being found out, and she felt as if her house of cards were about to suddenly come crashing down. She realized that she had become helplessly controlled by a potentially self-destructive way of life and decided to seek help.

BEHAVIORAL MANIFESTATIONS OF BULIMIA

Using strictly behavioral criteria *DSM-III-R* defines bulimia as follows:

A. Recurrent episodes of binge eating (rapid consumption of large amounts of food in a discrete period of time).
B. A feeling of lack of control over eating behavior during eating binges.

C. The person regularly engages in either self-induced vomiting, use of laxatives or diuretics, strict dieting or fasting, or vigorous exercise in order to prevent weight gain.
D. A minimum average of two binge eating episodes a week for at least three months.
E. Persistent overconcern with body shape and weight. (pp. 68–69)

Essentially, bulimia encompasses two distinct, opposing, and seemingly irresistible behavior patterns against the background of a persistent overconcern with body shape and weight.

The first pattern is a compulsion to eat, the binge. The term bulimia, meaning ox hunger in ancient Greek, originally was limited to this feature of intake of large quantities of food, not followed by purging.

However, current diagnostic use of the term bulimia includes the second pattern, which is a compulsion to purge in order to avoid weight gain, the inevitable consequence of overeating. The purging method can be vomiting, usually by manipulating the gag reflex but also by "willpower," or the use of laxatives (and enemas) to promote a rapid emptying of the bowels, or the use of diuretics to promote excretion of water through the kidneys.

Other frequently used methods of avoiding weight gain after binges include periods of strict dieting or fasting and vigorous exercising to burn up excess calories.

DIFFERENCES AND SIMILARITIES BETWEEN BULIMIA AND OTHER EATING DISORDERS

At first glance, the behavioral features of bulimia indicate that this condition has some clinical characteristics in common with two other eating disorders, obesity and anorexia nervosa.

First of all, there is the most prominent feature of excessive food intake, which is typical of obesity. Though considered mostly a condition caused by genetic and biological factors such as fat cell physiology, obesity clearly also has a psychological component. Obese people have a tendency to increase the amount of food taken in and to reduce the time intervals between meals, not unlike an addict who has to overcome tolerance by increasing drug dosage or shorten the intervals between drug use.

But, as discussed earlier, anorectics also start off with a tendency to overeat before they decide to go on a diet. Therefore, with regard to this impulse to overeat the three conditions—anorexia nervosa, bulimia, and obesity—are not as different as many believe. However, there is one difference. The bulimic and the obese person give in to this impulse, while the anorectic, who experiences this drive prior to going on a diet, steadfastly resists it from the day dieting has begun. Since this drive to eat is a universal response to distress, and food intake has a calming effect on the mind, the personality traits of many bulimics and obese people tend to be much more given to satisfying urges and impulses than anorectics. In this regard obese and bulimics are much closer to the drug user and abuser than the anorectic.

To their dismay many anorectics find out how strongly they are affected by this urge to eat when in the course of recovery this drive again becomes very powerful, thus confirming their worst fears of "getting fat." As discussed in Chapter 4, this has to be of great concern to the therapist and every effort has to be made to help the anorectic refrain from bingeing so that she does not feel the need to engage in purging as well. Unfortunately, many anorectics leave treatment early and wind up becoming bulimic.

Second, the bulimic is usually normal weight, if not suspiciously close to what our society considers "ideal weight." In contrast, the anorectic progressively loses weight and soon looks gaunt and emaciated, and the obese person is conspicuous by virtue of her overweight. Here, the bulimic occupies a place between obesity and anorexia nervosa not only in terms of absolute weight but also behaviorally, in that she would be obese if she did not purge and emaciated if she did not overeat.

Related to the issue of weight is the frequency of these conditions and people's acceptance of their respective eating disorders. The absence in bulimia of the societal stigma of being over- or underweight explains the extremely large number of young women affected by this condition and especially the incredibly large number of "secret" bulimics. To make matters worse, many bulimics secretly feel that they have found the ideal method of attaining a perfect weight and of enjoying the societal reward that goes with it.

Third, the bulimic's intermittent episodes of strict dieting and fasting and the use of vigorous exercise as a means of burning excess calories are clinical features resembling closely those of anorexia nervosa.

These similarities of bulimia with anorexia nervosa suggest the possibility that the motivational forces behind the strict dieting and exercising behavior of bulimics are linked to endorphin reward mechanisms. The fact that bulimics frequently change from one reward mechanism to the next, including the use of addictive substances, supports this idea.

But what about the most characteristic feature of bulimia, the three different purging behaviors: vomiting, laxative and enema use, and the use of diuretics? Do they constitute addictive behavior and are they biochemically linked to reward mechanisms as well?

The evidence, from two lines of inquiry, is quite strongly in favor of answering these questions yes. One is the evidence derived from examining the clinical features of bulimic behavior for signs of reward and other features characteristic of addictive behavior. The other line of evidence deals with biochemical data in support of the notion that bulimia, like anorexia nervosa, is mediated by reward mechanisms. It appears from these data that binge-purge cycles are in some ways related to endorphins; however, of greater interest is circumstantial evidence that all modes of purging may stimulate the endorphin system. Let us begin with a discussion of the clinical features and then proceed to a review of the biochemical evidence in support of endorphin mediation of bulimia.

ADDICTIVE FEATURES OF BULIMIA: CLINICAL EVIDENCE

The Binge-Purge Cycle

In examining the clinical evidence for addictive behavior in bulimia, we will start with the binge-purge cycle, the basic unit of bulimic behavior, which many bulimics go through many times in the course of a day. Since vomiting constitutes the most widespread method of purging, we will initially confine ourselves to this mode of "undoing" the binge.

If a bulimic is asked about her understanding of why she has to go through the binge-purge cycle, about a theory to explain her behavior, she will usually give the following answer. First, she feels an irresistible urge to eat, sometimes caused by hunger sensations but often just "for the head." Almost with the precision and rigidity of so-called instinctual behavior, she gives in to this "drive" and consumes large amounts of food, often of a consistency carefully chosen to facilitate vomiting. During the binge she experiences some satisfaction, but her guilt over eating and her fear of getting fat rise to extreme levels. Then, the bulimic would tell you, she induces vomiting to get rid of the food, whereupon she feels better and relieved that she averted getting fat. In other words, her theory is that she vomits out of guilt over having eaten too much.

But is this really all there is to it? The answer is no. There is much more to the vomiting part than most bulimics realize. Let's take the case of Kirsten, one of the first patients I treated. Her parents would actually instruct her to binge and vomit when their tolerance with her irritability, nervousness, and disagreeable bickering and arguing had reached a limit. I asked the parents, "What happens after she vomits?" They answered, "Well, she would be cheerful, calmer, easier to live with—at least for a while, maybe an hour," the parents said.

This suggested to me at the time that vomiting itself—not just the intake of food during the binge—might have a calming and relaxing effect on the mind. As I examined this possibility in the experiences of other patients, it became obvious that many bulimics are able to stop after eating just a little bit more than people would normally eat. But they extend their meals to a binge so that they are able to vomit.

If we combine the observations that vomiting has a calming effect and that meals are extended to binges to facilitate vomiting, it suggests that the act of purging may actually be very important—perhaps more important than the binge. The calming effect of the purge on the mind may actually be a reward stronger than that of food during the binge.

To the reader who has read the previous chapters on anorexia nervosa this must sound like a familiar theme. If there is a major shift from a state of aversive feelings, such as anxiety and/or anger, prior to engaging in a binge-purge cycle, to a state of relative calm and contentment after the purge, bulimic behavior would constitute a form of self-regulatory reward-mediated behavior. If this is so, then it is not surprising that this behavior is so irresistible and can lead to the full clinical expression of addiction, in which a person's life is dominated by daily binge-purge cycles.

Johnson and Larson (1982) conducted a quantitative study of behavior and moods of bulimics that confirms this pattern. The authors found that immediately prior to bingeing patients feel more irritable, weak, and constrained, feelings that get worse during the binge. However, after purging patients reported a state of alertness and absence of anger. Based on these findings the authors proposed the idea that bulimia is an attempt to modulate dysphoric mood states by excessive eating as well as purging, a behavior that can become addictive.

In fact, from a purely clinical point of view, without asking for a moment which biochemical substance may mediate this behavior, several reward mechanisms appear to be involved in the binge-purge cycle. Let us take a microscopic view of the typical cycle and see what a bulimic might notice if she observed her own behavior from the point of view that the binge cycle affects her feelings in a positive way. In other words, what reward mechanisms would she observe?

Most bulimics are able to identify this pattern of interaction between negative feelings and binge-purging behavior. However, for many bulimics this cyclic behavior is automatic and unreflected. In fact, many bulimics would like to shun responsibility by viewing their behavior as "seizure-like" activity during which they do not know what happens. If that is the case, delaying every step of the cycle for a while and turning one's observing functions inward towards feelings will reveal the pattern more clearly.

THE BINGE

Every binge-purge cycle starts with a state of negative feelings, a state of nonreward. These feelings may be a form of depression, emptiness, and dissatisfaction calling for a "vicarious reward." This is the case, for example, of the single working woman who after a day's hard work returns to her apartment and has nothing to look forward to—no children, no boyfriend, no date, not even women friends. Or the hard-driving student who returns from class in the late afternoon and has to muster the discipline to do extensive homework.

But the negative feeling state can also be one of nervousness and anxiety—in other words, a state of internal imbalance or disequilibrium that needs to be calmed down by a "psychological corrective reward." An example of this may be the same single working woman mentioned, who finally has a date, about which she is happy. However, she finds herself initiating a binge-purge cycle, this time because she is nervous about the evening and worries whether her date will like her.

A "corrective reward" is also needed if the negative feeling state is one of anger, tension, or hostility. For example, if anger is directed at the boss or co-worker who was critical of the bulimic's work, or if there is tension and hostility at home, often covert and unresolved, these aversive feelings demand some form of corrective reward.

There is a third form of reward that, often in conjunction with the above rewards, can trigger a binge. It is the "biological corrective reward" underlying the regulation of feeding. While the first two forms of reward mentioned above are "psychological" in nature, the third is a biological mechanism that is triggered by anyone fasting for more than about four to six hours, let's say. This mechanism is experienced as plain hunger, strong appetite, and an irresistible desire to eat, especially once food intake is begun. Most bulimics trigger this biological mechanism by delaying their first meal of the day to the late afternoon hours and are surprised that they are overcome by voracious hunger.

A brief experiment serves to illustrate this mechanism. The patient is asked to sit back, relax, and breathe regularly. Then she is told to hold her breath as long as she possibly can. When she virtually turns red in the face and gets the signal to start breathing again, she is asked to observe her breathing. Of course, she is hyperventilating and can't speak for a few seconds. When she compares her fast breathing with the pattern just before she stopped breathing, she realizes that hyperventilation is not her normal pattern. Rather, it is a physiological response of the breathing centers of her brain to compensate for the lack of breathing earlier in the experiment.

This situation confronts any dieter who abstains from food, including the bulimic who starves herself for the better part of the 24-hour day. Her body triggers compensatory mechanisms that force her to eat more than if she were to keep her food intake sufficient and steady. This corrective biological mechanism sometimes remains the only reinforcement that keeps a bulimic bingeing. Especially restricting bulimics of lower than ideal body weight yearn for the one daily binge when they indulge in food, even if anxiety and depression have receded as a result of therapy. All dieters, then, must accept the fact that no matter how powerful social fads may be, our bodies will set limits on the degree to which we can manipulate them, whether for the short or long term.

Let us return to the binge. The bulimic is confronted with the power of the need for any of these rewards, or a combination of them, and finds it difficult to resist. Food is the most ubiquitous gratifier and often the cheapest reward of last resort when all other forms of reward are unavailable. Food not only satisfies and thereby serves as vicarious reward, but also calms a person, probably due to some very simple mechanisms of digestion, if the person keeps it down.

But the reward of food satisfaction is of little help to the bulimic who fears getting fat. Therefore, her guilt and anger at herself increase as she eats and are kept under control only by her single-minded determination to get rid of the food afterwards. Without this assurance she might not binge. Furthermore, from previous experience her mind "knows" that after the purge she really feels better, an additional incentive to purge at all cost.

The nature of the binge food is not that important, except that its choice is quite fixed and idiosyncratic for every bulimic, often contains a large proportion of carbohydrates, and is selected for its ability to be thrown up easily.

THE PURGE

The methods of purging vary greatly and often bulimics use a combination of them.

Vomiting is the most widely used form of purging. Needless to say, bulimics find vomiting as disgusting and embarrassing as non-bulimics, so much so that most will avoid the word "vomiting," using "getting sick" or other euphemisms.

As is the case for all addictive behavior, the process has to be primed before it becomes habitual. Therefore, the circumstances under which a person learns to vomit can vary and have little to do with the maintenance and perpetuation of this behavior. Thus, a stomach virus leading to nausea and vomiting, sea or motion sickness, or "food poisoning" may be natural events after which the bulimic may get the idea of using this method after overeating. Unfortunately, the word-of-mouth mode is the most frequent method of initiating the binge-vomit cycle. In fact, many bulimics report group "pigging out" sessions in high school or college that have vomiting on the agenda as well, for vulnerable individuals a virtual induction ceremony to the bulimic club.

The method of vomiting induction varies as well, but often it is quite frantic and forceful if the bulimic fears that she might not succeed. Therefore, injuries to the fingers or the pharynx are not unusual, and the swallowing of a toothbrush is not unheard of. Only rarely are bulimics capable of inducing vomiting by triggering the nausea/vomiting mechanisms mediated by the autonomic nervous system through sheer willpower.

The beneficial anti-anxiety effect of vomiting on the bulimic's mind is not easily discernible. This is mostly due to the fact that the act of vomiting itself is a quite violent reversal of the normal functioning of the digestive apparatus causing an upheaval of the autonomic nervous system. However, beyond the physical stress involved, the bulimic feels disgusted and ashamed of herself, despite her satisfaction in having undone the binge. Underneath this satisfaction, though, hides the sense of calm and internal balance that constitutes the "psychological corrective reward" so much needed by the bulimic.

The use of laxatives as a purging method also begins in a variety of ways that are removed from their eventual addictive abuse. Serious dieting can lead to constipation, for which reduction of dieting, not the use of laxatives, is the treatment of choice. From this it is only a small step to thinking that laxatives can relieve an overextended stomach and that flushing food through one's digestive system will keep it from turning to fat. To what degree the digestive apparatus is a system of habit becomes evident when one realizes that some bulimics habitually use up to 40–60 laxatives a day, which have the same effect on them as one or two laxatives would have on the occasional user.

Similarly, the use of enemas often follows from the use of laxatives, but can become a highly ritualized procedure and a habit very difficult to break. The use of enemas can even become an addictive disorder by itself, not necessarily preceded by binges. For ages enemas have been used for the treatment of all kinds of medical ailments, and to this day enemas are part of the treatment plan of many spas and natural healing philosophies. However, the healing is more psychological than medical and, in view of the danger of priming an addiction, a high price to pay for a short-lived effect of feeling better.

The case of Rosalind illustrates this point. A 36-year-old, attractive woman, Rosalind was riddled by anxiety and anger, mostly related to her emotionally abusive husband, whenever she attempted to give up her addictive use of enemas. Several enema procedures now took up most of her morning, since she developed a delusional obsession that she had to make absolutely sure that not a speck of stool remained in her rectum after an enema, ostensibly to avoid getting fat. Towards this end she checked the inside of her rectum with her finger and other devices many times over. Nevertheless, whenever she had the physical sensation of stool remaining in her rectum, a sensation that easily could be caused by injuries to her badly tortured rectum, she was unable to resist taking another enema.

This otherwise perfectly healthy and non-psychotic woman developed this compulsion out of a pressing need to reduce her anxiety/depression. She became dependent on the physical manipulation of her bowels to achieve the desired anti-anxiety effect. Only secondarily did she form the obsessional delusion of having to check her rectum to justify to herself the many daily procedures. To make matters worse, since her habit interfered with a job, she was unable to support herself and had become dependent on a marriage that was devoid of rewards and replete with abuse and hostility.

A special variety of enema use is the self-administration of coffee enemas. Here the additive power of the usual plain water enema reward is magnified by the added effects of caffeine absorbed through the bowels. Caffeine is a known habit-forming stimulant which can lead to the condition of caffeinism. The effect of coffee enemas is described by patients as a unique calmness and sense of internal balance, quite different from the feeling of tenseness and "being wired" the same patients report after drinking coffee. Giving up the habit of coffee enemas is especially difficult because of the combined reinforcing power of enemas and coffee.

The use of diuretics, the third method of purging, produces a major shift in the body's fluid balance. Diuretic medication is usually prescribed to eliminate excess water from the body when the natural systems regulating fluid balance do not function, e.g., in cardiac conditions. Diuretics often are prescribed by physicians for the treatment of water retention occurring during PMS, the premenstrual syndrome. Unfortunately, some "diet doctors" prescribe diuretics for weight loss, which is not a medical indication for their use and is totally ineffective as a weight reduction method.

Diuretics are welcomed by bulimics in need of a magic pill that satisfies their need for instant weight loss on the scale. Even if the loss of 1–2 lbs. is the result of water elimination that is just as quickly reabsorbed by the body, the bulimic wants diuretics and cannot get enough of them. Since bulimics are intelligent and not easily fooled in many aspects of their lives, we must assume that some form of reward makes diuretics so desirable, perhaps the same "psychological corrective reward" that was discussed in conjunction with other modes of purging.

Binge-Purge Activity over Longer Periods of Time

So far we have taken a microscopic view of the binge-purge cycle and discussed evidence to suggest several reward mechanisms at work, of which the anti-anxiety effect, the "psychological corrective reward" after the purge may be the most important.

Now let us examine other features of the addictive process as it occurs in heroin addiction and see if they apply by analogy to the bulimic binge-purge cycle over the course of a longer period of time. Since these features of addiction were discussed extensively in Chapter 2, here we will make only a brief comparison to anorexia nervosa.

Essentially, the frequency of binge-purge cycles can serve as a measure of addictive behavior in bulimia the way weight loss serves as a measure of addictive behavior in anorexia nervosa.

VULNERABILITY

Before we discuss the long-term clinical manifestations of bulimia, let's look at how and where this condition begins. First there is the issue of vulnerability to addictive reward processes.

Bulimics are just as vulnerable as anorectics, by virtue of either their constitutional sensitivity or their distressing life situations, such as unhealthy family interactions or difficulties in adjusting to a new life situation. Bulimics also share certain personality characteristics with anorectics, such as narcissistic personality traits, self-esteem problems, and difficulties in negotiating their social environment.

However, bulimics are said to differ from anorectics along the dimension of impulse control. Bulimics are considered more self-indulgent and impulsive in their personality makeup, a view that closer analysis reveals to be not entirely correct. Bulimics and anorectics share the same precursor syndrome, a tendency to overeat in response to stress and distress. While the anorectic at some point decisively resists this impulse to overeat and goes on a strict diet, many bulimics give in to this impulse and soon adopt a mode of purging to avoid gaining weight. This has not always been the case, however, as is evident from the time before extensive media coverage publicly identified anorectics as sick. Then, most bulimics had a history of at least one bout of serious weight loss, if they had not actually succumbed to anorexia nervosa at some point in their lives.

This observation suggests that the personality differences between bulimics and anorectics may not be that important. What is called the overly indulgent trait of bulimics is just the flip side of the coin of overly restrictive anorectic behavior. Furthermore, restrictive behavior in anorexia nervosa is not a sign of health and may just be another form of "indulgence," the desperately needed pursuit of endorphin reward by starvation to cope with anxiety and depression. Thus, one can say that there is a "restricter" in every bulimic.

FIRST EXPOSURE: SLIMNESS AS A SOCIALLY ACCEPTABLE WAY OF FEELING BETTER

The setting in which the bulimic is first exposed to the idea of slimness is identical to the setting that predisposes anorectics-to-be to go on a diet. The values of the bulimic's family and social environment are identical, in that they emphasize slimness as a sign of social status and desirability and condemn any chubbiness. Thus, the first time a bulimic vomits or uses laxatives or diuretics after a binge, she does so with the intention of averting the dire consequences of her distress bingeing. And for the occasional binger the use of purging towards that end is not in itself addictive. However, the bulimic-to-be does not know that, by accepting purging as a mode of staying slim despite high calorie intake, she makes herself vulnerable to slipping into an addictive process.

TOLERANCE

If one takes a history covering years of a bulimic's life, one often makes the following observation. The frequency of binge-purge cycles varies greatly over stretches of months or longer, sometimes years. If one inquires about other events in the bulimic's life, one finds that low frequencies of binge-purge cycles or abstinence occur when things are going well, and highly active bulimic behavior occurs when the bulimic experiences serious distress or a high degree of anxiety and depression.

It appears that the need for reward derived from the binge-purge cycle is quite responsive to the overall reward state of the person involved. It also seems that the bulimic resorts to it only when there is a dire need for reduction of anxiety or a serious lack of satisfaction in life leading to depression. It is as if the bulimic pops a pill to make herself feel better when the chips are down.

When distress sets in, overeating is the first response, followed soon by a panic feeling over "getting fat," calling for the need to purge. The purging act, which may have been used only occasionally before, now becomes the principal reinforcer as anxiety and depression demand some form of relief. A vicious cycle is set into motion, as tolerance for the rewarding effects of the binge-purge cycle requires more and more frequent binge-purge cycles to achieve the needed correction.

The relatively short-lived reward effect of bingeing/purging may be the reason why this behavior fluctuates with other states of nonreward and reward in a bulimic's life. The fact that many bulimics will go through the elaborate and lonely procedure of binge-purging many times a day, taking up hours of free time, indicates that the rewarding effects of one cycle are relatively inefficient, indeed. Further, bulimia also has less momentum of its own than anorexia nervosa, where the addictive process tends to maintain and perpetuate itself even if external and internal causes of distress have lessened or disappeared. The fact that many bulimics, nevertheless, give a history of years of uninterrupted daily binge-purging, shows how chronically entrenched many bulimics are in depressing, distressing, or anxiety-provoking life situations from which they seem unable to extricate themselves.

DEPENDENCE

The change of values, beliefs, and moral standards occurring under the influence of rewarding substances or brain mechanisms, on which the person has learned to depend, is observable in bulimia as in anorexia nervosa and drug addiction.

It is interesting to note, however, that bulimics do not seem to develop the self-idealized belief system found regularly in anorectics around ideas of being superior and morally better than others. This should not take us by surprise. Bulimics primarily view their problem as one of indulgence in food and are very ashamed of their manipulations of their bodies for the purpose of purging. In that sense they are much closer to drug addicts or alcoholics, who are hard-pressed to see anything superior in their addiction—except the occasional alcoholic, perhaps, who hides his addiction behind the pride of being an exquisite connoisseur of fine wines and liquors.

Closest to a self-idealized belief system is the phenomenon of secrecy, to which most bulimics are devoted. They spend a great deal of thought and energy guarding their secret. To attribute this secrecy to shame and guilt does not quite tell the whole story. Many bulimics feel that they have a good thing going for themselves as far as the social advantage of slimness is concerned. To blow the cover on this secret would in the bulimic's mind not only cause her to lose the admiration of others but would condemn her to the category of sick and devious people. Therefore, most bulimics seek the solitude of their apartment or room and, often not without a sense of ceremonial pleasure, go through the ritual of a binge-purge session.

To illustrate the importance of secrecy, let us listen to the story of Laurie, a college student, 24 years of age, who "confessed" to me how her preoccupation with keeping her bulimic activities secret had ruined her life. After years of hiding, she now felt ready to do something about her addiction. Laurie always wanted to be liked and feel special in the eyes of others—teachers, female friends, boyfriends, and family—and she was willing to do anything for this approval, often to her detriment. But her bulimia had its own agenda. In college she was so busy keeping track day and night of all the lies she had told her women friends as to where she was and what she was doing that studying became impossible. She failed courses and was asked to leave college after a fair period of probation. Although she was popular and was wanted as a friend, long emotional arguments and discussions were necessary to mend her friendships. Some girls felt so confused, neglected, and hurt by her evasiveness that they gave up on their friendship with Laurie. To top it off, her boy friend, whose presence she had sought in college as a way of abstaining from bingeing and vomiting, finally called it quits, distraught and rejected, feeling that she was no longer interested in a relationship after having caught her in lies about her free time and whereabouts.

While she had almost grown accustomed to her parents' and sisters' distrust and suspicions about her secret bulimic life, her boyfriend's decision to leave her finally opened her eyes. In her words "everything important to her was gone"—college degree, friends, family, and boyfriend. It was time to abandon her bulimia.

Thus, bulimic dependence is evident from the way bulimics organize their lives around the ability to binge and purge, unimpeded by other people and activities. No matter how much they detest their addictive life-style, they find excuses to continue it and secretly wish that the world would change to accommodate their addiction.

However, bulimic dependence manifests itself in several other ways. First, there is the abandonment of responsibilities, such as job, school, and other obligations. Second, there is the funnel effect described previously, the forgoing of other forms of pleasure and reward, such as friends, hobbies of all kinds, and of other enjoyable activities, for the sake of food, the "best friend" of the bulimic. Similarly, manifestations of the reverse funnel effect are observable as well.

Third, there is the failure to recognize the real dangers of bulimia, not only in terms of financial losses and endangerment of a career. A sign of dependence is the persistence of severe bulimic behavior despite obvious real dangers to its victim's health. The most prominent danger is electrolyte imbalance, a shift in the concentration of body salts that maintain the body's internal chemical milieu and play a part in the conduction of nerve impulses. Bulimics know that changes in these electrolytes can produce abnormal heart rhythms and heart failure leading to sudden death, yet their persistent fear of such effects does not help them give up their habit. Their lives are also threatened by stomach rupture and esophageal bleeding from overextension. Most visible and disconcerting to the appearance-conscious bulimic, however, is a permanent damage to her teeth, the destruction of tooth enamel by the acidic gastric juices brought up with vomitus.

It appears paradoxical that bulimics, known to be health conscious and afraid of disease, will use the powerful defense mechanism of denial so typical of the state of dependence. As a consequence these serious dangers to their health do little to weaken the addictive power of bingeing and vomiting.

Of special interest are two signs of dependence unique to bulimia. These are shoplifting and hoarding, mostly related to food but often extending to other items as well, two frequently occurring behavior patterns that seem irrational, as bulimics readily admit. Habitual shoplifting and hoarding can also occur independently from bulimia and essentially follow the dynamics of yearning for and securing material goods. The paradoxical nature of this behavior is best described by St. Augustine, who in his *Confessions* (370 A.D.) admits, ''Yet I lusted to thieve and did it compelled by no hunger, nor poverty'' (Goldman, 1991).

Shoplifting is often considered a character flaw; it is not right morally and is against the law to boot. Likewise the bulimic must take full responsibility if and when she steals. Nevertheless, shoplifting in the context of bulimia must be understood as abnormal, illness-related behavior. The bulimic brain, having become dependent on a steady and large supply of food, will exert its powerful influence by causing the bulimic to secure the addictive substance, no matter what the consequences are.

Additionally, the extreme fluctuations of the nutritional state, shifting rapidly between excess and depletion, leave the brain centers regulating food intake in total disarray. Because of the predominance of a metabolic state of starvation caused by purging activity, it is not surprising that these centers signal the need to secure more food, no matter by what means, and to hoard food as well. Thus, the events in the central nervous system of bulimics leading to stealing and hoarding of food are not much different from those in the hibernating hamster, which gets the signal to hoard food as the days shorten and winter nears.

WITHDRAWAL AND CRAVING

Withdrawal and craving, the effects of abstinence on the mind and body of the addicted person, are the principal hallmarks of addiction. Not much has to be said about bulimia in this regard. The feelings of panic and agony experienced by the bulimic if she only attempts to delay the various steps involved in a binge-purge cycle are testimony to the addictive power of this habit. The pervasive sadness and sense of deprivation felt by the abstinent bulimic make her and any empathic observer truly believe that she has given up her best friend. Often there are endless attempts to renegotiate the acceptability of bulimia and a helpless subordination to the reinforcing powers of the binge-purge cycle.

If the bulimic's experience during withdrawal is not enough

evidence for the addictive power of bulimia, the reader is reminded that so far bulimia has been very resistant to treatment, especially over the long term. This is the case despite a wide armamentarium of conventional treatment approaches, including psychotherapy, family therapy, and medication. Awareness of the addictive principles governing this condition gives the bulimic the willpower to renounce her habit and to overcome the effects of withdrawal and craving during abstinence. However, before we proceed to the discussion of withdrawal and craving in the section on treatment of bulimia, we will review the biochemical evidence for the notion that this condition is mediated by brain reward mechanisms.

ADDICTIVE FEATURES OF BULIMIA: BIOCHEMICAL EVIDENCE

In examining the biochemical features of bulimia we will focus on the special role endorphins may have as the biochemical substrate of the addictive binge-purge cycle. At this point we do not have firm evidence that endorphins are the underlying addictive substance. However, just as in anorexia nervosa, there is considerable circumstantial evidence from animal and human studies that brain reward mechanisms play a role in bulimia as well. These studies are reviewed for the interested reader only and are not essential for the understanding of the treatment of bulimia.

As we review the existing literature on this subject we will take two different approaches. The first deals with general clinical investigations, in which either endorphin levels were measured or the therapeutic effects of endorphin receptor blockade were observed. The second, purely speculative approach deals with the question of whether the different modes of purging might have a physiological link to endorphin mechanisms and could thus explain any reward function purging may have on the bulimic.

Clinical Studies

Fullerton, Swift, et al. (1986) studied the plasma beta-endorphin response of vomiting bulimics to the ingestion of 100g of glucose solution. Their hypothesis was that bulimics may respond the way obese subjects were found to respond to glucose ingestion in an earlier study (Getto, Fullerton, and Carlson, 1984). However, unlike the response of obese subjects to glucose ingestion, which was a significantly higher rise of beta-endorphins than normal controls, bulimics did not have a beta-endorphin response to glucose higher than normal. But these bulimics showed an elevated level of plasma beta-endorphins before and during the experiment, unrelated to glucose ingestion. To examine this elevation of beta-endorphins in these vomiting bulimics further, Fullerton, Swift, et al. (1988) applied the same protocol to nonvomiting bulimics and found that beta-endorphins were not elevated, matching those of normal subjects.

This experiment indicates that bulimics differ from obese subjects in their normal beta-endorphin response to glucose ingestion. But more importantly, bulimics who vomit, unlike those who do not vomit, seem to have a steady-state elevation of plasma beta-endorphins compared to normal controls. Although these studies were not designed to examine the direct effect of binge-purge cycles on beta-endorphin levels, the results suggest that the elevated endorphin levels observed are related to vomiting in some ways.

Waller, Kiser, et al. (1986) found lower plasma beta-endorphin levels in ambulatory bulimics. However, because of loosely defined inclusion criteria and no mentioning of purging activity, nothing can be learned from this study about the interplay between the binge-purge cycle and endorphin activity.

Several studies addressed the question of endorphin mediation in bulimia from the vantage point of opiate receptor blockade. For example, Mitchell, Laine, et al. (1986) found that opioid receptor blockade with naloxone significantly decreased the amount of food consumed during bingeing episodes. Equally important is their observation that the effect of CCK-8, a synthetic octapeptide of cholecystokinin known to be a satiety factor, failed to significantly suppress binge-eating behavior in the same subjects. This finding tells us that bingeing is not due to a failure of the satiety mechanism, as some investigators maintain, but rather due to an activation of reward systems.

Jonas and Gold (1988) studied the effects of naltrexone, an oral opiate receptor blocker, on the frequency of binge-purge cycles of outpatient bulimics. Elaborating on an earlier study of theirs, the authors compared the efficacy of two dose ranges of naltrexone given for six weeks. They found that blockade of endorphins significantly reduces the frequency of bingeing and purging. Furthermore, they showed that the higher dose (200–300 mg per day) was much more effective than the lower dose (50–100 mg per day). Thus, the authors made an important point. The blockade of endogenous opioids requires much higher doses of a blocking agent than the blockade of exogenous opioids, which is known to occur at a dose range of 50–100 mg naltrexone a day. This fact was little known in earlier endorphin research and the cause of many ambiguous results.

Modes of Purging and Their Link to
Endorphin-Mediated Mechanisms

In the absence of studies directly examining the effect of purging activities on the endorphin system, it may be useful to review what is generally known about the role of endorphins in the physiology of vomiting and the physiological effects of laxatives, enemas, and diuretics.

First, it is noteworthy that all purging methods have one common feature. They produce a massive and sudden loss of body fluids irrespective of the different sites of action—stomach, bowels, or kidney—and different compartments of the body—stomach content, bowel content, and body water and electrolytes. Based on this observation, we can ask what happens if the body suddenly loses body fluids? Is there any model or physiological response that would shed some light on the role of endorphins in this situation?

One possible model is cardiovascular shock, which can occur after massive blood loss, but also as the result of bacterial products that render blood vessels incapable of moving blood through the circular system. Faden and Holiday (1979) have demonstrated that endorphin receptor blockade with naloxone is effective in counteracting the decrease of blood pressure associated with these conditions. These findings, which were confirmed by Gurll, Vargish, et al. (1981) and Allgood, Gurll, and Reynolds (1988), are suggestive of a role of endorphins in cardiovascular shock.

With these data at hand, one might ask the question whether, just like the loss of blood, the loss of body fluid from purging might evoke a similar stimulatory response of the endorphin system. At this point we can only say that the cardiovascular shock model may serve as an interesting analog for the fluid losses from purging and provide a useful hypothesis to be studied.

Similarly, the evidence for endorphin involvement in the physiology of vomiting is far from established. However, Kobrinsky, Pruden, et al. (1988) show that endorphins have an inhibitory role in the regulation of nausea and vomiting in cancer chemotherapy. Similarly, Lang and Marvig (1989) provide evidence that endorphin receptors may mediate inhibition of vomiting in another experimental design. If one generalizes from these specific experimental settings, one can postulate that, if endorphins have a suppressing function on vomiting, they might be triggered in response to the nonphysiological act of self-induced vomiting.

Let us now turn to the interaction of laxatives and enemas with the endorphin system? Certainly enemas (like blood-letting) have been used in the treatment of a variety of maladies and diseases since antiquity. And it is a good rule of thumb that, if humans used a certain treatment method for a long time, it must have done some good, even if the indications for such procedures were hair-raising by today's standards. Could it be that these procedures had a non-illness-specific, if only temporary, benefit mediated by the stimulation of endorphins? Maybe; we cannot yet tell.

But we do know that cells of the endorphin system are heavily represented in the guts. And we also know that for centuries the principal treatment of diarrhea was tinctura opii, an opium preparation, and that exogenous opiates cause constipation.

Therefore, it is likely that the endorphin system is part of the regulatory mechanisms of bowel functions. In fact, according to Hedner and Cassuto's (1987) review, endogenous opioids influence gastrointestinal motility and fluid/electrolyte transport, as well as gastric acid secretion. Thus, it is conceivable that the use of laxatives and enemas, essentially methods of artificially shifting bowel functions into the direction of diarrhea, will trigger the anti-diarrhea function of endorphins.

Finally, the use of diuretics: These drugs cause the kidneys to excrete more water than they normally would by interfering with the tubular reabsorption of sodium chloride. In other words, they produce a diuresis, an increased flow of urine, which in a body like the bulimic's, not burdened by excess water, creates abnormal physiological conditions. One of the many reactions to this event may be the secretion of vasopressin, a hormone that has a corrective effect on lowered blood pressure, as the name indicates, but that has also an anti-diuretic effect. Therefore, it probably is secreted to "correct" the diuresis caused by the pharmacological effects of diuretics.

The diuresis created by bulimics is of interest in the context of anorexia nervosa. Gold, Kaye, et al. (1983) documented a deficiency of plasma and cerebrospinal-fluid vasopressin in anorectics, who have long been known to suffer from diuresis. Bulimics who abuse diuretics seem to create the same diuretic condition as found in anorectics by virtue of their starvation-related low vasopressin levels.

Now, one might ask, where and how do the endorphins enter the picture? While endorphins have been shown to have a suppressing effect on vasopressin in rats (Van Wimersma Greidanus, Van Ree, et al., 1981), their effect on the regulation of vasopressin in humans seems to be gender-specific and to depend on the presence of female sex hormones (Johnson, Bower, et al., 1990).

While the information gained from these studies is limited, it becomes clearer from reviewing the literature on the physiology of body fluid loss that a triangular pattern emerges between fluid loss, vasopressin, and endorphin secretion. We saw that vasopressin and endorphins are released in response to a variety of changes in the circulatory system, although their mutual effects are not yet clear. Furthermore, it is possible that the vasopressin deficiency in anorectics is due to increased endorphin activity secondary to self-starvation. On the other hand, in bulimics the elevation of vasopressin levels secondary to diuresis may bring about a corrective suppression of vasopressin by increased activity of the endorphin system. Thus, the endorphin system may be stimulated by the use of diuretics, a speculative but intriguing possibility nevertheless. We will know if this is truly so when the direct and immediate effects of purging on the endorphin system are investigated.

I wish to end this section by citing a small study by Abraham and Joseph (1986–87), which was designed to examine directly the interplay between the binge-purge cycle and endorphin activity. More studies of this design are needed. The investigators measured in one patient before and after four binge-purge cycles the effects of naloxone versus normal saline on pain tolerance (probably in lieu of unavailable direct measures of endorphin activity), euphoria, depression, and anxiety using visual analog scales, as well as ACTH, cortisol, prolactin, and luteinizing hormone. The authors found that pain tolerance was increased by vomiting and blocked by naloxone, but not by saline. Vomiting was also associated with a decrease of depression and anxiety and an increase of ACTH and cortisol. These findings are highly suggestive of an endorphin-mediated reinforcement mechanism operative in bulimia. They will carry more weight once they are replicated in a study that includes additional measurements and more subjects.

This report makes another point as well. It shows that just listening carefully to the patient's experiences may sometimes produce very useful clinical insights, as well as research hypotheses. It seems that researchers often are guided in their design of studies by what their impressive, but also very expensive, laboratory equipment can measure, rather than by careful knowledge and control of clinical parameters.

THE TREATMENT OF BULIMIA

The principles of the treatment of bulimia are derived from understanding the underlying mechanism of addiction and have much in common with the treatment of anorexia nervosa. Therefore, it is suggested that the reader become thoroughly familiar with Chapters 4 and 5 on the treatment of anorexia nervosa. This discussion will mention only those aspects of bulimia in which the treatment differs significantly from anorexia nervosa.

Obviously, bulimia differs from anorexia nervosa with regard to the behavior triggering the mechanism of reinforcement or reward. The reinforcing role played by self-starvation in anorexia nervosa corresponds to the binge-purge cycle in bulimia. Aside from this difference and its practical implications, the treatment of bulimia does not depart substantially from that of anorexia nervosa. To facilitate parallel reading between the chapters on treatment of anorexia nervosa and this discussion, the same format and order will be used.

The treatment of bulimia entails the therapeutic triad, three distinct parts, all of which are equally important for an optimal outcome. The first two parts deal with the treatment of the bulimic state and include learning about the addictive process of bulimia and giving up binge-purge behavior. The third part of the triad deals with the treatment of the bulimic trait; this involves the therapy of faulty family dynamics as well as individual therapy.

Part One of the Therapeutic Triad: Learning about
the Addictive Process of Bulimia

When Jacqueline came for help, she had no understanding at all of the psychological and biological events that brought her to this point. Full of self-loathing, depression, and hopelessness, she had become a victim of a process that took over her mind and body once she had initiated it. When she had started to vomit to undo the effects of overeating, she knew that it was dangerous. But no one had told her *how* it might be dangerous.

The first step of therapy is to learn how the addictive process works. This task requires combining an intellectual, cognitive approach with an experiential one. The bulimic has to experience the reinforcing power of bingeing, but even more so the reinforcing power of purging, by observing the interplay between bulimic behavior and its effects on the mind.

Since denial and distortion are so powerful in any addictive process, the bulimic must agree to keep a daily log in which she records the nature and amount of food and fluid taken in, purging, states of mind, and exercising. The log is best kept on a letter or legal size sheet that has 24 hours marked down the left, short edge of the paper and provides columns for seven days of the week. Such an arrangement allows the therapist to scan each week for days and hours of highest bulimic activity and to focus on the distress the bulimic experienced during those times. This kind of log also serves as a reinforcement for the recovering bulimic when she observes the progression from sheets filled with entries indicative of heavy bulimic activity and emotional turmoil to sheets indicating greater control, distinct healthy meals, and less emotional trouble.

However, many bulimics find it difficult, if not impossible, to keep such a log. Whatever the reasons for these difficulties, they have to be overcome before there can be any progress in the treatment of bulimia. Acceptance and faithfulness in keeping a log are so important that the readiness of the bulimic for treatment and to some degree its outcome can be estimated from it.

Helping the bulimic see the connection between mood states and bulimic behavior requires some time and some experimentation with the various behaviors that compose this cycle. For example, the patient must learn to observe her various states of mind before, during, and after the binge. What state of mind makes bingeing such an urgent matter? Is it nervousness and anxiety, exhaustion from a day's work, loneliness, anger, worry, depressed feelings? What kinds of thoughts go with these feelings? What exactly makes her nervous, angry, lonely, or depressed? During bingeing, are there some calmer feelings at all, some form of reward from eating? If these feelings are overshadowed by guilt feelings and self-hate, look underneath them and observe what other feelings are there.

After bingeing she must learn to delay vomiting for a while and observe what thoughts are going through her mind, what she feels while she has those thoughts. Often these thoughts are apparent to the bulimic as they arise towards the end of the binge. However, they will become clearer if the bulimic is capable of delaying the purge. Strong feelings of anxiety, sometimes panic, associated with guilt, anger, and self-depreciation, are experienced by the bulimic while holding off.

While the bulimic may correctly relate these feelings to her fear of getting fat, something else is going on that may be of equal importance. These feelings and thoughts of panic are very much like those experienced by the anorectic when she eats more than her usual starvation diet. Bulimics are frequently in starvation mode as well, as Pirke, Pahl, et al. (1985) observed. The metabolic state of starvation may be caused by periods of starvation, by exercising, or by the metabolic effects of the previous purge. It is abruptly ended by the binge. Therefore, it is quite possible that the bulimic, like the anorectic, is momentarily withdrawing from whatever endorphins she stimulated during the state of starvation and experiences the panic and fear associated with withdrawal.

Finally, the bulimic has to observe her feelings and thoughts after whatever method of purging she uses, be it vomiting, laxatives, enemas, or diuretics. The "beneficial," rewarding effects of the purge on the mind are not easily discernible. But with some help the bulimic is able to identify feelings of calm and serenity beneath her feelings of guilt and disgust, a marked contrast to the anxiety, distress, and despair she felt before her binge.

Part Two of the Therapeutic Triad: Behavioral Aspects of Giving Up Bingeing and Purging

As the bulimic is experimenting with her binge-purge behavior and observes herself, she gains insight into its reinforcing and addictive nature. This process produces the first therapeutic results. It gives her a sense of cognitive control over her experience—she no longer feels victimized by some unknown psychological or biological dysfunction. The interplay of thought and feelings with the habitual manipulations of her body becomes understandable and even predictable.

However, her experimentation with and better understanding of her addictive behavior also set the stage for changing this behavior. And change in addictive states occurs only when the patient systematically eliminates one element after another of the behavioral repertoire that constitutes addiction, piece by piece.

Notwithstanding many promises made to bulimics, there is no easy or magic cure. The process is as difficult as anything bulimics have experienced in their lives. Nevertheless, it can be done and it must be done; there is no alternative.

Behavioral work on withdrawing from binge-purge cycles has to focus simultaneously on the two basic elements, the binge and the purge. Whatever method of purging the bulimic uses, it is easily identified as addictive behavior and she must abstain from it. However, in order to achieve this goal, the bulimic first has to abstain from bingeing. And that poses a major problem, since food is not easily identified as an addictive substance.

For the bulimic food is both a healthy and life-supporting substance, as for any non-bulimic, and a "bad" addictive substance. The bulimic finds many paths from using food in a healthy way to employing food as an addictive substance. Food has its own rewarding properties; it also plays an essential role in the addictive pursuit of the reward brought about by purging. Without food there is no vomiting. It is crucial to help the bulimic differentiate clearly between these two aspects of food.

To circumvent this problem patients receive several fixed daily menus of three small meals and a snack adding up to 1200–1400 kilo calories. These menus are prepared by a dietitian from the patients' preferred foods in such a way that they satisfy basic nutritional requirements. These menus constitute healthy non-addiction-related food, which the patient is instructed to eat at the prescribed times without modification. Second, this healthy diet secures the intake of essential nutriments, a deficiency of which the body would attempt to satisfy by demanding excessive food intake.

If the patient is unable to limit her food intake to this healthy diet and is compelled to binge, as would be expected initially, she is instructed to separate her bingeing activity from her healthy food intake by at least one hour. Rigidly maintaining this regimen prevents the bulimic from extending a healthy meal to a binge with all its consequences. Such an arrangement serves the purpose of clearly drawing a line between addictive behavior and healthy eating; she always knows when she is giving in to food as an addictive substance.

Once the patient is able to separate addictive from healthy food intake, half her battle is won. She can nourish her disordered body and mind with a balanced diet. By isolating her binge-purging activities she can examine them and reduce their frequency.

Reducing the frequency of binge-purge events inevitably leads to withdrawal from the addictive reward. Here everything applies that has been said about withdrawal from drug addiction in general and anorexia nervosa in particular. The patient enters a period of stormy emotions, struggling between the wish to give up her dependence and the wish to retain the addictive behavior.

This also is the stage where the temptation to lie and cheat is the greatest, calling for an attitude of acceptance and support by the therapist. It is important to remember that the patient is embroiled in an internal conflict fought by the healthy and addicted parts of her mind. Often the patient will externalize this conflict by attacking her therapist, parents, mate, or dearest friend with a variety of angry complaints. Taking these attacks personally and withdrawing from the patient is not the answer in these situations. An understanding and supportive stance, but without room for negotiation or compromise, is most helpful to the patient in overcoming her addiction.

Part Three of the Therapeutic Triad:
Treatment of the Bulimic Trait

By the time the bulimic approaches the withdrawal stage she should have achieved some understanding of antecedent psychological difficulties and her personality traits. This will give her a framework within which to see the evolutionary steps leading to her current dilemma. It also may already give her some sense of direction out of the life situation that caused her bulimia.

Most bulimics are somewhat older than anorectics and usually have left their families, if only to attend college or to pursue a working life. While the bulimic often lives independently, she is by no means independent from her parents emotionally or financially. She at best is pseudo-independent.

Much therapeutic work can be done individually, but often the patient's problems turn out to be deeply affected by her relationship with her parents and events of the past. Nevertheless, the patient—and unfortunately more often her parents—will resist the idea of family therapy. Every effort has to be made to overcome this resistance in the interest of the patient's long-term recovery.

Therapeutic work on acute life situations leading to anxiety or depression—or on personality traits—follows standard psychotherapeutic theories and methods and is based on the psychodynamics of the individual patient. Therefore, no further elaboration is necessary beyond the discussion in Chapters 4 and 5. However, to illustrate the therapeutic issues involved in the treatment of the bulimic trait, let us consider again the case of Jacqueline. Her therapy is summarized here to give an example of how one of the many possible psychological constellations leading to bulimia was resolved.

Jacqueline clearly was very depressed and hopeless when she came for treatment and started taking fluoxetine hydrochloride (Prozac), 20 mg a day, after her second session and continued for about six months. The medication significantly improved her ability to cope. However, Jacqueline also was very determined to make maximal use of therapy.

She realized how her self-esteem problems were at the core of her addictive bulimic behavior, in that she was riddled by anxiety when confronted with many aspects of her adult life. She may have had some genetic tendency to be oversensitive. But more troubling, she was exposed to, and had to live by, her father's depressive perception of life. She learned to feel deeply inadequate and unloved by him whenever she failed to meet his demands for a life of punitive work schedules, devoid of pleasures and full of paranoid vigilance to avert any possible danger.

Despite superior intelligence and willingness to work hard, she had developed four forms of unhealthy dependence. The most deeply rooted was her dependence on her parents. She had not yet developed emotional independence and autonomy, although financially she was totally self-supporting. Second, she was very dependent on her boyfriend, which contributed to the unhealthy relationship in many ways. Third, she had become dependent on her job out of fear of interviewing and leaving a safe place, even though the job offered her little opportunity for advancement. Fourth, she had become dependent on bulimic self-manipulation to cope with her depression, only to realize that her bulimia was about to ruin her life.

In the course of therapy she overcame her fear of interviewing and changed her job twice within a short period of time. She found a position where she was able to do the kind of work she had hoped to do, was respected by boss and peers alike, and earned twice the salary she had received on her first job. With her newly won confidence she also reassessed her relationship with her boyfriend, found it lacking, and left him. Her salary allowed her to leave the one-bedroom apartment she shared with two other roommates for an apartment of her own. Towards the end of therapy she met a man with whom she seemed to have a very good relationship and made plans to marry. She took the most difficult and biggest step towards emotional independence and autonomy when she stood her ground in the face of her parents' disapproval of her new boyfriend. In the end she actually managed to help her parents overcome their fears and threats of abandoning her and to accept the man with whom she wanted to spend her life.

Jacqueline had essentially given up her bulimic behavior soon after she started the second job. However, she tended to return to it with daily binges and vomiting whenever she was distressed by a new challenge, or when there was serious tension with her parents. However, towards the end of treatment she was able to handle major stresses, such as her parents' objections to her new boyfriend, without resorting to bingeing and purging.

At that point Jacqueline decided to stop treatment and to try it on her own. While Jacqueline had accomplished her initial goal of giving up bulimia, ideally she would have continued therapy to work on her driven and perfectionistic personality. However, most therapists would probably agree that, since Jacqueline was free of major symptoms, this was a good time to end therapy. Jacqueline needed to explore, live, and consolidate all the changes in her life.

Other Aspects of the Treatment of Bulimia

MEDICATION

As in anorexia nervosa, specific symptomatic drug treatment may be advisable should the patient be overwhelmed by anxiety or depression as she attempts to give up her pathological coping mechanisms. If the symptom of distress is primarily anxiety, an anti-anxiety agent may be indicated; for primarily depressive symptoms a selective serotonin reuptake inhibitor, such as fluoxetine hydrochloride (Prozac) or sertraline hydrochloride (Zoloft), is the drug of choice. From my experience, these compounds reduce the reactivity to the patient's individual stressful situation, as well as to the ubiquitous stresses of everyday life. Therefore, the patient's coping power, estimated on the basis of her reactivity to intrapsychic and outside events, serves as a useful measure of the drug's efficacy.

HOSPITALIZATION

Hospitalization should be considered only if a prolonged trial of outpatient treatment fails to bring about withdrawal and abstinence from bulimic behavior. Since the cases requiring inpatient treatment are most severe in terms of the underlying psychopathology, family therapy during and after admission in addition to individual therapy is essential to improve the chances for a successful outcome.

GROUP THERAPY FOR BULIMICS

Group therapy can contribute significantly to the treatment of bulimia and add to the treatment three features not available through individual sessions.

First, the bulimic has the opportunity to observe other bulimics at various stages of their treatment. This allows the bulimic to "look ahead" by observing how others deal with issues that she will face at some point. The bulimic also will "look back" to previous stages of her treatment as she helps novice group members to manage issues that she has learned to cope with previously. Thus, the group permits learning by modeling after others, and teaching as reinforcement of the therapeutic process.

Second, the group serves as a support network for its members. Mutual support and the benefit of calling on group members in times of severe distress are useful to the bulimic in view of her sense of shame and social isolation.

Third, just as the group process fosters support, it also leads to confrontational modes of interaction, from which addicts, including bulimics, benefit. Many bulimics find being confronted regarding issues of denial, rationalizations, and other behavior typical of dependence easier to accept from their fellow patients than from a therapist. The give-and-take of the group situation makes a confrontation less authoritative but equally effective.

7

Other Reward-Mediated Behaviors and Addictive Behavior Disorders

Hans Selye, known for his research on ACTH (adrenocortico-tropic hormone) and stress, once said that important discoveries in medicine are characterized by three criteria: The discovery is unexpected, the discovery is true, and the discovery can be generalized. He said this in 1976 when he accepted the International Kittay Award and reflected on the events surrounding major discoveries in the history of medicine.

Selye illustrated this idea with the story of the discovery of penicillin. At the time, Selye was working in a laboratory that was full of Petri dishes, small glass plates, containing several gel-like substances in which bacteria could grow. These growth cultures enabled physicians to identify which bacteria were causing the infectious illnesses suffered by their patients. From time to time unwanted molds would settle on these dishes and grow uncontrollably, much to the dismay of the scientists, since the laboratories had to be emptied, repainted and refitted before work could go on.

According to Selye, researchers in at least five different centers in the world had experienced the destruction of their bacterial cultures by fungi. It occurred only to A. Fleming in England that what appeared to be an unwelcome laboratory accident could point the way towards developing a medicine to kill these and other bacteria.

This is what Selye called "unexpected": an idea that resulted not from a long sequence of logical steps based on previous knowledge but rather from an entirely new way of interpreting and understanding the significance of an observation. Selye himself, like many others, had noticed those small areas where bacteria in Petri dishes had been killed and dissolved by the mold. But it was Fleming, unencumbered by existing concepts and knowledge, who made the leap into seeing a new significance in it and, by doing so, into a whole new era of medicine.

The second point Selye made about significant discoveries is that they have to be true. In other words, the scientific community must prove that an innovative concept is valid. In the case of antibiotics, Fleming and many other investigators later showed that certain fungi are indeed lethal to bacteria, a discovery that constituted the basis for all anti-bacterial treatment to come.

The third element characteristic of major discoveries is that they are generalizable. Fleming observed the antibiotic effect in the Petri dishes that he worked on. However, by seeing his observation in an entirely new light, giving it a new significance, he started an entire science of modern antibiotic therapy that had major ramifications regarding the knowledge of bacteria in general.

Selye's reflections were often on my mind as it slowly became apparent to me that the unexpected concept of endorphin involvement in anorexia nervosa might well be true, even though further proof and validation by the medical community are required. Suddenly all clinical features of this condition, as previously described by others, fell into their proper place. Like Hilde Bruch, many therapists had heard patients describe their addicted state when in the thralls of anorexia nervosa. But we missed the significance of our patients' descriptions. Only with the discovery of endorphins in general, and their functional link to starvation specifically, do the accounts of our patients make sense.

The initial surprise when a new concept is discovered and then seems to be true is enhanced by Selye's third characteristic, "generalizability," to which the next two chapters are devoted. It appears that the concept of endorphin stimulation as an unconsciously learned behavior to correct internal states of anxiety and depression, including its potential for addictive dyscontrol, can be applied to other human activities as well.

There is a dual and mutual benefit in exploring the interplay between other human behavior and anorexia nervosa regarding the role of endorphins. Some phenomena to be discussed fall outside of the immediate clinical context of anorexia nervosa but seem to support the notion of endorphin involvement in anorexia nervosa either by analogy or by clarifying certain aspects of this condition. On the other hand, the concept of endorphin reward in anorexia nervosa will shed new light on some forms of human behavior that are very different from anorexia nervosa, but may also be mediated by endorphin reward.

With that in mind, let us consider some examples of human behavior in which endorphins seem to play a motivating role. We will begin with behavior in which endorphins are stimulated by physical means. Afterwards we will venture into the more speculative field and discuss examples of human behavior in which the stimulus for endorphin reward is not physical but mental.

The Hunger Striker

Throughout history, imprisoned people have fasted, some to their deaths, as a powerful way to protest their imprisonment. One particularly dramatic event of this kind was the death of Bobby Sands, imprisoned for political reasons in Ireland.

Self-starvation is perhaps the most powerful political statement a person can make while in prison because it exposes the helplessness of captors. Except for being politically motivated, the mental process triggered in Bobby Sands by starvation was identical to that in anorexia nervosa. Quite possibly the distress and depression of prison life contributed to the perpetuation of his self-starvation because he felt less depressed and demoralized while fasting. He died when the authorities decided not to intervene by force-feeding him.

His tragic death is evidence that there is no brain mechanism to automatically stop self-starvation and reverse weight loss, even at the point of severe physical deterioration. With the onset of the final stage of coma, there is no conscious mental mechanism to halt the process. Nor does there seem to be a last resort physical mechanism to preserve life.

THE FAMINE VICTIM

General states of starvation or semi-starvation have occurred historically and continue to occur because of drought, political turmoil, or other reasons. This tragic human situation gives us the opportunity to observe the effects of starvation on the human mind and body under conditions other than anorexia nervosa.

Researchers of anorexia nervosa generally agree that there are few, if any, important differences between anorexia nervosa and other states of starvation regarding the effects on mind or body. In their book, *The Biology of Human Starvation*, Keys, Brozek, et al. (1950) extensively discuss biological and psychological features of starvation observed in the Minnesota Experiment, a study of starvation in human volunteers to benefit American soldiers during World War II. In their review of accounts of human behavior during famines of historically large proportions, a few consistent themes stand out.

One such theme is the ubiquitous preoccupation with food found among starving people. What is quite perplexing and unde- sired in the self-starving anorectic is more plausible in the context of imposed starvation. Anorectics know the power of this mecha- nism, which drives them to fantasize and read about food, to shop for and handle food, to do whatever they can to satisfy their mind's demand for food without actually eating it. This preoccu- pation is an adaptive brain mechanism that occurs in response to lack of food and proper body nutriments. Its survival value in famine becomes obvious if we think about general patterns of eating and food choice.

It is likely that one's childhood exposure to certain kinds of food establish preferential patterns for life. When people are starving, however, the incessant preoccupation with food helps them overcome these established food patterns, so that "inedible" foods become edible, if not appetizing.

Starving people constantly talk about food and engage in food-related activities, but also search for and gather food more intensely. For example, Keys et al. quote an account by Digby about the Indian famine of 1876–1878, where he observed women working for six to eight hours to secure a few handfuls of grain from ant holes. Preoccupation with food allows starving people to gather and eat grass, roots, insects, rodents, and other seemingly inedible substances. In some cases, to preserve life their brains command them to overcome taboos like eating human flesh or drinking urine. If we consider how deeply most societies honor such taboos, we can see how powerful this brain mechanism becomes when survival is at stake.

Not surprisingly, a second predominant theme is the reduction and cessation of sexual activities, including courtship, as well as the suppression of all activities incompatible with food-seeking efforts, such as marriage and social gatherings. These observations support the concept of the funnel effect of anorexia nervosa, only in reverse. In the case of famine victims we observe a reduction of all rewards for the sake of one reward, food.

A third observation of interest here is the lack of aggression and hostility. On the one hand, the accounts speak of a clear-cut disintegration of the social fabric, where children are abandoned and people desert their homes, moving around restlessly in search for food. Although this is a situation clearly conducive to aggression, suicides were rare. Rather, starving people were described as apathetic and dull, which Digby attributed to their physical debilitation. But when he describes people attempting to stay alive by picking up the grains that fell from rice carts, one might ask, what stopped these people from attacking the rice carts to get their hands on a real supply of food? Why this passivity and placidity?

In my view, famine victims do not lack aggression because of physical debilitation only. Rather, their minds are calmed and dulled by the universal survival mechanism mediated by endorphins. The effect on the mind of this mechanism may be twofold—a reduction of a sense of suffering and despair coupled with an exclusive focus on searching for food.

The reduced sense of suffering is evident in an almost humorous observation made by a visitor to a relief camp and quoted from Digby's account:

> I was very much struck with the grumbling, fault finding, quarrelsome spirit of the people. Some were quiet enough; they evidently had no strength to grumble or fight. But others, hundreds of them, swarmed round the visitors and complained of almost every possible thing. The quantity was not enough, the rice was not good enough, the addition to the rice was not tasty enough, the meals were not punctual enough. . . . Quarrels too were going on. (Keys et al., 1950, pp. 788–789)

Does that sound familiar to those treating anorectics? These people were grumbling while around them people were dropping dead—30 of 3,000 each day in one camp by Digby's account. The denial of danger evident in their complaints shows how far removed from the perception of death's reality they must have been.

Even the central nervous system arousal of phase III of anorexia nervosa seems to occur in states of famine starvation, as indicated in an account by Howard, quoted by Keys et al. (1950, p. 787). Writing about the semi-starvation in London, 1837–1838, Howard observes: "Notwithstanding general languor, however, the patient sometimes manifests a highly nervous state; he is startled by any sudden voice and worried by the most trifling occurrences."

In summary, people stricken by famine experience the same

physical and mental effects as do anorectics, but they benefit from this survival mechanism both physically and mentally. From all that we know to this date, the endorphins mediate an impressive array of adaptive changes that permit survival, or at least increase its chances. In contrast, anorectics selectively seek the benefit of endorphins for their anti-depressant and anti-anxiety effects on the mind.

THE JOGGER

Excessive physical exercise, especially in the early weight loss phase, is a ubiquitous behavioral feature of anorexia nervosa. During later phases of self-starvation exercising is reduced because of physical weakness; however, it is frequently resumed during recovery, often in an addictive fashion.

The earliest indication that endorphin secretion is stimulated by physical stress, specifically injury, was reported by Guillemin et al. (1977). Since then Carr et al. (1981), Farrell, Gates, et al. (1982), and Elliot, Goldberg, et al. (1984) have shown that physical exertion, both endurance and burst activities, are powerful triggers for endorphin release.

This link to the reinforcing effects of endorphins explains why joggers experience behavioral and mental effects that can become entirely consistent with addictive behavior. In fact, Yates, Leehey, and Shisslak (1983) suggested that, based on behavioral similarities between "obligatory runners" and anorectics, there may be a common reinforcer for both conditions, i.e., increased endorphin activity. The authors support their contention by showing that a small sample of anorectics had plasma endorphin levels much higher than chronic pain patients, known to be depleted of endorphins, but somewhat lower than women in labor, known to have high endorphin levels.

Responding to Yates et al. (1983), Blumenthal, O'Toole, and Chang (1984) conducted a comparative study of runners and anorectics based on the Minnesota Multiphasic Personality Inventory (MMPI). They showed that obligatory runners differ from anorectics in the degree of psychopathology; yet, they did not control for the severity of addictive behavior displayed by their subjects. They failed to appreciate that most obligatory runners are comparable to "obligatory dieters," who engage in dieting behavior but never reach the level of anorexia nervosa. These are the phase I anorectics, who do not feel depressed and are behaviorally quite similar to runners. In two case reports, Katz (1986) illustrated how serious long-distance runners can switch to addictive running under the impact of depression, a behavior comparable to anorexia nervosa.

The value of jogging and strenuous physical exercise is not an invention of our times, as is evident from the Latin saying, *mens sana in corpore sano*, that is, a healthy mind is in a healthy body. These few words express the wisdom of the old Romans, which prompted them to value athletes and physically active individuals. It is only today that we understand the biochemical basis for this idea, which has resulted in Western society's increased interest and obsession with working out to keep in shape.

When the interest in jogging developed 15 or 20 years ago, few people understood the secret benefits that joggers derived from their long, often lonely runs. Many people criticized and ridiculed joggers for spending so much time and energy on a seemingly useless and unproductive activity, which often resulted in injuries.

While strenuous physical exercise in moderation is health-promoting and highly desirable, it can become addictive very quickly in a vulnerable and distressed individual. Once the jogger, or anyone engaged in a serious aerobic sport, overcomes his/her initial reluctance to exercise, the activity becomes self-motivating, driven by the desire to overcome tolerance to endorphin reward. Very soon, as the endorphin effect takes hold and dependence sets in, a powerful thought invariably forces itself on the jogger's mind: "What if I could run the marathon!" This potentially addictive thought enters in the disguise of one of the most virtuous and heroic legendary events, Phidippides' run from Marathon to Athens, a feat that is commemorated at all Olympic games.

HEAT AND COLD STRESS

An integral part of the health and fitness movement is the exposure to heat in saunas and steam rooms. Originally cultures as geographically diverse as, for example, the Scandinavians, especially the Finns, and some North American Indian tribes made regular exposure to high temperatures a custom. Some people are also known to alternate their sauna bath with a swim in the ice-cold lake, thus exposing themselves to cold stress.

Could it be that these peoples found an effective, natural method of increasing their endorphins to promote their physical and mental well-being? It is quite possible, as demonstrated by Holaday, Wei, et al. (1978), who were among the first to show a link between endorphin stimulation and heat stress. Similarly, Bodnar, Kelly, et al. (1978) found that cold-water stress is a trigger for endorphin secretion, as measured by a reduction of stress-induced analgesia by naloxone.

It is not surprising that the use of sauna heat stress for the sake of general well-being became most firmly established in northern countries. The relative lack of sun in these countries is believed to be related to the high rate of alcoholism and suicide, a sign of greater vulnerability. Today the popularity of sauna bathing all over the world indicates that the reward mechanism involved is enjoyed irrespective of number and length of sunny days per year. A sauna bath alternating with a cold shower (just imagine the lake) appears to be a healthy and almost effortless means of achieving endorphin reward. The recovering anorectic may want to use this method instead of dieting, though she has to be cautioned because she has some intolerance for heat and cold stress if she still suffers from weight loss.

SEX

One would assume that sex, a function serving as important a purpose as reproduction and survival of the species, is biochemically linked to endorphin reward. In fact, Graber, Blake, et al. (1984) documented an inhibitory effect of opiate receptor blockade on male sexual response, and Murphy, Checkley, et al. (1990) found that naloxone inhibits oxytocin normally released by orgasm. This link between the opioid system and oxytocin is of special interest in view of the recently discovered importance of oxytocin in the regulation of sexual behavior (Caldwell, 1992), other phases of reproduction from pregnancy to lactation (Jirikowski, 1992), and maternal behavior (Pedersen, Caldwell, et al., 1992). Most exciting, though, is the observation that oxytocin promotes mother-infant bonding as well as social interaction and closeness (Carter, Williams, et al., 1992), thus linking endorphins to psychological phenomena.

Sexual activity can become addictive in vulnerable individuals, resulting in obsessive pursuit of sexual gratification irrespective of the quality of relationships or harmful consequences. Similarly, compulsive masturbation is a form of seeking frequent and habitual endorphin stimulation by achieving orgasm without a sexual partner.

PAIN AND TOUCH

If endorphins are part of the body's natural pain-killing system, one would expect that pain itself is a stimulus for endorphin secretion. One of the earlier studies supporting this notion was done by Willer, Dehen, and Cambier (1981). And Catlin's (1977) group was one of the first to document the pain alleviating effect of beta-endorphin intravenous infusion in cancer patients. However, it appears that only acute pain will cause a rise in endorphin levels, and that chronic pain patients suffer from an endorphin depletion.

This natural pain-killing mechanism is likely to be the underlying principle in a variety of behaviors that have the common feature of being self-injurious or self-stimulatory. The more severe forms of this behavior are self-injurious in nature and are rare (Winchel and Stanley, 1991). But painful stimulation of the body surface appears to be the principal aim of a variety of widespread habits and practices.

Trichotillomania, or pathological hair pulling, is one example of painful stimulation of the body surface, a grotesque and habitual behavior resistant to change (Christenson, Mackenzie, and Mitchell, 1991). The diagnostic criteria in *DSM-III-R* include an irresistible impulse to pull out one's hair, resulting in noticeable hair loss, and increasing tension immediately before pulling out the hair followed by a sense of gratification and relief afterwards. These criteria tell the whole story, if one conceptually links this painful activity to endorphin stimulation and views it as a form of self-medication.

However, there are milder forms of habitual stimulation of the pain receptors of the skin. These are usually caused by a need for tension reduction as well. These ubiquitous behaviors include "neurotic" habits such as nail biting, playing with hair, compulsive plucking of eyebrows, and the squeezing of pimples and other skin blemishes. The gratifying and irresistible nature of these activities, usually engaged in during states of nervousness or anxiety, suggests a link to some calming reward.

The skin is replete with sensors receptive to painful stimuli. As one would expect, these receptors are designed to monitor when the endorphin system has to be activated to control pain. Thus, even if pain is self-inflicted, the endorphin system is triggered, and with it the calming reward function of endorphins.

The good news is that these sensors also respond to very light stimulation, such as gentle stroking. The back rub or massage appears to be the most popular form of experiencing pleasure by skin stimulation and muscle stretching. But a slight, feather-light touch to the skin promotes an endorphin-mediated sense of pleasure far superior to any gratification derived from self-infliction of pain. It seems that a stroking session should be a regular part of our daily pursuit of well-being.

SEXUAL MASOCHISM

If the physiology of both sexual orgasm and pain includes stimulation of the endorphin system, it is not surprising that various behaviors aim at potentiating the endorphin effect by incorporating pain into sexual practices. One example of the infliction of pain to heighten sexual arousal is sexual masochism, in which the pain can be inflicted by oneself or others.

The case of Lola, a married woman in her forties working out of her home as a writer, illustrates this point. In the course of treatment for depression, we had discussed on several occasions that she frequently masturbated as a way of reducing her anxiety whenever she had to write magazine articles or proposals. One day, she revealed to me tearfully, with great embarrassment and shame, that she was inflicting pain on herself while masturbating. She had to hurt her nipples and vagina with surgical tools, sometimes to the point of bleeding, in order to achieve orgasm. She told me that she hates herself for this sick behavior and has not revealed it to anyone, including her husband.

After exploring her experience further, I told her that in light of the role of endorphins in pain and sexual arousal, her habit made perfect sense as a way of forcefully bringing about the much needed relief from anxiety. Lola realized that this behavior did not make her "crazy" or "depraved," as she thought. This permitted her to explore other ways of reducing her anxiety, which included an improved sex life with her husband.

THE BLUE BOY

"Autoerotic Death of Youths Causes Widening Concern," warns an article by Jane Brody in *The New York Times* of March 27, 1984, describing the death of teenage boys by self-strangulation. Sheehan and Garfinkel (1988) found that one-third of all adolescent deaths by hanging are not by suicide, as they are often labeled. These deaths are accidental and result from the sexual practice of depriving oneself of oxygen close to the point of asphyxiation by strangulation with a noose. The "blue boy" is a colloquial term for this behavior, which *DSM-III-R* refers to as "hypoxyphilia," the love of lack of oxygen. This latter term hints at the reward motivating this behavior.

Hypoxia is likely to constitute another form of physical stress to which the endorphin system responds with increased secretion. There is experimental evidence for this physiological interaction; for example, Stark, Wardlaw, et al. (1982) showed that hypoxia in sheep is a potent stimulus for the release of beta-endorphin.

PREGNANCY

The endorphin system seems to play a role during pregnancy and delivery. For example, Csontos, Rust, et al. (1979) found elevated plasma beta-endorphin levels in pregnant woman, while Demura et al. (1982) found higher beta-endorphin levels in placental trophoblastic tissue. Measuring plasma endorphin and ACTH levels during delivery, Furuhashi et al. (1983) found elevation of both substances in comparison to normal controls. Thus, it seems that endorphins play a physiological role in facilitating the course of pregnancy and during delivery.

However, if endorphins are increased during pregnancy, they have to come down again, which, in part, may be the cause of postpartum depression. It is likely that this sudden state of serious depression occurring in some women after delivery may be related to the precipitous withdrawal of endorphins.

On the other hand, the endorphin effect during pregnancy might be why some women would be happy to be pregnant many times over if it did not involve bringing up another child.

For some women pregnancy can serve as a form of self-medication against serious depression. For instance, a couple sought my help for their marital difficulties. Their problems centered on the wife's singular desire to go on having children after their sixth child. This desire was not shared by the financially exhausted husband, who took the long-term view and calculated his earliest retirement age by adding 30 years to each recent addition to his family. However, the wife had good reasons for her wish to have more children. The family history revealed a strong genetic disposition for serious depressive illness, and the wife admitted that throughout her adult life she felt best during the times of pregnancy and nursing. In a way she had become addicted to the state of pregnancy.

Another woman, Abby, illustrates how higher endorphin activity during pregnancy can affect a woman with bulimia. Abby had been very sensitive as a child and, since late adolescence, had suffered from many anxiety attacks associated with thoughts of doom and gloom. She had a history of bulimia for several years prior to treatment with me, but told me that while she was pregnant and nursing her first child she did not have to go through her binge and purge cycles. And, she said, it was not through willpower, to protect the baby from the ill effects of bulimia; rather, it came quite easily. However, as soon as she stopped nursing she felt "blue" again; the anxiety attacks returned and with them the need to binge and purge.

In treatment Abby soon was able to abstain from bingeing and purging, but she continued to suffer chronically from quite severe anxiety. When she became pregnant again with her second child, the anxiety attacks promptly stopped, except for an occasional, not unusual worry or fear about the health of the baby she was carrying. After she stopped nursing her second child, her anxiety returned with greater frequency and intensity, and she was afraid that bingeing-purging might become irresistible again. But she was able to resolve some of her personality difficulties and, with the help of regular exercises and learning to pace herself, left therapy with a sense of mastery over the symptoms of her past.

8

Anorexia Nervosa and
the Convent

WHEN I REFLECT on my years of treating patients with anorexia nervosa and bulimia I realize that most patients left me with a few lasting impressions. Naturally, of the many reasons for making an encounter unforgettable a frequently occurring one is that I learned something new and important.

One of these encounters was a family session with Cecil, age 16, and her parents, very religious Catholic people. While the parents were struggling to come to terms with their daughter's relentless pursuit of thinness and the personality changes that go with it, her father exclaimed, in despair, that if their daughter were not an anorectic, she would make a perfect nun.

This spontaneous observation appeared surprising, since the notion that anorexia nervosa might be in some way related to sisterhood in a religious order appeared truly farfetched. But at the same time it somehow rang true. Little did this father know at the time—nor did I—that his observation would turn out to be the point of departure for my venturing into an entirely new area of reward-mediated and potentially addictive behavior.

It is quite striking that many anorectic women display patterns of behavior and personality changes that are very similar to those conventionally ascribed to women devoting themselves to a life in a religious order. In fact, it appears that most anorectics will almost naturally fit into and benefit from the lifestyle of nuns in a convent. Let us examine these features.

FEATURES OF CONVENT LIFE

Spiritual Life

We will start with the spiritual life and religious content, the most important feature and principal purpose of convent life, although the reader may find linking this feature to anorexia nervosa conceptually most difficult. It encompasses a set of religious beliefs within which members seek to devote their life to God, seek faith, and are promised salvation and rescue from falling from God's grace.

However, there is a conceptual link. The attitudinal and spiritual practices fostered and strived for in a religious order have their counterpart in the anorectic's belief system, which she develops as a result of her dependence on endorphins. She becomes convinced that she is pure and beautiful, unencumbered by a life of human mediocrity and desires of the flesh. This self-idealizing belief system justifying her abstinence from food is of major importance to the anorectic's newfound identity and, in fact, is a cause worth the role of a martyr.

The Vows of Poverty and Chastity

The vow of poverty, the renunciation of worldly goods and other pleasures, and the vow of chastity or celibacy, the abstinence from sexual activity, are principal precepts of most Catholic orders. They constitute the basis of an ascetic life-style found in different forms and to various degrees in other religions as well. Asceticism serves one purpose, the withholding of worldly rewards for the sake of pursuit of one singular reward, the reward of spiritual enlightenment and/or salvation.

Similarly, anorectics deprive themselves not only of the pleasure of eating but also of many other enjoyable aspects of life.

Without a religious motive in mind, anorectics experience the funnel effect, a contraction from the usual range of worldly pleasures and rewards to the singular pursuit of endorphin reward. As her pursuit of endorphins becomes the primary motivating force in her behavior, the anorectic treats almost all pleasures as if they were food. The anorectic abstains from sex, not only for reasons of discomfort with intimacy or for the sake of moral purity, but also as a result of the mental and physiological effects of reduced sex hormones.

Giving to Others

Giving to others—more than one takes—is another important ingredient of the spiritual life of convents. Serving and helping one's fellow man and accepting tasks that are shunned by others have been part of the calling of virtually every sisterhood and order.

We observe the wish to give to others in many varieties in anorexia nervosa as well. For example, anorectics not only hold demanding jobs, but strive for superhuman feats of performance while eagerly absorbing every possible menial task from their co-workers. Outside of the workplace they derive much moral satisfaction from exhausting themselves in helping troubled family members or friends far beyond the call of duty and their emotional and physical strength. However, they do not engage in this behavior just to seek a high level of physical activity or to counteract their restlessness and take their minds off food. Rather, these are signs of the reverse funnel effect, causing the anorectic to need—and justify—an ever greater endorphin reward to compensate for her hardship.

Fasting and Penance

Fasting is a regular element of the ritual life of convents and religious life in general. In fact, fasting has an almost ubiquitous role as a means of spiritual enlightenment in the history of mankind. All major religions, however different from each other, know of the beneficial effects of fasting on the mind.

Fasting, the hallmark of anorexia nervosa, is used by the anorectic as a physical means of stimulating the endorphin system to enhance her coping power. The universal inclusion of fasting into religious life suggests that physical means to improve coping have been adopted to complement the spiritual message of salvation.

Another example is penance, the ritual of undergoing punishment to redeem oneself for sins after confessing to a Catholic priest. If intense physical exertion is chosen as penance, its calming effect on the mind may be as much related to the stimulation of endorphins as the religious significance of redemption.

A powerful illustration of penance by enduring physical exertion and pain is given in the beautiful movie, *The Mission*. It tells the story of a Catholic missionary's desperate attempts to defend a tribe in the Amazon, converted by him to Christianity, against the land interests of the Spanish throne. The missionary's only and closest ally in this battle is a Spaniard from the provincial capital. This man had killed his brother in an act of jealous vengeance and had gone into a deep depression. He undergoes penance in the form of dragging a huge weight, made up of heavy metal pieces, many times up and down the jungle cliffs bordering the water falls near the mission. Finally, when he breaks down in exhaustion and tears, he finds his peace of mind as he is absolved for his sins. He later becomes a priest himself, but loses his life in a fierce battle defending the mission and the tribe against eradication by Spanish soldiers.

This form of penance, the endurance of physical exertion solely for the purpose of promoting physical exhaustion rather than serving God or the community in some way, makes it obvious that the endorphin-releasing nature in the interest of the penitent's peace of mind is of primary importance. Thus, the religious ritual of penance incorporates a form of natural therapy for the relief of guilt and depression.

The Vow of Obedience

Religious orders rigidly structure a novice's spiritual life, not only regarding religious content, but also concerning her conduct, attitudes, and values. This takes place in a well-defined hierarchy in which all nuns vow obedience to the mother superior.

Such an environment would fit the needs of the anorectic extremely well, since she usually is racked by concerns over good and bad. Furthermore, being relieved from making decisions by the structure of convent life would comfort the anorectic, who lives with so many self-doubts that decisions are not easily made and never seem right once they have been made.

The Nun's Protection by the Order

The order protects its members by providing for all needs of daily life—shelter, food, and financial security. It is very likely that, in the past, this factor entered into the considerations of some young women, or their families, in contemplating a life devoted to sisterhood.

Many anorectics, especially those afraid and anxiety-ridden over entering adulthood, would find a sheltered life appealing. The order would support them and provide for all phases of their life cycle, including their social life. All possible fears and anxieties about living independently from the family and establishing an identity within the adult world would be averted.

The situation of a young woman unfit for autonomous adult life is very beautifully depicted in the play and movie, *Agnes of God*. It tells the story of a young, child-angel-like nun, Agnes, who as a child was traumatized by neglect and abuse and found shelter and protection in a convent under the leadership of a wonderfully wise and humane mother superior. When Agnes becomes mysteriously pregnant, she delivers the baby secretly in her room and kills it in a state of psychosis. The incident is investigated by a court-appointed psychiatrist, a smart, dedicated, energetic and attractive woman, who stands with both feet in the world.

The story is an outstanding example of the interpersonal dynamics between these three prototypical women, who, it seems, have found a place in life that meets their needs. With her vulnerability Agnes would not have felt anywhere else as protected as in a convent; the psychiatrist, a life-embracing, independent woman capable of fending for herself, probably would have found convent life difficult; the mother superior had experienced a full life, but had chosen at some point to devote her life to God by entering the convent.

To summarize: given the basic tenets of sisterhood, the anorectic might not find it difficult to become a nun. She actually would benefit from the lifestyle of a convent. Has she not implemented some of the rules for herself, without ever being initiated into a religious order? In the past the choice of entering a convent may have offered the vulnerable young woman a socially acceptable alternative to living an independent adult life. Today such a woman is more likely to succumb to anorexia nervosa once she initiates weight loss to "better" herself, as she fights her overeating associated with depression and distress.

Two Saints

Is it possible that in the past many women, who devoted their lives to sisterhood, not only were as vulnerable as anorectics but were in fact anorectic without ever having been identified as such?

Certainly the step from fears and anxiety over growing up to some form of asceticism is not a big one. In our times many adolescents deal with their sexuality and freedom of choice over many issues of conduct by becoming overly moralistic or religious, as many clerics will testify. And changes in dietary habits, such as abdication of meat and various degrees of vegetarianism, are often undertaken for ethical reasons but can lead to or become a disguise for anorectic behavior.

In fact, there are historical examples of women who chose a religious ascetic life and became anorectics (if diagnosed by today's clinical criteria).

Lacey (1982), for example, discusses the thousand year old legend of St. Wilgefortis, the bearded saint. She was the daughter of the cruel and tyrannical King of Portugal who spoiled her father's plan to marry her to the Saracene King of Sicily by giving her life to God. She overcame her appetite as an expression of selfless love of God. According to one source quoted by Lacey, "she begged the Lord to deprive her of all beauty and God granted her prayer" by causing her to develop a hairy body and grow a beard. She renounced her femininity by starving herself "in order to preserve her virginity." Hence her name, St. Wilgefortis, derived from "virgo fortis," the strong virgin. She was crucified by her father but word of her overcoming of "the passion that encumbrance all women" (things suffered by all women) spread as a cult around Europe.

As her name changed to St. Ontkommena in the Netherlands, St. Kummerniss in Germany, St. Uncumber in England, St. Liberata in Spain, she became the patron saint for women's problems. Lacey wonders, though, whether St. Wilgefortis is not one saint with many names but the story of many young women with different names, who had developed a similar illness with similar clinical histories, namely anorexia nervosa. My guess is that St. Wilgefortis is one saint with many names. But the spread of the St. Wilgefortis cult over Europe is an indication of the appeal her choice of life had for many women of the times who, as most names indicate, were "deeply burdened" (cumber, Kummer) by the role of being a woman.

St. Wilgefortis abdicated worldly pleasures such as food and sex and devoted her life to God in order to avoid a prearranged marriage. We assume that she became anorectic because she grew a beard, a form of masculinization well-known in chronic anorexia nervosa. This legend is also a testimony to the powerless status of women and the dependent role of children at the time, two forms of social injustice that have, sadly, survived to our times.

We have a second, more reliable report, which is the biographical account of the ascetic life of St. Catherine of Siena, a 14th-century virginal saint. She wrote her own life story, which also was recorded by her confessor, Raymond of Capua. According to Rampling (1985), St. Catherine of Siena had all the classic symptoms of anorexia nervosa. The antecedent factors leading to her anorexia nervosa were a strong symbiotic relationship with her mother, who anxiously watched over her daughter's physical appearance as the road to marriage, and Catherine's rebellion when she abstained from food to avert the "sin" of attractiveness.

Catherine's motive for self-starvation differed from the usual motive of contemporary anorectics, who seek attractiveness through weight loss. But the results were the same: The addictive cycle of self-starvation was initiated. Not only did Catherine starve herself but, despite her confessor's attempts to dissuade her, she was compelled "to let a fine straw or some such thing be pushed far down her throat to make her vomit." In other words, St. Catherine was also bulimic. Catherine's description of her starvation-induced ecstacy, as she experienced the yearned-for union with the Lord, is much more vivid and brilliant than any account of the endorphin induced "high" an anorectic of our times might give.

Now, as we have established a link between anorexia nervosa and elements of religious life in the convent and two saints, one might ask: How does this add to our understanding of anorexia nervosa?

First, we see that the mental benefits of fasting are not unique to anorexia nervosa. It has been practiced for ages in many religions as part of the armamentarium to achieve a sense of mental well-being.

Second, the Church has long known about the dynamic interactions of reward. Depriving a person of the pleasures of the world and flesh is essential if one is to induce him/her to pursue the singular reward and pleasure of a life for God. The anorectic unconsciously adopts the same principle when she falls under the control of endorphin addiction. Her rescue is not God, but the endorphins.

Third, the behaviors and attitudes members of a religious order strive for are not in themselves signs of addiction, despite their similarities to anorectic behavior and attitudes. One can assume that in sisterhood there is usually moderation in applying the precepts of the order, and that the novice is guided in her handling of potentially addictive behavior. One could imagine, however, that excessive, addictive pursuit of any of the precepts discussed might occur with some regularity, especially among those sisters who are vulnerable because of depression. As the examples of two saints show, unguided exposure to behavioral and spiritual precepts of religious life can lead to profoundly addictive behavior.

Now what about the reverse: How does our knowledge about anorexia nervosa add to our understanding of religious life?

In most general terms, religious beliefs, customs, rituals and institutions have traditionally provided what any vulnerable person, including the anorectic, is yearning for, i.e., rescue. Being exposed to depression and anxiety, the anorectic has inadvertently learned to provide rescue for herself, albeit in an unhealthy, self-destructive manner. To illustrate this point, let us briefly recapitulate the four elements of our basic model of anorexia nervosa:

1. The anorectic vulnerability, her difficulties and fears of dealing with adult life, and the ensuing states of anxiety and depression that demand a remedy.
2. The learned behavior of physical self-manipulation by self-starvation to achieve endorphin reward, and the improved coping resulting from it.
3. As the anorectic becomes addicted and dependent on endorphins, the development of an idealized belief system of self-rescue justifying her starvation state.
4. Eventually, the realignment of the anorectic's hierarchy of rewards and values by subordinating previous rewards and values to the pursuit of endorphin reward.

Now, if we compare these with some basic aspects of religious life, as exemplified by a convent, we find the four elements of our anorexia nervosa model represented. However, like a mirror image, they take on the form of meeting the anorectic's needs, or those of any vulnerable person:

1. Provision of shelter, a social setting with hierarchic structure, and rules of conduct.
2. *Physical* means of achieving endorphin reward as part of religious customs and rituals that include fasting.
3. Provision of a *psychological* form of reward, a message of salvation, and guidance in living a life for God as a means of rescue from sins and human frailty.
4. A realignment of usual rewards and values by subordinating these to the specific psychological and physical rewards offered by the convent.

Using these four elements of convent life as a point of departure, we will expand on the concept of reward-mediated behavior and its potential for addictive dysregulation. As the reader will see, this exploration will establish a link to serious clinical conditions associated with religious and nonreligious life, which encompass a blend or variations of one or several of these four elements. These conditions are notoriously resistant to treatment, unless they are identified as belonging within the conceptual framework of reward-mediated behavior.

Without doubt, life in a convent is beneficial to its members once one accepts its basic premise. The question arises, however: How is it beneficial? Do these basic elements of convent life constitute some form of brain reward—perhaps related to the endorphin system in some ways?

One probably would find few problems with the *physical* means of endorphins stimulation, of which fasting and physical penance are examples, but which include many more religious practices, ranging from chanting, dancing, and dance-induced trance states, to self-flagellation and other forms of self-afflicted pain and injury, which are practiced in Christian and other religions.

PSYCHOLOGICAL MEANS OF ENDORPHIN STIMULATION

However, how about the provision of an ideational, spiritual belief system that promises rescue for the believer and gives a sense of hope? It is easy to see how spiritual life constitutes a form of reward. However, the role endorphins play in this form of reward is more problematic. Religious belief, faith, and hope are mental phenomena that reside entirely outside of the physical realm. How could they be linked to physiological reward mechanisms?

We all experience some form of mind-body interaction, of which one example is the anxiety reaction. For many people a simple thought of a frightening situation can suddenly cause heart palpitations, hyperventilation, butterfly feelings in the stomach, all physical changes brought about by a plain thought. Similarly, we know that reassuring, pleasant, and unworried thoughts are capable of calming those same feelings of anxiety. In other words, our body, the anatomical site of good and bad feelings, also reacts to calming thoughts, expectation of relief, and hope. The following experiments illustrate how these reactions might be mediated by reward centers of the brain, some of which involve endorphins.

The Placebo Effect

This elegant experiment, conducted by Levine, Gordon, and Fields (1978), documents a psychological trigger mechanism for the pain-killing action of endorphins. Several volunteers, who had undergone impacted wisdom tooth extractions, were told that they would receive morphine, placebo (a tablet that tastes like medicine but contains no pharmacologically active ingredients), or naloxone (the endorphin-blocking agent). All subjects were asked to indicate on a visual analog scale how much pain they felt at various points during the experiment. Later on, the subjects who had received placebo were given naloxone and again asked how much pain they felt.

The results were remarkable. Those who had received morphine reported fairly little pain, as would be expected from the known analgesic property of morphine. Of those who had received placebo about one-half reported little pain, as if they had received morphine, and the other half felt considerable pain, as if they did not receive an analgesic. The test came when both placebo groups received naloxone. The group that had felt a placebo pain-killing effect reported a marked increase of pain after receiving naloxone. The group that had not felt a placebo pain-killing effect continued to feel considerable pain.

This experiment indicates that the placebo responders, those who expected and "believed" in pain relief from the placebo pill, secreted endorphins, which when blocked by naloxone became ineffective so that the subjects felt pain again. The subjects who did not have the capacity to respond to the placebo, the "doubters," did not trigger endorphins, and therefore, they felt pain from the beginning of the experiment without being affected by naloxone.

This intriguing experiment, validated by Grevert, Albert, and Goldstein (1983) in a different study design, indicates that the placebo effect of pain control may be due to the expectation of relief from pain, a psychological trigger of endorphin secretion. Clinicians have long known about the great variety of individual responses to pain, the role of the mental state in the perception of pain, and the placebo effect, but only now do we have some idea of the mechanism behind these clinical observations.

Meditation and Prayer: The Relaxation Response

The second example for the attainment of brain reward by psychological means is the effect of calming thoughts on the body mediated by the relaxation response. Prayer and meditation are an essential ingredient of spiritual and religious life and there is little doubt that the altered state of consciousness experienced during meditation and prayer does have a calming effect on the mind. Benson (1976) has shown that this calming effect on the mind has a physical equivalent, a calming effect on the body.

In his book, *The Relaxation Response*, Benson reports on the relaxing effects of meditation. He shows how practitioners of Transcendental Meditation are able to calm body functions, such as breathing, heart rate, and blood pressure, and to improve oxygen consumption. These body functions tend to respond to excessive stress in an unhealthy way, thus contributing to the development of hypertension and other stress-related illnesses. Benson postulated that there is an innate physiologic response in humans, the relaxation response, that protects against, and is diametrically opposite to, the fight-or-flight response triggered by "over-stress."

While the relaxation response can be observed through measurable changes of body functions, its effects on the mind are subjective and result in an altered state of consciousness. Practitioners of meditation have described this altered state of consciousness as feelings of pleasure, peace of mind, total relaxation, clairvoyance, and ecstasy.

Most fascinating, though, is Benson's observation that the instructions for meditation recorded in the spiritual literature of all ages are very similar, no matter how far apart and different the religions are. Thus, one finds common elements in meditation techniques taught by the great Eastern religions and philosophies, such as Yoga, Zen Buddhism, Taoism, as well as by Western Christian teachers, such as St. Augustine, Martin Luther, the monks on Mt. Athos, Greece, as well as those taught by Judaic traditions.

Out of these teachings Benson developed a simple and effective technique of bringing about the relaxation response. The procedure essentially has four elements: a quiet environment, an object to dwell on (such as the word "one" said silently while concentrating on breathing), a passive attitude, and a comfortable but not sleep-inducing position. This technique is very useful to simply relax or to treat clinical conditions such as high blood pressure and other stress-related illnesses.

Thus, Benson established a physiological link between meditation and prayer and their calming effect on a variety of body functions. Benson conducted this research in the pre-endorphin era, but later explored the role of endorphins in the mediation of the relaxation response. He found that naloxone administration interfered with the subjects' capacity to achieve a state of meditation deep enough to produce relaxation (personal communication). While the rewarding nature of prayer and meditation on mind and body is without question, this observation does not shed light on the role of endorphins in this process.

Now, if we apply the clinical observations of the placebo effect and the relaxation response to the religious realm, we arrive at a useful model for the achievement of brain reward by spiritual, psychological means. "Expectation" of pain relief translates to "hope" and "faith," a mental attitude of confidence and trust that we will attain what we desire. Meditative relaxation has its equivalent in peace of mind, if not joy and ecstasy. In religious life the message of salvation or rescue gives the believer hope, a most reassuring feeling for the worried and anxious mind.

With this model in mind, let us explore conditions in which the pursuit of reward in religious life has become excessive, i.e., addictive. This is of interest, since such conditions shed light on a vast variety of everyday-life obsessions and addictive behavior.

Religious Obsession

The well-known condition of religious obsession illustrates how some individuals escalate their religious pursuits to ever more intense levels. This is similar to the overcoming of tolerance in drug addictions, when any given amount of a drug soon has to be increased to achieve the desired reward effect.

As a result, religious pursuits can assume such excessive proportions, often in the form of persistent preoccupations and rumination, that they qualify for the clinical condition of obsession. In these cases it often requires the services of a minister or priest to confront the person with the excessiveness of his pursuit of faith. As many therapists and priests know, to argue the virtues of this behavior does little to change this obsession. However, viewing these obsessions as an addictive pursuit of self-rescue through faith, in order to overcome depression and distress, provides a rational, cognitive framework for the treatment of these conditions.

Examined more closely, the principal pursuit of religious obsession is the attainment of absolute religious certainty. However, religious certainty is a contradiction in terms, almost a perversion of religious attitude and experience. Religious life does not lend itself to certainty, no matter how strictly the seeker abides by the precepts, and no matter how angry his demands for certainty are. This is illustrated in the following clinical vignette.

Ken is a very likable, gifted young man, 23 years of age, who suffers from a morbidly low self-esteem evident from his difficulties with peers and overidealization of people in authority. At age 12 he became overly religious, by his own account spending hours and days wondering and ruminating how to become acceptable in God's eyes, especially how to know that he is in God's grace. Ken also suffers from serious anxiety states alternating with bouts of depression.

These conditions have driven him to periodic binges of heavy alcohol consumption whenever his depression or anxiety become unbearable. Or, to lift himself out of the depth of self-hate, he gambles excessively in the hopes of accomplishing the superhuman feat of predicting the unpredictable and winning big. If he has a winning streak he reaches a feeling of ecstasy, unfortunately only short-lived, and never a reason to stop playing. Now, being an excellent student in divinity school, he focuses all his attention on the theology of salvation, trying ceaselessly to find the elusive answer to the question: How he can be sure that he is accepted by God?

Of special interest here are his own views of his behavior patterns. He has always been an outstanding student, in high school and college, and he accomplished this with hard work. So much so that he would qualify as a workaholic as well. However, he derives absolutely no satisfaction from his superior performance, acknowledged by teachers and peers, explaining: "I worked for it." On the other hand, catching a winning streak and raking in the chips under the excited cheers of fellow gamblers gives him a feeling of ecstasy because: "I don't work for it, it's the ultimate of just being me, it's given to me."

Ken's self-esteem problems can be traced back to constitutional sensitivities and, even more so, to his disturbed relationship with his parents. In his search for rescue from these difficulties he has pursued two avenues, religion and gambling. His rescue is the reward of establishing once and for all that he is an acceptable person, about which anyone knowing him would hardly have any doubt. However, his criteria for success, knowing that God accepts him or scoring a big win in the casino, are virtually unattainable. Nevertheless, in his mind they are potentially within immediate reach, as he escalates his search and keeps trying over and over again, virtually day and night.

Missionary Zeal

Proselytizing and recruiting new members is practiced almost universally by religious groups, ostensibly for reasons of sharing with one's fellow man the benefits and blessings experienced by its members. Each group may have its specific reasons for this desire to spread "the word." But the motives for this widespread practice might also originate in the specific brain reward purveyed by the group.

For one, humans seem to have an innate desire to share with fellow humans their secrets of well-being. There is something exciting and joyous about a newly discovered remedy for one's fear and anxieties. Even the use of a new drug spreads among drug takers by word of mouth through the "try it, you will like it" method. Or a jogger might tell his friends how running has made him feel physically and mentally healthier. Similarly, anorexia nervosa and bulimia spread among young people by word of mouth. Many patients report that a suggestion by a friend prompted them to begin their rigorous diets or bulimic behavior.

Second, consistent with the notion of brain reward and addiction, the dependent mind tends to secure a steady supply of the rewarding substance. The bulimic would like everybody to be bulimic and hoard food; the anorectic would encounter fewer challenges if she were surrounded by anorectics; obese people would like the whole world to be obese. What better way of guaranteeing the availability of a given reward than to expand its use among an ever larger part of the population? The larger the segment of the population subscribing to a particular belief system, the broader the power base, and the less likely the possibility of forceful withdrawal from the reward.

Third, the change of personality and identity of individuals dependent on a particular form of reward demands constant reaffirmation of the rightfulness of their pursuit. Recruiting new members and making believers out of nonbelievers serves to foster this reaffirmation and to bolster the newly found identity. This process can take on addictive patterns, in that recruitment and expansion can become a never-ending process, like the overcoming of tolerance in the process of addiction.

How these reward-driven motives can lead to addictive behavior is illustrated by Nina, the self-appointed missionary. Nina, age 19, the only daughter of a wealthy but abusive couple, came for treatment under duress, at her parents' insistence. She had gotten into serious trouble on several occasions when she had set out to save the world from sin and debauchery and had chosen appropriate and—more recently—not so appropriate settings for her mission. Initially she had given speeches and sermons on street corners, in subways, and from park benches, but did not succeed in attracting receptive listeners. Instead, she sought out captive audiences by entering restaurants and bars or speaking up in movie theaters to deliver her fiery evangelical calls for repentance. This, of course, did not sit well with the owners of these establishments, and soon the police became involved. At the time she came for treatment she had been in court on several occasions and her parents were sued as well. Worse yet, on her ventures to spread the word into streets and bars controlled by drug pushers and pimps, she had been mugged, beaten, and slashed with a knife, though not, according to her, raped.

While Nina was sitting in my office telling me her side of the story, her big brown eyes were fixated at me, as if to accuse me of sin as well, but also "knowing." "Let me tell you something," she started, "my parents kicked me out. I lived in the streets. I was on drugs and got drunk. I offered sex for money, food, and shelter. You know what changed me? God, I found God."

Nina went on to tell me about her turbulent life in the past three years. Her trouble began actually in junior high school; it simply did not interest her, she was not able to concentrate or apply herself. From then on her saga was one of many disappointments, abusive relationships, alcohol and drugs—anything she could get her hands on—a hopeless life with no way out.

Her parents were of no help at all; her father was busy earning money, her mother had gone back to work when Nina was young, to pursue her own career. There was no time for family life, joint meals, holidays and birthdays, no time for talking or caring. When the situation exploded in high school, Nina's home had become an emotional battlefront, from which her father soon withdrew, blaming the mother for everything. The parents' marriage almost broke up over disagreements caused by Nina's rebellion. Then the father read a book about "tough love," advising the parents to let the daughter leave the family and "survive" on her own.

One day, while walking the streets aimlessly, Nina was rescued. An evangelical group was conducting worship to which everybody from the street was invited. For the first time she heard of hope again, of forgiveness, and of being loved. The group gave her shelter, food, community, even helped her pass the test for the high school equivalency diploma. Strict rules, no drugs, church services every morning and prayer sessions every night. Nina ended her story. "What do you say, is that a reason to go out and preach, or not?"

Nina was not psychotic, nor was she manic-depressive; she simply had to hold onto the reward of her rescue with every fiber of her body and mind. She did what many of us would do if we were rescued and "born again." This is especially true for the helping professions, psychiatrists and therapists alike. We try to help others with what has helped us. Like other converts, however, we sometimes go overboard; we become intolerant of others and intrusive, even radical—to the detriment of our patients.

Nina had become dependent on what had lifted her out of her misery and sustained her in pursuing a life free of drugs and sexual promiscuity. Indeed, she had become addicted to sharing with others her mode of rescue, without regard for the risks involved. Not even the group succeeded in persuading her to abstain from her dangerous ventures. Ironically, in her missionary zeal she exposed herself to some of the same dangers that had threatened her life prior to being rescued. However, her addicted mind did not know of danger, nor was it concerned over creating a public nuisance or getting into trouble with the law. Nina found it very difficult to accept that her missionary activities were excessive. However, once she recognized how her experience of being reborn again was linked to her depression in adolescence and her wayward life away from home, she was able to channel her experience into less dangerous pursuits.

Everyday Addictions to Beliefs of Self-Rescue

Religious beliefs are not a prerequisite for the development of obsessional, addictive pursuits. Whenever we are troubled, a variety of corrective rewards impose themselves on our mind. Let us now examine nonreligious, everyday situations in which this form of reward comes into play.

Powerful beliefs as an expression of hope for one's future, of goals in life, and of means to achieve them are the driving force behind much of our thinking life. The reward we are seeking with these beliefs is not religious or spiritual; nevertheless, it is of a similar nature, in that these beliefs and ideas constitute some form of rescue from real or irrational danger, conscious or unconscious.

Like all reward-mediated behavior, if the need for a rescue is most pressing, beliefs and ideas of rescue can become irresistibly compelling. They can reach the level of obsessions that constitute a coercive and all encompassing ideational system governing our behavior every minute of our lives. In other words, normal healthy ways of defining and going about one's goals can become unhealthy addictive pursuits. The unhealthy power of these ideas of rescue often is compounded by their increasingly unrealistic and unattainable nature, something we observed in Ken's attempt to achieve absolute certainty that he is acceptable in God's eyes.

FINDING THE WHITE KNIGHT

Let's take the example of Wesley, a very attractive woman, age 25, working in fashion design. During her school years she struggled with the educational and emotional consequences of a learning disability. Although quite gifted in art and design, her idea of rescue was to marry a wealthy man from one of the "best families" in the country, so that she would not have to ever work or worry about a "happy" life and financial security. This idea of self-rescue was easily traced back to her mother, who had implanted this goal in her mind from early childhood on. As if her mind was preprogrammed, she pursued this goal: She was very weight-conscious and became anorectic in high school, attended several debutante balls, developed bulimia in college, became a young socialite, was seen only in the "best" circles, was photographed for newspapers and magazines on a regular basis, and, in the process, used drugs and became an alcoholic.

A turning point in Wesley's life came with her hospital admission at age 22, when she became abstinent from drugs and alcohol. She has stayed sober since. What she has not achieved abstinence from is her idea of being rescued by a "white knight." Although she has established herself quite well in the fashion industry and for several years has been seeing a good-looking, caring, hardworking, and potentially successful man her age, she continues to be obsessed with her search for the "white knight." In her eyes, no one has been perfect so far. Her relationship with this man runs hot and cold, her moods swing between depression and short moments of elation, mostly depending on the way she feels about her looks and the amount of attention she receives. On the job she is guided only by the goal of being recognized by her boss, although she is easily incensed by orders given by superiors.

There is no doubt about this woman's narcissistic personality and behavior. But the source of her narcissistic needs is a battered self-esteem that demands corrective compensation. Once we identify this core deficiency in her emotional makeup, her design for rescue by marrying a "white knight" makes sense. To argue that her rescue plan is unrealistic and unattainable misses the point. She is leading a life full of depression and self-loathing, she may lose any day a career that she has created and earned with her skills, and she may lose a man with whom she feels quite comfortable and compatible in many ways. Only if she comes to accept that her master plan of self-rescue is a mental form of addiction will she be able to give up her obsession the way she once gave up her addiction to alcohol and drugs.

THE LOSS OF A PRINCESS

The active pursuit of self-rescue is not the only form of ideational addictive behavior. One also observes the principles of addiction in the state of withdrawal or loss. In those cases it becomes a form of pathological mourning that can only be successfully treated if the patient understands and accepts that his/her obsession with the lost object is a form of ideational addiction.

Let's take the example of Stan, a handsome, athletic, and successful man, age 28. He had broken off a rocky relationship when his girlfriend insisted on getting married, for which he was not yet ready. Although later he tried to mend the relationship by agreeing to the marriage, she refused to take him back and found someone else. For about three years after the breakup Stan obsessed about his former girlfriend, viewing her as the ideal wife whom he should never have given up. He was chronically and seriously depressed, often talking about suicide, and he was full of self-hate and recrimination, refusing to date or become interested in any other woman. His preoccupation with her and ruminations of self-accusations and remorse had started to interfere with his work and prospects of promotion, which added to his sense of hopelessness and despair.

Stan had been very uncertain of his role as a man and, while otherwise very successful and self-sufficient, he had not had any lasting relationships until the age of 24 when he met this woman. Only after he had broken up with her did his frustrations with her turn into the opposite: She became the answer to his life, the perfect wife, a rescue from his fear of not being enough of a man to please women. He was not able to accept that the same woman, who was too much to handle during the relationship, had in retrospect become a rescue fantasy. He would not let go of this ideational reward and refused to see the reality; in short, he had become dependent on his overidealized beliefs. As a result, his judgment became distorted so that, in his thinking, his former girlfriend's considerable irritating traits turned into assets. Stan's mourning for this woman had become pathological as a result of his addiction to a corrective reward for his fear of women.

SHELTER, PROTECTION, AND STRUCTURE

Let us now proceed to the third element of convent life, shelter, protection, and structure. How are these features related to endorphin reward?

The degree to which we experience anxiety and distress, the prerequisite for the need for a corrective reward, follows a simple equation. Given a fairly fixed coping system, the amount of distress we experience corresponds to the degree of distressing events, real or perceived. Since life invariably presents with a steady amount of stressors, we will try to reduce the amount of stress we are exposed to—but often we will find it difficult. However, when faced with serious distress we have two choices to reestablish equilibrium. We can either attempt to stimulate the endorphin system to increase our coping power—as many of us chronically do—or we must reduce exposure to the stressors of life. Sometimes we have to seek shelter and protection in a less stressful environment as, for example, a convent.

Therefore, the relationship between a sheltered and protected life and the need for endorphins is an inverse one. The more sheltered and protected our life is, the less our coping system is taxed and the fewer endorphins we need.

Although not related to endorphins, shelter, protection, and structure provide significant reward in that these factors contribute greatly to a peace of mind, especially for those who seek a reduction of anxiety and fear. Because of this reward effect, life in a communal setting, such as a convent, fosters dependence. As in drug dependence, the dependent mind will seek to justify it, will retain it as long as possible, and will be in turmoil and riddled by anxiety and fear once it is given up or taken away. In other words, the need for protection and structure can become addictive.

Withdrawal

How addictive the reliance on protection and structure—and on the spiritual elements of a group—can become is often apparent only when a member decides to leave his/her religious group or movement, no matter how valid the reasons for leaving. We know from other reward mechanisms that the mental benefits of a particular reward mechanism become most apparent when the reward subsides, whether due to voluntary renunciation or to outside forces. This is reflected in the adage: Absence makes the heart grow fonder. Whatever makes us feel better is noticed most when it is gone. At this point the coping difficulties a person experienced prior to joining the group will return with full might, often even with greater force than prior to joining.

This feature is similar to what psychiatrists observe in patients—and warn them about—when a minor tranquilizer is discontinued. The clinical rule is that the very symptoms that were alleviated by the medicine will be temporarily magnified during withdrawal, beyond the level prior to taking the medication. Once the patient's own coping mechanisms are activated again, the symptoms will recede to at least their pre-medication level, if not be reduced much more because of changes resulting from psychotherapy.

Similarly, one observes in people withdrawing from a religious movement a degree of turmoil, marked by guilt, doubts, anxiety, and depression, that often exceeds the degree of distress prior to joining. Why is this so? This phenomenon can be fully understood only on the basis of the reward principle. If a person leaving a spiritual organization has experienced reward in the form of relief from anxiety and self-doubts and has become dependent on it, he/she feels terrorized at the thought of having to live without it. This inner turmoil is further intensified by attempts of fellow members to keep the absconding member in the fold. Since their and the group's belief system is challenged by a departing member, they will do everything in their power, not only in the form of arguments, but sometimes also threats and actual physical retention, to foil the decision of a member to leave.

Take the case of Linda, who had decided to leave a communal setting associated with the Fundamentalist Church: Linda, an intelligent and attractive nurse one year out of nursing school, suffered from depression and anxiety related to her ability to live an independent adult life, especially after she had lost two brief jobs because of poor performance. At the time she was totally alienated from her parents, feeling that she was not worthy of their love.

She came for treatment of severe bulimia, but it became apparent during the first consultation that she was most distraught about her struggle to leave a sisterhood associated with the Fundamentalist Church. She had turned to that group hoping that she would be rescued from her failures and misery if she devoted herself to a radically different life, a life for God as defined by the Fundamentalist Church. She had tried to abide by all the rules, including abandoning her boyfriend, a young man she had known since early high school. She had not found peace of mind, however; her bulimia had gone completely out of control during her life with this group.

The degree of her mental turmoil almost defies description. Linda was riddled by guilt and anxiety over leaving the protective setting provided by this group; her thinking swayed back and forth between self-incrimination that she should have tried harder and a sense that the group was not the answer to her problems. She had hoped to get control over her need to indulge, be it drinking, overeating, or sex. But she wound up thinking of suicide as a way out of this group and her misery. Members of her group virtually bombarded her day and night with phone calls and personal encounters, frightening her with the most terrible warnings of hell and suffering should she decide to leave. And each of these warnings fell on the fertile ground of a mind that was full of self-hate; she was distraught and totally confused.

In therapy Linda was able to accept the connection between her dependency needs and her fear of leaving the group. Once she understood her tumultuous experience from the perspective of withdrawal, she did manage to cut her ties to this group. She was able to give up her bulimia and resolve some of her difficulties with her mother. She also gained insight into the interplay of her dependent personality trait and addictive behavior, especially as these tendencies interfered with a healthy relationship to her boyfriend. She eventually married him and, as of her last Christmas card, she is a happy mother of two children.

Because of the addictive dependence promoted by some religious organizations, many "deprogramming" services and self-help organizations have sprung up. One of them is Fundamentalists Anonymous, an organization that has chapters all over the country and is modeled after Alcoholics Anonymous. At least by name, this organization correctly recognizes the addictive nature of the process experienced by many people trying to extricate themselves from the fundamentalist movement.

Everyday Addictions to Protection and Shelter

The importance of the protective element of communal settings becomes apparent when we consider other, nonreligious settings, in which we find the same degree of dependence without any religiously motivated spiritual reward.

Shelter and protection from the uncertainties of adult life are universal forms of reward. Their pursuit only becomes problematic when a person, despite his/her adult stage in life or ability to live independently, remains in a dependent situation, not by choice, but as a result of fear. It becomes truly pathological when an individual remains in a setting dependent on another person at the expense of his/her emotional and physical integrity. If we observe people in everyday life, we frequently find these patho- logical situations.

Let's take, for example, the woman who stays in an abusive relationship, only for the sake of financial protection and a com- fortable life-style. Or the man who stays in an intolerable marriage out of fear of managing the tasks of everyday life without the assistance of his wife. Or the person who would not even consider leaving a job, despite enormous frustrations and emotional or physical strain, and/or sex or ethnic discrimination, and/or lack of fulfillment or personal growth and no opportunities for future advancements or promotions.

The main reason given for not leaving such a relationship or job is the desire to keep one's life-style and financial security. The bottom line, however, is the reward of protection and shelter. The consequences for victims of this addictive dependence on a protective setting are sad. Staying in such demeaning situations destroys a person's self-esteem and leads to self-hate and doubt. Eventually, these negative self-images produce distress and de- pression, which lessen still further the likelihood of taking neces- sary action. Even long after the benefit of protection and shelter is gone, the addictive process perpetuates this state and eventually destroys the person spiritually if not physically.

Secular Movements and Cults

On a larger scale, the issue of dependence on shelter, protec- tion, and structure is also relevant to secular movements and cults. Contrary to widely held beliefs, cults do not differ greatly from communal religious settings with regard to the four elements of convent life under discussion. In fact, sometimes the transition from religious movements to cults is fluid. Cults often include some form of worship and rituals, but differ from religious groups in their dogmatic, sometimes fanatical belief system.

Although not always acknowledged, the object of worship is often the leader of the movement or cult to whom the members devote their lives. And no matter how high the declared spiritual aim of the group, many leaders succumb to the temptation of making themselves the center of the group's spiritual life. If this leader promises relief from constitutional and acquired anxieties, he greatly adds to the group's attractiveness.

Cults and many secular movements tend to be associated with the practice of mind control and brainwashing. As individuals become involved in such groups, they undergo drastic changes in their values and attitudes. One can observe a transformation towards accepting, justifying, and even defending the life-style and belief system of the group, no matter how different from previous values. This is often associated with breaking off contact with family and friends.

The irony is that in mind control the mind treats a given situation as if it were beneficial to the person as long as there is one benefit that overrides all disadvantages. The mind wants to feel better now and often disregards the price the person has to pay for it later. In situations truly beneficial to the person, no harm will come from this; it can, in fact, be regarded as a form of positive adaptation. However, in abusive settings mind control becomes dangerous. Brainwashing, as practiced in some cults, can be brought about by procedures of alternating severe forms of physical and emotional deprivation with offering the member acceptance and rewards specific for the particular group or cult. These methods are usually used to subdue a person and break his/her independent will. Even in those situations mind control is spontaneous and often not recognized by the victim.

Whatever the given philosophy of a group, it is important to remember that dependence and mind control is the final outcome of the dynamics between the need for protection and structure of the individual and the mind controlling efforts of the group. The great popularity of some cult like movements is a testimony for the degree to which people—mostly young people—yearn for the benefits conveyed by shelter, protection and structure.

I wish to sum up this chapter with an observation that applies to all addictive states, but is best illustrated by the tragic events surrounding the demise of the Rev. Jim Jones cult that shocked the world in 1978. A visit by members of Congress to inquire about possible abuse of human rights resulted in mass suicide and murder among the members of the Peoples Temple in Jonestown, Guyana. It makes it clear that all addictive states of mind, including those found in cult life, are very delicate, fragile mental structures. Any heavy-handed interference and threat to the pursuit of addictive reward can lead to catastrophic mental and moral disintegration of the people involved. It is important that anyone dealing with addictive behavior keep this in mind, be it family, friends, or therapists of people afflicted by addiction.

9

Treatment of
Addictive Behavior Disorders

IN PREVIOUS CHAPTERS we have identified many forms of human behavior that are motivated by brain reward. The degree to which
we can be certain that endorphins are the underlying reward substrate in these activities ranges from reasonably certain to likely.

SUMMARY AND REVIEW OF REWARD-MEDIATED BEHAVIOR

Reward-Driven Behavior or States

If we reflect on these forms of behavior and conditions, identifiable patterns or groupings emerge. The first group involves behavior in which endorphins are stimulated by physical means, a
form of reward fairly easily recognized by anyone engaging in this
behavior, even if not addicted.

Basic Behavior	Addictive Behavior
Fasting	Anorexia nervosa
	Excessive religious fasting
Purging	Bulimia
Exercising	Excessive exercising
Heat and cold exposure	Excessive sauna use

Sex and orgasm	Sex addiction (nymphomania)
	Compulsive masturbation
Pain and touch	Hair pulling (trichotillomania)
	Nail biting and others
	Obsessive sexual masochism
Oxygen deprivation	Hypoxyphilia (blue boy)

A second group comprises purely mental activities that often are part of a belief system, not only religious, spiritual or philosophical, but also related to everyday obsessional thoughts and rescue ideas.

A conceptual and physiological link between brain reward of ideational nature and the endorphin system was established in the previous chapter. The link is the placebo effect, experimental evidence of endorphin involvement in the phenomenon of expectation, and hope for a "painless," peaceful state of mind. The brain reward achieved in this group stems from an inner conviction of attainment of peace of mind by spiritual and ideational means. Unfortunately, in their unhealthy addictive forms the ideational goals are so distorted and unrealistic that they are not attainable, or attainable only for a fleeting moment.

The behavior in this group is so mental that we have evidence for its rewarding effect only when it becomes excessive or when we observe the consequences of withdrawal.

Basic Behavior	*Addictive Behavior*
Seeking faith	Religious obsession, e.g., seeking religious certainty
Feeling special or safe	Self-rescue obsessions, e.g.:
	Finding the white knight
	Loss of a princess
	Pursuit of stardom

A third form of reward relates to the benefits of shelter and protection. We have identified this form of reward as an important element of the communal life of religious organizations and cults, but it is also an important factor in individual relationships, marital or otherwise.

This reward derives its power from reducing the need to cope with independent adult life. In that sense it takes on a role diametrically opposite to endorphin reward. The more we are protected and sheltered, the less we need endorphins for special coping power.

Basic Behavior	*Addictive Behavior*
Depending on group	Addictive dependence on communal life
Depending on partner	Addictive dependence on partner

A fourth group of reward-seeking behavior includes conditions that we identified in the discussion of bulimia and in the previous chapter. Although these conditions appear quite unrelated on the surface, they can be reduced in some ways to the reward of eating, if we define "eating" in the wider sense of acquiring and taking in material goods or substances. In that sense they also resemble drug addictions to some degree. On the other hand, these conditions share an ideational element of reward, like the rescue fantasies of group two. They are known to be serious conditions and notorious for their resistance to treatment.

Basic Behavior	*Addictive Behavior*
Eating	Compulsive overeating
Shopping	Compulsive shopping
Securing supplies	Compulsive hoarding
Being given something for nothing	Compulsive stealing (kleptomania)
Gambling	Pathological gambling
Working	Workaholism

Differentiating Obsessive-Compulsive Disorders from Addictive Disorders

When we review the lists of reward-motivated behavior above, we find several references to conditions that contain the word "obsessive" or "compulsive" to describe the symptoms of irresistible thoughts and action. Even anorexia nervosa could be called "compulsive dieting" or "obsession with thinness." The terms "obsessive" and "compulsive" also denote a disease with many faces called obsessive-compulsive disorder (OCD). Therefore, the reward-mediated behaviors on the list could be falsely understood as clinical variations of OCD. It is important to keep reward-mediated conditions apart from OCD.

The psychiatric diagnosis of OCD is limited to obscure, often secret thoughts and actions that represent attempts to control or neutralize unacceptable impulses. Obsessive-compulsive symptoms can be understood as ineffective ways of controlling the anxiety associated with these impulses. Typical obsessions are related to fears of contamination, infection, or dirt, or sexual or criminal thoughts. Typical compulsions are excessive cleaning and grooming, orderliness, and checking on things and people. Recently, obsessive-compulsive disorders have become the focus of a great deal of attention, especially since a new medication, clomipramine (Anafranil), has been helpful in the treatment of these conditions.

It has become customary, however, to use the term OCD more generously by including many more forms of behavior of compelling nature under this diagnosis. For example, Steven Levenkron (1991), in his book: *Obsessive Compulsive Disorders*, included excessive running, working, shopping, anorexia nervosa and bulimia, together with the classical OCD "excessive showering" under this diagnosis. While Levenkron gives us valuable insight into the cause for their rising occurrence in our society, most of these conditions fall under the more general category of *behaviors* that are obsessive and compulsive. They are not obsessive-compulsive *disorders* in the traditional sense.

The main difference is that the addictive conditions listed at the beginning of this chapter are compelling because they are driven by an identifiable brain reward mechanism that promotes an effective, albeit often unhealthy, method of achieving well-being. In contrast, traditional obsessive-compulsive symptoms are highly ineffective, and are ways of controlling anxiety only.

The second major difference is that the patient with an obsessive-compulsive disorder realizes that his behavior does not make sense. In contrast, the patient with a behavioral addiction will insist that his behavior makes sense and defend his actions as long as he can. Only at the very end, during the burn-out phase, will he admit to the futility of his efforts—perhaps.

Indications for Treatment

Since the abnormal addictive conditions in our four groups are excess states of basically normal behavior (except stealing), one might ask: What makes them unhealthy conditions requiring treatment?

A jogger goes for his long runs for a thousand reasons. To name a few, he may run for health reasons, social reasons, pride in his body, looks, to prove his youthfulness, to compete with his father, wife, brother, sister, neighbor, friends, to prove his masculinity, for better sex, to worship the runner of Marathon, to prove to himself and others that he is not a "wimp." Whatever reasons the reader may wish to add to the list, it may never be complete. But he also runs because it makes him feel better, and endorphins produce this effect.

An important rule of human psychology is that our behavior has multiple determinants; that is, there are many reasons for us to engage in particular actions or behavior. Therefore, all of the reasons for jogging mentioned are valid, but none of them will cause a person to become addicted to it, except for the underlying endorphin mechanism.

In other words, the identification of reward mechanisms, endorphin reward or otherwise, underlying certain behavior patterns is not a sign of addiction. Quite the opposite is true. Reward mechanisms of the brain are essential for life and are part of nature's many ways of maintaining and preserving life. For example, we abstain from food for a while after a big meal; the body may respond to indigestion with the vomiting reflex; certainly we engage in many physical activities even though we experience physical pain. We engage in many sports and enjoy the exhaustion afterwards. We even get used to it, like the jogger gets used to running, increase the frequency or intensity of it, and become dependent on it for our good feelings. The normal use of rewarding behavior, like jogging, remains healthy, unless the dependence on it becomes addictive.

Then, one might ask, how does dependence become unhealthy, addictive dependence, and when is this point reached?

In the case of the jogger, the transition to addictive running is likely to occur under one condition—when the jogger is or becomes vulnerable because of mental distress or depression. In the presence of distress, anxiety, depression, or any other mental state especially benefitting from brain reward, the pursuit of this reward becomes primary and all other reasons for running lose importance and become secondary. Singular pursuit of this anti-anxiety and anti-depression effect will lead to addictive dependence with all its consequences for the mind and body of the jogger.

We speak of addictive dependence when the jogger cannot abstain from running—or even escalates his running—although it causes harm to body and mind. The harm can be physical injury, which sometimes forces him to abstain. But often the harm is less obvious, when his addicted mind causes him to neglect responsibilities to his job, family or friends, or to abandon other important goals and interests. This is the point at which jogging, a healthy physical activity, has become a condition requiring treatment.

We can apply the experience of the jogger to all other forms of reward-seeking behavior and identify the interplay of two factors that push a person into a state in which treatment becomes necessary. One is vulnerability, such as anxiety or depression, the signs of which have to be watched out for, to avoid being trapped by addiction. The other factor is the addictive process, the end result of which is the state of addictive dependence.

The stage of addictive dependence has been reached when reward-seeking behavior continues—or even escalates—despite the presence of harm and serious danger. This is the point at which the person ought to stop and must stop. When it becomes apparent that the person has lost the capacity to choose between engaging in addictive behavior and abstaining from it, treatment becomes absolutely essential.

Harm to the addict affects the body and the mind; it is sometimes life-threatening. Sometimes harm also involves serious emotional and sometimes physical injury to people close to the addict. Irrespective of the specific reward-seeking behavior, harm can be defined narrowly or widely, and often will include moral considerations and repercussions for the person's self-esteem. Since addictive dependence distorts judgment and insight, people close to the addict have to accept the thankless task of confronting him with his destructive behavior and insisting on treatment.

Special Situations and the Issue of Adaptation

The criterion of harm to differentiate between dependence and addictive dependence is very useful regarding reward-driven behavior in general.

For example, this concept can be applied to drug addictions, albeit with one proviso. The inevitable physical harm from regular use of drugs makes every state of dependence almost instantly a harmful addictive dependence. This issue is, however, of interest in view of recent calls for liberalization of drug laws that would permit certified drug addicts to receive drugs by legal means. Such a change of public policy would reduce a secondary form of harm from drug addiction, which is the criminal means by which the addict currently has to secure his drug supply. This element of criminality is harmful to the addict and the public at large. If drugs were made legally available to the certified incurable drug addict, the dangers of addictive dependence would be reduced to some form of acceptable dependence.

But let us return to behavioral addictions. When we review the forms of reward-driven behavior listed at the beginning of this chapter, the presence of harm as indication for treatment appears valid for all conditions listed. The differentiation of dependence and addictive dependence appears especially poignant, though, in situations of dependence on a sheltered and protective life, communal or individual.

These situations bring up the issue of adaptation, the adoption of a life-style that is in the interest of a person who is not equipped to deal with the rough and competitive life of independent adulthood. In those cases dependence on such a life-style is adaptive. But it is only adaptive if the criteria for addictive dependence do not apply; that is, the setting is not harmful or abusive, emotionally or physically.

This applies to religious and secular group settings, but also is relevant to individual relationships. In the latter, the stage of addictive dependence is reached if the healthy give-and-take for both sides and a fair and mutual complementarity of the partners' personality assets and liabilities become seriously unbalanced. Then relationships turn into situations in which one partner reaps most of the benefits from the relationship and the other is emotionally or sometimes physically abused.

The issue of adaptation versus harm is also relevant with regard to the important dimension of time. It is one of the hallmarks of reward-mediated behavior to want the reward now and to worry about the consequences later. Too often, however, what is found to be adaptive and beneficial now turns out to be maladaptive later. Usually one realizes the consequences when it is too late.

For example, often decisions and choices affecting a person's life in a major way are made with only one question in mind: "What helps me now?" In fact, without any conscious effort, our mind may come up with apparently good solutions to a present and pressing problem. The defense mechanisms of the mind are activated to reestablish instant balance, if at all possible.

However, many solutions turn out later to have been based on a need for immediate peace of mind rather than a true answer to the problem. As much addictive behavior shows, these immediate solutions often lose their efficiency later on and leave the person stranded at some point in life. In those situations the transition from dependence to addictive dependence has usually occurred much earlier than the time at which the person realizes the harmful consequences of earlier, seemingly adaptive choices. At the point of realization people often feel trapped and victimized; however, with courage and hard work they can free themselves from entrapment.

PRINCIPLES OF TREATMENT OF
ADDICTIVE BEHAVIOR DISORDERS

The principles of treatment are derived from an understanding of the underlying mechanism of addiction to brain reward. Recovery is brought about by reversing the behavioral process by which the addiction came into being. For this reason, knowing precisely the biochemical substance promoting brain reward is unnecessary. Even if we knew very little or nothing about endorphins as the substance mediating many or all of these addictions, the course and other clinical features of these conditions would be evidence enough to identify them as addictions and to treat them by reversing the behavior.

Treatment of addictive behavior disorders was derived from the treatment of anorexia nervosa. Therefore, it is suggested that the reader thoroughly familiarize him/herself with Chapters 4 and 5. This discussion will mention only those aspects in which the treatment differs significantly from that of anorexia nervosa.

Obviously, behavioral addictions differ from each other with regard to the behavior triggering the mechanism of reinforcement or reward. The reinforcing role played by self-starvation in anorexia nervosa corresponds to the multitude of specific behaviors or ideas characteristic of a particular behavioral addiction. But this difference and its practical implications are about the extent of substantial variations in the treatment of anorexia nervosa and other addictive disorders.

The treatment of an addictive disorder entails the therapeutic triad, three distinct parts, all of which are equally important for an optimal outcome. The first two parts deal with the treatment of the state of behavioral addiction and include the process of learning about the addictive process and the behavioral aspects of giving up the addictive behavior. The third part of the triad deals with the treatment of the behavioral addict's trait and the underlying mental conditions; this involves individual therapy and the therapy of faulty family dynamics wherever possible.

It is important to note that this breakdown of treatment into three parts reflects the progression in time of the major focus of treatment. In the typical clinical setting elements of all parts may come up in the course of any session.

PART ONE OF THE THERAPEUTIC TRIAD:
LEARNING ABOUT THE ADDICTIVE PROCESS

We begin the discussion of the therapeutic work involved in learning about the addictive process by looking at situations in which the reward is *actively* pursued. These conditions consist of states of actual endorphin pursuit as listed in group one, such as jogging or sex addiction. Also included are other compulsive behaviors, such as compulsive shopping, hoarding, stealing, and gambling, as well as ideational pursuits of brain reward, such as religious obsession and "the white knight," as well as states of dependence on groups or individuals.

Let's put ourselves in the situation of someone who seeks help for one of these conditions. He is usually at a loss to explain how he got to this point. But he knows how it all started.

For example, most likely the jogger initially started jogging to get his body into better shape. In addition, he may have been motivated by any or all of the reasons mentioned earlier. If asked he will tell you that he runs to get his body into shape, no matter how many injuries he has suffered. If he is very perceptive, he may also admit that he keeps running to avoid feeling the unpleasant effects of withdrawal. But he will never tell you that he has become addicted to running to treat his depression or anxiety.

The jogger usually does not know that he is suffering from anxiety or depression or from any other adverse mental states. All he knows is that he used to feel very good from jogging and that "it does not work anymore." He very likely will also have experienced some physical or emotional harm from jogging; otherwise he would not be asking for help. But how or why it happened is unclear to him.

Therefore, the first step of therapy is to understand how the addictive process works. The patient has to learn how each step of the addictive process applies to his personal experience. This learning process, though, cannot occur only intellectually. The patient has to experience for him/herself the reinforcing power of the addictive behavior by observing the interplay between the behavior and its effect on the mind during active pursuit of brain reward, but even more so during withdrawal.

The Log

Since denial and distortion are so powerful in any addictive process, the first task is to establish some objectivity, at least to the degree possible. The patient must agree to keep a daily log in which he/she records his/her addictive behavior and the mental states before and after engaging in this behavior. The log is best kept on a letter or legal size sheet that has 24 hours marked down the left, shorter side of the page with 12 noon in the center, and columns for seven days of the week arranged from left to right. Such a design allows the therapist to scan each week for days and hours of highest addictive activity and to focus on the distress experienced by the patient during those times.

This log also serves as positive feedback for the recovering patient. He/she observes the progression from sheets heavily filled with entries indicative of heavy self-reward activity caused by emotional turmoil, to sheets indicating greater control, distinctly healthier patterns, and an emotionally less troubled life.

However, many people find it difficult, if not impossible, to keep such a log. Whatever the reasons for these difficulties, they have to be explored and overcome before there can be any progress. The acceptance of the log and faithfulness in keeping it are so important that the readiness of the patient for treatment and the speed of recovery can be estimated from the patient's compliance with this task.

Learning about Reward/Reinforcement

Enabling the patient to experience the connection between mood states and addictive behavior requires some time and some experimentation with the various behaviors that comprise this cycle. For example, the patient must learn to observe his changing states of mind before, during, and after engaging in self-reward activity. This is possible only if the patient focuses simultaneously on his vulnerability, aversive feelings, and moods that demand correction.

What state of mind makes seeking the reward such an urgent matter? Is it nervousness and anxiety, anticipation of the day's schedule or of anxiety-provoking encounters on the job, or is it exhaustion from a day's work, loneliness, anger, worry, depressed feelings? What kinds of thoughts go with these feelings? What exactly makes the patient nervous, angry, lonely, or depressed?

During or after engaging in the behavior, are there some calmer feelings at all or some sense of feeling better or stronger? If these feelings are overshadowed by feelings of guilt, fear, or self-loathing, the patient might try to look underneath them and observe what other feelings are hidden.

Learning about Tolerance

Another important technique in learning about the reinforcing power of addictive behavior is to abstain from it briefly, to engage in it less often, or to do it with less intensity. The goal is to provoke the tolerance phenomenon.

If nothing has convinced the patient so far of the reinforcing power of reward, he/she will be surprised by how difficult it is to stop. The patient is urged to observe all the feelings and thoughts that come up. These may be slightly anxious feelings or a touch of being "blue." Or they may be strong feelings of anxiety, some-times panic, associated with anger and a sense of loss, if not outright depression. Remember, the addiction is already under attack and is reacting with great sensitivity. The slightest chal-lenge brings about explosive reactions.

The patient may relate these feelings to his/her fear of giving up this behavior, like the anorectic's fear of getting fat. Weren't there many good reasons to engage in this behavior at the begin-ning? It's like losing a "good friend."

But how good is this "friend" really? Controlling the patient's life, making the patient do things that physically and mentally harm him/her, hurting family, friends, spouse, and ultimately ruining the person in a very selfish way—is that a friend?

These feelings of fear and anxiety are real, but they are not caused by the loss of a "friend." The patient is momentarily expe-riencing the loss of whatever brain reward he/she would have stimulated. This, of course, becomes more apparent when the patient experiments during a time of the day when he/she usually engages in the addictive behavior most urgently.

Another way of understanding the tolerance phenomenon is by looking back over a long period of time, back to the beginning of the addiction. The patient will recall how the rewarding behav-ior escalated. Marked by either greater intensity of the behavior, or greater frequency, or both, the escalation of addictive behavior is usually easy for the patient to remember. Any increase or de-crease of this behavior in response to the waxing and waning of stress during the months or years prior to treatment provides further insight into the interplay of stress and reward-seeking behavior.

Learning about Dependence

Similarly, the feature of dependence is understood by reflecting on how the patient's life has changed since the beginning of the addictive process. As mentioned before, dependence is not always detrimental; it can be quite positive, sometimes even representing some form of adaptation. Yet, attitudes and values have changed nevertheless. And these changes have evolved slowly and taken on shape, eventually forming the mind-set that powerfully resists relinquishing the behavior when it becomes harmful.

A careful analysis of the transformation of life-style, views of self and others, fantasies, and moral values and priorities during dependence is necessary. Often it will reveal that the harmful consequences of the behavior began much earlier than the patient thought. He/she might find that the reward behavior was not a real solution to the problems it was supposed to solve. For example, the jogger who is in an unhappy job situation may have viewed running as the answer to his need to cope better with stress. A true solution might have been to leave the job before his performance suffered or his hostile dealings with his boss precluded a positive letter of reference.

Learning about Addictive Dependence

Finally, the patient will engage in the struggle within him/herself to sort out the harm and injury that have resulted from engaging excessively in reward behavior. It is a struggle because the patient is of two minds. On the one hand, his mind is controlled by dependence on the reward behavior, a way of thinking that refuses to recognize harmful repercussions. On the other, residues of healthy judgment, no matter how faint, will enable him to see the harm done.

A thorough assessment of the harmful consequences of addiction is essential, because these consequences will be the only rational reasons to abandon a behavior pattern that has to come to an end. Only if the patient is sufficiently convinced that this behavior is his "enemy"—not his "good friend"—can he muster the willpower and energy to defeat his unhealthy method of obtaining brain reward.

Withdrawal States

So far we have discussed situations in which the person is actively pursuing brain reward by engaging in reward-stimulating behavior. But the list at the beginning of this chapter includes conditions in which the person comes for help while he/she is in the state of withdrawal, voluntarily or involuntarily. Whether the reward was from an active endorphin-stimulating behavior like jogging, from compulsive shopping or gambling, or from a protective setting like a spiritual movement or individual relationship, it was attainable and experienced. But in some situations the rewards are illusory, are the product of a mind craving for reward, and have not been attained, such as the pathological mourning for a lost "princess."

One would assume that patients seeking treatment while in the state of withdrawal from brain reward would have little difficulty recognizing the mental benefits actually attained by their behavior or situation; they simply entered the learning process at a later stage of the addictive process. But that is not quite so. For one, these patients forgo the cognitive benefit of experimenting with the effects of reward on the mind. And this makes the process of gaining the necessary insight and conviction about the addictive nature of their behavior more difficult, especially when the nature of reward is ideational and illusive.

An additional disadvantage is the state of mind during withdrawal. Whatever the severe reaction is—anxiety, depression, agitation, anger, despair—the mind is in turmoil and craving, a state extremely unsuitable for learning.

Equally complicating the learning process is the "flight into health" phenomenon, when a patient just beginning treatment quickly gives up the addictive behavior. This often short-lived abstinence is a form of resistance to avoid acknowledgment of the seriousness of the addiction and the underlying psychological problems.

In these situations it is sometimes necessary and advantageous for the patient to engage in some of the addictive behavior for a while if the withdrawal was voluntary and the situation is reversible at all.

Many readers may find it appalling that a therapist recommends resuming addictive behavior that a person has already given up and may have to relinquish totally. However, the cognitive and emotional acceptance of the validity of the addictive process is so important for the outcome of treatment that this step, no matter how risky it may appear, is of critical importance. If the reward nature of addictive behavior is not firmly established, the therapist may find him/herself engaged in fruitless discussions about the merits of the behavior to be relinquished, session after session. This is of no help to the patient at all.

If the situation of withdrawal is not reversible, as is the case for individuals who leave a communal setting or an individual relationship, cognitive learning by reflecting on the rewards of group life versus independent life often has to suffice. A useful technique is to reconstruct the lost state of reward by using hypnotic methods or imagery, to revive the experience of brain reward by helping the patient to visualize being in the rewarding situation.

PART TWO OF THE THERAPEUTIC TRIAD:
BEHAVIORAL ASPECTS OF GIVING UP
ADDICTIVE BEHAVIOR

While the patient experiments with his addictive behavior and observes himself, he gains insight into its reinforcing and addictive nature. This process produces the first therapeutic results. It gives him a sense of cognitive control over his experience; he no longer feels victimized by some unknown psychological or biological dysfunction. The interplay of his thought and feeling states resulting from his habitual manipulations of body or mind becomes understandable and predictable.

His experimentation with and better understanding of his addictive behavior also sets the stage for changing this behavior. However, change in addictive states occurs only when the patient systematically eliminates one element after another of the behavioral repertoire that constitutes addiction.

Notwithstanding many promises made to people with addictive behavior disorders, there is no easy or magic cure. The process is as difficult as anything they have experienced in their lives. Nevertheless, it can be done and it must be done; there is no alternative.

A Battle Strategy

In the process of learning about the addiction the patient has already learned much about his enemy, the addiction. By experimenting with the addictive behavior the patient has already challenged the addiction in many ways and kept it in a state of constant alert—and confrontation. In getting ready for the battle of withdrawal, patient and therapist have to form an alliance and collaborate closely. Therefore, we will proceed here as if the patient were in treatment and is addressed directly by the therapist.

If the word "battle" makes you think of war, it is intended. It is a battle between two forces that we will personify. One is the good guy who wants health and normal life; the other is the bad guy who goes to bat for the addiction. To personify these two forces is not as farfetched as you may think. They both have a splendid mind, are inventive and capable. They can even implement all kinds of actions, make things happen or not happen. How come? Very simple, these two guys in combat with each other reside in you, in your mind and body. They represent the two sides of you, the health-seeking side and the addiction-seeking side.

When you, the person who wants to recover, take action for the good guy, you are up against a formidable enemy. The bad guy has the most powerful weapon known to humans. It is the reward system of the brain that is capable of making you do anything, literally anything! The bad guy's addicted reward center of the brain is the headquarters of your enemy. It has come to control you in a systematic fashion, influencing every part of your mind and body, as well as your life-style and relationships.

This is what the good guy is up against. He has been in

retreat for a long time and is about to be defeated. He needs all the strength he can get. Therefore, the good guy in you has to apply the same clever systematic approach to combat that the bad guy has used, an approach that will affect every part of your mind and body, as well as people around you. You devise a plan of battle in written form with the help of a booklet.

It is a booklet of one-half composition book size that will serve for a variety of entries that are meant for only your eyes and those of your therapist. It will become the ongoing record of your work towards recovery. And as a record it must retain all entries of your work with your therapist and yourself. Tearing out pages is not permitted. Sometimes it is important to remember what you have written down previously, even though you may hate it. Starting with the second page, count the pages and divide the book into ten equal sections to be used for different kinds of entries. This booklet will become an important weapon in battling the addiction.

  1. *Know your enemy: Identify all behavior associated with the addiction.*

Addictive behavior disorders are not confined to just one type of action, such as running in the case of jogging addiction. We have seen that addictions tend to structure a person's life so that many different activities are subordinated to one goal, to facilitate the addictive behavior. For example, the jogger usually attends races or meets with other joggers, reads books or magazines about jogging, buys running clothes and shoes, and may do stretching and other exercises to become a better runner. These are the behaviors that evolved out of the principal reward behavior, in this case running.

List these behaviors and activities in the first section of the booklet starting with the *second* page. They will serve as a reminder of what kinds of behavior have to be given up to get the addiction under control. The addicted jogger, for example, will have to reduce all activities related to running. If he does not succeed in reducing, he may ultimately have to sever all ties to the lifestyle associated with running.

The same applies to all people associated with the addiction. They are part of the enemy and will have to be abandoned. Usually, they have a vested interest in your addiction; often they are addicted themselves. Unless they have joined your fight, you have to reduce their influence as much as possible. List their names, explain to them why you have to sever ties, and wish them good riddance.

> 2. *Know the disguises your enemy uses: Identify all elements of mind control by the addiction.*

We have discussed many ways the addiction-dependent mind changes its values and standards. These are forms of brainwashing or mind control. Remember the anorectic who in her state of dependence developed different kinds of self-idealizing fantasies, trying to justify her self-starvation by creating new values and priorities. These are ways of thinking that will tempt you to engage in more addictive behavior if you are not vigilant.

List all examples of mind control caused by your addiction as soon as you recognize them. Start recording these in the second section of the booklet. Also, make a big poster for the wall and list these features under the heading: *Warning!* Enter the most important ones on a small calling card that you carry with you in the wallet.

> 3. *Never forget why your enemy is your enemy: List all forms of harm your addiction has caused you.*

Identify all the harm and suffering your addictive behavior has brought into your life—to you personally, mentally and physically, and to others, mentally and physically.

Give all the reasons why the addictive behavior is not your "good friend" as the bad guy would like you to believe. Think about this question a lot and enter features in the booklet as they come up. Harm is not easily identified by a dependent mind, but it can be used as one of the most powerful weapons against your addiction.

List all instances of harm and suffering in your booklet, starting in the third section. Make a poster and hang it on the wall as a steady reminder of why you have to give up your addiction. Also, write the principal forms of harm on a calling card for your wallet.

4. *Know your weak points: List all signs of mental distress during tolerance and withdrawal.*

List your specific signs of mental distress, whether anxiety, depression, anger, hopelessness, or some other. Observe how they become evident in thoughts, behavior, and feelings of the body. Use this list to recognize your reaction to tolerance and withdrawal. The occurrence of these forms of distress may weaken your resolve to continue combat against the bad guy.

Enter these signs in the fourth section of your booklet. List them also on your log sheet, with just one or two words, when they occur.

5. *Know your fellow soldiers: Identify what situations used to give you satisfaction before you became addicted.*

The funnel effect of addiction has caused you to abandon many small ways of getting satisfaction. Remember, life without reward is impossible to sustain. So, list the sources of pleasure and contentment from the time before the addiction took over. They may be the same now as in the past. But you may be able to think of additional activities that would give you good feelings. Go for them actively. It is your way of fighting back the funnel effect and with it the addiction.

Make sure, however, that these forms of reward are *not* related to your addictive behavior. It is not always easy to tell. List them in the fifth section of your booklet.

> 6. *Know who your friendly troops are: Identify interests and life-styles from before your addiction.*

Consistent with the funnel effect, the reward experienced from special interests, hobbies, or life-style activities has been slowly undermined. Now is the time to recover these interests, although they may not be easily remembered or implemented, having been wiped out of your conscious thinking under the influence of dependence.

List those interests and abandoned life-styles in the sixth section of your booklet. Add new ones to enrich your life to its fullest. Go for them and discover that you still can feel as passionate about them as you did years ago.

> 7. *Know who your allies are: Identify people who support your fight against addiction.*

At times of distress and temptation you have to reach out to others for comfort, understanding, and distraction. Think hard to name those individuals who were most troubled about your addiction, openly or covertly. Come out with your decision to quit your habit and enlist their help.

People who are part of a therapeutic group or self-help organization may qualify as long as you are vigilant about their attitude towards their addiction and yours.

List the names of your allies in the seventh section of the booklet. Add telephone numbers and other relevant information. Call them for help whenever you need an ally.

> 8. *Know your current position: Define the basic units of addictive behavior and record your current level of addiction.*

In drug abuse the habit is measured by the amount of a substance taken within a given time. Analogous to that, we define a unit of addictive behavior as the number and/or intensity of actions taken in a given time. For example, in anorexia nervosa an addictive unit was the action of not eating during mealtimes, or eating less than required. Units can be many or few, depending on the addictive behavior. For example, in bulimia one addictive unit may be a binge or a binge-purge cycle, usually ranging from once every three days to three to seven times a day. A jogger may take a mile as a unit, and his units may be many miles a day.

The definition of a unit of thought or ideational addiction follows the same principle, although often it is more difficult to define and control obsessive thoughts and wishes. There is a way, however; these thoughts translate into behavior. Consider, for example, the woman who is waiting for her "white knight." That fantasy defines her life-style, going out every night, dressing up, displaying a certain demeanor, doing whatever she thinks will attract that perfect man. These activities are basic units of her ideational addiction that have to be systematically reduced.

The same applies to religious obsession. The basic wish behind a religious obsession is religious certainty, a state of mind that is aimed for but is never—or only rarely—attained. Therefore, the basic unit of religious obsession is represented by any behavior that aims at achieving religious certainty. A religious life-style forms the larger context of religious obsession and offers many opportunities for excess pursuit. These excessive behaviors, but not necessarily a religious life-style, have to be radically reduced.

In dependent relationships, the basic addictive unit is defined as how many times a person depends on the partner for daily needs that are not part of a mutual give-and-take of a partnership or marriage. Another similar measure is the number of times a person tolerates abuse from a partner without putting a stop to it. The same principles apply to addictive dependence on groups.

Define your basic unit of addictive behavior as accurately as possible. Specify all associated behaviors and set the criteria for a basic unit. Enter these in section eight of your booklet.

In addition, record your current level of addictive behavior based on units of activity within a certain time. Include all forms of associated behavior and specify how often within a given time you are currently engaged in them.

> 9. *Know your objective: Define your goal, the extent of withdrawal.*

In deciding on the extent of withdrawal, the principal goal is the elimination of harm and suffering associated with your addictive behavior. From our discussion of the indications for treatment it follows that your least objective must be to transform your addictive, harmful dependence to a harmless dependence. If we reflect on the beneficial aspects of the basic reward-mediated behaviors summarized in the beginning of this chapter, this goal appears to make sense. Certainly, some people may consider their habit outright sick and may wish to give it up altogether. But aren't others healthy and accepted sources of pleasure and peace of mind?

However, if you define as your goal a reduction of addictive activities to a level harmless to yourself and others, it may not be enough. You may find yourself having to reach for a more radical goal, the total elimination of all behavior related to your addiction. Why should this be so? As every addict knows from personal experience, addictive habits follow the all-or-nothing principle; it is virtually impossible to maintain a middle of the road approach, since the powerful reward mechanisms of the brain always demand more. This principle is also reflected in two rules governing recovery from drug abuse.

The first rule says that the drug has to be given up totally and the addict has to stay absolutely clean in order to succeed in his goal of being free from his habit. Although this may sound harsh, punitive, and unrealistic in view of the many beneficial effects of these behaviors if pursued in moderation, the validity of this rule cannot be overestimated.

The other rule of drug abuse treatment is that the ex-addict must never allow himself to use the drug again, even if it is only in smaller doses and occasionally. While it is easy to accept this dictum for drugs, it does not seem to make sense for behavioral addictions. But, why this rule of permanent abstinence?

To paraphrase Freud's famous statement that the brain never forgets, the brain of the behavioral ex-addict will always remember the mode by which brain reward was achieved. The risk of sliding from occasional use back into an addictive pattern is enormous whenever one's mind is distressed. This point cannot be emphasized enough.

It seems, though, that the concept of addictive behavior as antidote against depression and anxiety allows us to redefine the permanent abstinence rule somewhat. Psychotherapy for trait conditions constitutes one of three legs that recovery stands on. It reflects the importance of treatment for the mental conditions that make a person vulnerable to addictive disintegration.

With this in mind, the lifelong abstinence rule can be redefined: If you have truly made extensive changes in the handling of personality problems, attitudes, and way of life—in other words, if you have gained some degree of mastery over your symptoms of anxiety and depression—some of the truly rewarding forms of behavior may be taken up again after some period of total abstinence.

In conclusion, a realistic first goal—one that is even useful for the learning process—is to reduce the addictive behavior to a level at which no harm comes from it. Make every possible effort at succeeding so that you can benefit from the rewards without harm. If you keep slipping into addictive levels, you must reach the conclusion, albeit very reluctantly, that you have to bring about a total withdrawal from the addictive behavior and prepare for a long period of abstinence, if not permanent abstinence.

After having made a thorough analysis of the first eight items, define the goal for your addiction and spell it out in section nine of the booklet.

> 10. *Define your strategy: Spell out your schedule of reduction.*

Define a schedule for reducing the units of addictive behavior as you have defined them. In the description of your current level of addiction under item 8 you came up with a number of addictive behavior units within a certain period of time, such as: "I am running on the average 60 miles a week, do work-out and conditioning exercises three times a week, and stretch daily." Or, "I am gambling three times a month and lose about $300 each time. I also bet on horses with a local bookie and spend another $200 weekly. I also meet with other gamblers at a local bar four times a week and check the daily paper for race results."

A realistic schedule of reduction would aim to withdraw within a period of 12–18 weeks or in 20–30 distinct steps, until the occurrence of addictive behavior reached the predetermined goal level or zero. For example, the jogger would reduce his running by five miles every week, his conditioning exercises by one day every month, and his stretching exercises proportionally to the reduced distance he is running. The gambler would reduce his visit to a casino and money spent by one visit and $100 a month. He would cut back playing the horses by $70 a week each month, reduce visits to the local bar by five every month, and decrease checking up on race results by 10 days every month.

Finally, once this task is accomplished, draw a big horizontal line under the last entry of items 9 and 10, indicating that these sections will not be modified at all. This is in contrast to all other sections, which will be added to and elaborated on as the withdrawal process progresses.

Enter your schedule of reduction in your calendar on the days the reductions have to take place. Also, enter a short version of your goal and of the schedule of reduction (item 9 and 10) on the first page of the booklet as a quick reminder of your task whenever you open the notebook.

You are ready to reduce your addictive behavior. Are you really? If so, put everything on hold, make your withdrawal the first priority in your life, and avoid any stressful situations and encounters. You need all the energy you can muster to succeed.

Learning to Live with Tolerance and Withdrawal

The patient faced with giving up the addictive behavior has to overcome two major obstacles. One is the power of the reward mechanism; the other is the mind-controlling effect of dependence. Together, these two factors will result in many distortions, justification of the addiction, and forceful attempts to hold onto the habit. While the power of the reward mechanism must be overcome by sheer willpower, the distortions must be controlled at all cost by careful record-keeping.

Reducing the intensity and frequency of the addictive behavior inevitably will lead to withdrawal from the addictive reward mechanism. Here everything applies that has been said about withdrawal from drug addiction in general and anorexia nervosa in particular. The patient enters a period of stormy emotions, struggling between the wish to give up his dependence and the wish to retain the addictive behavior. Without storm and turmoil there is no true withdrawal, and spouses, family members, relatives and friends have to be prepared for it.

This also is the stage in which the temptation to lie and cheat is the greatest, calling for an attitude of acceptance and support by the therapist. It is important to remember that the patient is caught in an internal conflict, which he may externalize by attacking his therapist, mate, family member, or dearest friend with a variety of angry accusations and complaints. Taking these attacks personally and withdrawing from the patient is not the answer in these situations. An understanding and supportive stance, but without room for negotiation or compromise, is most helpful to the patient in overcoming his/her addiction.

Inevitably, depressed and anxious feelings will emerge as the self-medication effect of the addiction slowly evaporates. Thus, these feelings have to be regarded as therapeutic, which the agonizing patient will find difficult to accept. Simultaneously, as depression and anxiety emerge, they can be understood and alternative solutions for the depressing or anxiety-provoking life situations can be found. They open the door to the exploration and treatment of the trait conditions that made the person initially vulnerable to addictions.

At this stage patient and therapist have to guard against the development of other forms of addiction, either excesses of other behaviors or drug abuse. The need for brain reward at this stage is so powerful that it takes major vigilance on the part of the therapist and enormous willpower on the part of the patient to avert inadvertently succumbing to another addictive habit.

The course of withdrawal should not be expected to go smoothly. There will be difficulties in staying on schedule and outright relapses into full-blown addictive behavior. If this happens, it is very important not to give up altogether, since this is only in the interest of the bad guy, the addiction. Slips and some degree of relapsing are so frequent that the speed of recovery from a relapse is a more meaningful sign of progress than the attainment of a consistent record of reduction.

Indeed, lasting abstinence is more likely to be achieved when the course of withdrawal is rocky and frequently challenged by relapses. On the other hand, what appears like smooth sailing during this phase more often than not turns out to be a disguise for noncompliance. If the patient expects smooth sailing he/she may be so disheartened when a relapse occurs that he/she may abandon treatment entirely.

PART THREE OF THE THERAPEUTIC TRIAD:
TREATMENT OF THE ADDICTIVE TRAIT

By the time the behavioral addict approaches the withdrawal stage he/she will have achieved some understanding of antecedent psychological difficulties and personality traits. This understanding will provide a framework within which he/she sees the evolutionary steps leading to the current dilemma. It may have also already given him/her some sense of direction out of the life situation that caused the addictive disorder.

Therapeutic work on the patient's unhealthy life situation or on personality traits follows standard psychotherapeutic theories and methods and is based on the psychodynamics of the particular patient. The individual dynamics or family dynamics found in the background of behavioral addictions are identical to those found in anorexia nervosa. Therefore, the reader is referred to the discussion of trait therapeutic approaches for anorexia nervosa in Chapter 5. However, brief mention of the different contexts of therapy might be useful.

Initially, treatment of trait conditions takes place in the context of individual therapy. The-one-to-one mode of patient-therapist interaction fosters the development of a therapeutic alliance and represents the principal setting within which the treatment of the addictive state takes place. It is also the best initial setting for the exploration of many life experiences and other therapeutic tasks.

However, any close analysis of trait problems leading to addictive behavior disorders will reveal that they are deeply affected by the person's relationship to his/her parents and events of the past. And family therapy is therefore an essential ingredient of any treatment plan. Nevertheless, both patient and family may resist a recommendation for family therapy. Every effort has to be made to overcome this resistance in the interest of the patient's long-term recovery.

A frequent argument for not engaging in family therapy is that the patient is a grown-up and independent from his/her parents. While most anorectics come for treatment in late adolescence, people with addictive behavior disorders tend to be young adults who have left the family to attend college. Or they are married and/or pursue a career. While behavioral addicts often live independently, they are at best pseudo-independent. They continue to be highly dependent on their parents emotionally and often financially, even though they live separately.

Additionally, there is a very useful third context within which therapy should take place. Most young adults are engaged in some form of intimate relationship or friendship, be it marital or otherwise. This constitutes the emotional and interpersonal environment of the patient and, in that sense, is an extension of his/her psychological makeup. The inclusion of that person in conjoint or couples therapy provides a valuable source of therapeutic insight and progress. It is advisable to include the spouse or friend regularly in sessions as soon as the patient can tolerate more taxing and challenging aspects of joint therapeutic work. Often patient and therapist will find that such work produces more valuable insight and problem resolution than numerous individual sessions.

OTHER ASPECTS OF TREATMENT

Medication

As in anorexia nervosa, the use of specific symptomatic drug treatment in addictive disorder may be advisable should the patient be overwhelmed by anxiety or depression as he/she attempts to give up the pathological coping mechanism. If the symptom of distress is primarily anxiety, an anti-anxiety agent may be indicated; for primarily depressive symptoms selective serotonin reuptake inhibitors are widely used, such as fluoxetine hydrochloride (Prozac) or sertraline hydrochloride (Zoloft). From my experience, these drugs reduce the patient's reactivity to his/her specific stressful situation, as well as to ubiquitous stresses of everyday life. A useful measure of the drug's efficacy is gained from observing the patient's coping power as it is expressed by his/her reactivity to intrapsychic and outside events.

Hospitalization

For reasons discussed in the chapter on the treatment of anorexia nervosa, hospitalization should be considered only if a prolonged trial of outpatient treatment fails to bring about withdrawal and abstinence from the addictive behavior. Since the cases requiring inpatient treatment are most severe in terms of the underlying psychopathology, family therapy in addition to individual therapy during and after admission is essential to improve the chances for a successful and lasting outcome.

Group Therapy and Self-Help Organizations

Many organizations have sprung up to provide people with addictive disorders with very useful information and assistance, as well as group and sometimes individual therapy. Attending groups is a very important feature of treatment for addictive disorders. As discussed in the treatment of bulimia, these groups bring to the treatment three benefits not available through individual sessions.

One benefit is that the patient has the opportunity to observe other behavioral addicts at various stages of their treatment. This allows the behavioral addict to "look ahead" with regard to the progression of his/her own treatment and to see how others deal with issues that he/she will have to deal with at some point. The behavioral addict also will "look back" to previous stages of her treatment as she helps new group members to deal with issues that she has dealt with previously. Thus, the group permits learning by modeling after others, and teaching as reinforcement of the therapeutic process.

Second, the group serves as support network for all members. Mutual support and the benefit of calling on group members in times of severe distress are useful in view of a sense of shame and not feeling understood by people not afflicted by addiction.

Third, just as the group process fosters support, it also leads to confrontational modes of interaction that any addict benefits from. Many behavioral addicts find it easier to be confronted by a fellow patient than by a therapist about denial, rationalizations, and other behavior typical for dependence. The give-and-take of the group situation makes a confrontation less authoritative but equally effective.

10

Some Theoretical Considerations
Regarding Reward-Mediated Behavior

SINCE THE DISCOVERY of endorphins much research effort has gone into understanding their role in human physiology and psychology. While a large body of knowledge has been accumulated about their role in the physical functions of the body, explorations into their role in human psychology have yielded few positive results so far, except for their effect on pain perception, perhaps, and the beneficial effect of physical exercise on the mind.

The identification of endorphins as the addictive substrate of anorectic self-starvation adds to this knowledge. But more importantly, our understanding of how the mind is affected by the endorphin reward in anorexia nervosa and many other forms of endorphin-mediated behavior has given us access to an entirely new dimension of human psychology and behavior. One could say, by revealing some of her secrets, the anorectic, ''the best little girl in the world,'' has taught us much more than the secrets of anorexia nervosa. She has opened the door to new knowledge about many heretofore poorly understood aspects of the human condition.

The concept of endorphin reward does not explain just pathological conditions, such as anorexia nervosa, bulimia, and other behavior in which the pursuit of endorphins has taken on addictive proportions. Chapters 7 and 8 described everyday ''normal'' behavior patterns that derive their motivational power from their link to endorphins. Only when these behavior patterns disintegrate into addictive pursuit of brain reward do we identify their reward-mediated nature and speak of pathological states or disease.

Let us here take a conceptual leap and examine and extract, so to speak, what we can learn from pathological conditions about the normal role of endorphin reward in the functioning of the brain and mind. Since endorphins are not the only biochemical substance mediating brain reward, we will speak of brain reward and nonreward in general, unless reference is made to behavior of which endorphins are, or most likely are, the mediating substance.

This chapter will demonstrate the importance of seeking brain reward and avoidance of nonreward in the psychology of everyday life. In fact, it will explain many known psychological constellations and behavior patterns much better than previous explanatory concepts. While some of these new concepts pose no particular challenge to the basic premises of behavioral science in general, and psychiatry specifically, others diverge considerably from established tenets. We will begin with a look at the role of reward systems in the regulation of basic biological and physical functions, and proceed to the higher realm of human psychology, thought, and behavior.

THE ARCHAIC BRAIN:
THE IMPORTANCE OF REWARD SYSTEMS FOR THE MAINTENANCE OF LIFE AND SURVIVAL OF THE SPECIES

The brain is commonly viewed as the central switching station for the regulation of many of the body's organs and functional systems. With the help of countless internal and external monitoring devices, the brain maintains equilibrium, also called homeostasis, for itself and the organism of which it is part. The organism uses the brain to respond to external and internal stimuli in such a manner that an internal balance is maintained within a narrow range of functioning.

The basic functions of maintenance of life and survival are governed by a part of the brain that is old in terms of the evolution of man, the "archaic brain." It is the part that regulates numerous basic, life-supporting functions of the body, such as breathing, heart rate, and blood pressure; it also governs more complex functions such as food intake and reproduction.

Because food intake and reproduction appear to be expressions of forces within the organism, these behaviors have been thought to be driven by "instincts." Instinctual behavior is rigidly patterned and takes care of more complex functions, such as self-preservation and survival of the species.

It has long been known that many of these functions are strongly influenced by mechanism of reward-mediated by "reward centers" of the brain. Together with other regulatory systems, such as hormones, these reward centers primarily motivate the organism to engage in complex behavior to secure maintenance of life and survival of the species. By linking these functions to powerful brain reward mechanisms, nature insures that these essential tasks are repeated over and over again. In other words, the organism does not grow tired of them, and thus the likelihood of the survival of the species is increased.

With the discovery of endorphins one of the biochemical substrates for the motivational role of reward centers was found. Thus, endorphin reward is closely connected to motivational forces governing maintenance of life and preservation of the species. Consequently, brain reward is not optional; life without reward is not possible. What holds true for this most basic level of organismic life is also true for higher levels of human behavior. This is contrary to the widely held belief that reward is always a form of indulgence that man can choose to pursue or withhold from himself.

Beyond the motivating role, however, reward systems of the "archaic" brain also turn out to have a far-reaching role in the protection of the organism from acute inside and outside dangers threatening its physiological equilibrium. Anorexia nervosa is an excellent example of the protective role of endorphins over basic functions of the body. To adapt to the state of starvation functions such as breathing, heart rate, and blood pressure are lowered under the influence of the endorphin system. Furthermore, the organism responds to pain and other physical stresses by stimulating endorphin-mediated mechanisms to reestablish equilibrium of body functions. Thus, corrective and adaptive mechanisms in response to excessive physical exhaustion, starvation, heat and cold stress, loss of body fluids, lack of oxygen—all seem to be mediated to some degree by the endorphin system.

Therefore, one could say that any form of imbalance in the body or in the brain itself is responded to by the reward system as if physiological imbalance were a state of nonreward that requires immediate corrective activation of the reward system.

It is important to remember, though, that these protective mechanisms are designed by nature to respond to these conditions acutely and to cease functioning once the stressful condition has subsided or the organism has removed itself from it.

Most species of the animal kingdom seem to fare quite well with these functions of the archaic brain that promote homeostasis, maintain life, and secure survival of the species.

The Thinking Brain:
The Importance of Reward Systems for the Maintenance of the Mind's Equilibrium

The human is distinguished by his/her cortex, a part of the brain that is a relative newcomer in evolutionary dimensions and very large in size and complexity by comparison to all other animal species. The cortex supplies us with the power to think, a highly complex but most economic form of functioning. Having the option of thinking various alternatives through, we do not have to translate them into action, material matter, or muscle activity; we simply try them out in our minds.

There is no doubt that the powerful ability to think has made us superior to lower species. Essentially, the large cortex has freed us from purely instinctual behavior. The human is a "homo sapiens," an intelligent being, although perhaps not as free from instinctual behavior as we would like to believe. Furthermore, humans have used their large cortex to create in an almost playful way external conditions of their existence that suit their need for equilibrium. The human has become, as Huizinga said, a "homo ludens," a playful, inventive being.

The ability of humans to think gives them greater freedom of thought and action. But with a greater range of choices comes greater freedom to get into difficulties. This makes the defenses of the mind so important. Just as the "archaic" brain provides protective mechanisms for physical functions, the thinking brain also benefits from many ways of maintaining equilibrium, some of which are "borrowed" from the archaic brain.

Here, anorexia nervosa serves as unique model because it is the condition of defense mechanisms par excellence. It offers examples of the two major categories of defense functions promoting mental homeostasis. To the first group belong the traditional psychological, purely mental defense mechanisms, such as denial of illness. But more importantly, anorexia nervosa has taught us about the mechanism of counteracting anxiety and depression by self-starvation, a mode of defense employing physical or bodily means of achieving homeostasis. These modes of keeping mental equilibrium will be called physical defense mechanisms of the mind.

Thus, our understanding of defense mechanisms can be greatly enhanced if we examine them in the light of our knowledge of anorexia nervosa and other reward-mediated states. We learn that all defense mechanisms, psychological and physical, are closely linked to the dynamics of reward and nonreward. Our mind experiences any form of disequilibrium of thought and feeling as a state of nonreward and is highly responsive to any sign of danger to a smooth functioning of its internal milieu. By taking instant corrective action in thought or by instituting corrective behavior, our mind attempts to reestablish homeostasis. Furthermore, these defenses are subject to the principles governing all reward-mediated behaviors, which include the danger of leading to addiction.

Let us briefly mention physical defense mechanisms, that is, the many forms of endorphin stimulatory behaviors that are the topic of this book. We now see where they have their place in the context of defenses of the mind. Just like alcohol and drugs, they represent the second line of defenses and are often used as a last resort to regain balance when psychological defenses do not suffice in establishing equilibrium of the mind.

Self-manipulation of the body to achieve brain reward is usually not initiated for the purpose of benefitting from endorphins the way drug users set out to take advantage of the mind-altering effects of drugs. However, once the endorphin-stimulating effect has been set into motion, the brain-rewarding effects are identical to those of drug addiction and can lead to addictive states as powerful as drug addiction, if not more so.

In contrast to the use of an external substance in alcoholism and drug abuse, endorphin stimulatory behaviors take advantage of an internal source of brain reward, the biological protective mechanisms of the archaic brain. While designed by nature to protect the organism from external, imposed stresses requiring effective adaptation, these self-regulatory mechanisms can be ''borrowed'' by the mind to promote a sense of well-being by natural, although sometimes very unhealthy, methods.

Let us now turn to psychological defense mechanisms and examine them in the context of brain reward. They are important ingredients of healthy as well as unhealthy behavior and thought. Health and illness are not that different with regard to the nature of defense mechanisms employed. Rather, the use of rigidly fixed patterns and excessive use of only a very few mechanisms of defense are typical of unhealthy behavior and thought. The same patterns used in moderation, in greater variety, and flexibly can be perfectly healthy. Because abnormal behavior often is a caricature, an exaggeration of basic features of healthy behavior, we learn about the nature of health by studying states of disease.

Not much has to be said about the traditional psychological defenses. They were extensively studied by Sigmund Freud, Anna Freud, and their disciples, and include the well-known defense mechanisms of repression, displacement, denial, isolation, undoing, and many others. They are automatic and mostly instant mental responses that serve to deflect conflict and anxiety. In this capacity they promote the reward of mental equilibrium and are governed by the dynamics of reward and nonreward.

However, much normal and abnormal human psychology is expressed in prolonged or repetitive behavior patterns that serve defensive functions. And it is in these patterns that we can apply what we have learned from anorexia nervosa and observe the dynamics of reward and nonreward activated for the purpose of maintaining or restoring mental equilibrium.

Many of these patterns are used in everyday healthy, adaptive ways. However, many appear adaptive to the individual but turn out to be ineffective and detrimental in the long run. Others are basically healthy but, consistent with their reward function, can disintegrate into excessive, addictive behavior.

The following examples illustrate how the dynamics of reward and nonreward can provide a better understanding of ubiquitous unhealthy behavior patterns and show the way towards change.

Delay of Nonreward: Procrastination

Procrastination can be viewed as a special case of the defense mechanism of avoidance. In procrastination our mind causes us to delay actions that produce stress or anxiety, states of mental disequilibrium. The avoidance is not total, but temporary.

Procrastination is an inefficient method of maintaining equilibrium, since the delay usually results in greater strain when the action has to be implemented. This greater strain, of course, is a reason for our mind to attempt delaying still longer the next time this action has to be taken.

For example, if the writing of a term paper causes anxiety or stress for a student, he/she is prone to procrastinate to the last minute, at which point he/she puts in an "all nighter" and writes the paper under enormous pressure. This stressful experience in turn causes the student to delay even longer the next time a paper is due. A vicious cycle is created in which a particular task is associated by the mind with more and more distress, leading to increasingly strong avoidance attempts by procrastinating. In addition, the mind is not really at ease while delaying necessary action. Everyone knows how burdensome to the mind it can become when many undone tasks have accumulated.

Often, procrastination is considered a character flaw or, for that matter, sheer laziness. However, once this behavior is understood in terms of avoidance of nonreward, it can serve as a signal that tells us under what circumstances our mind is taxed. We can use it as a door to understanding ourselves, a way to analyze our strengths and weaknesses. This, of course, is only possible if we do not choose an attitude of: "This *should* be easy for me." Obviously, many tasks eventually have to be done and will be done much more easily if one avoids getting entangled in this vicious cycle. On the other hand, if certain tasks tax and distress us chronically, we should find ways of making the task easier or seek alternatives to this repetitive exposure to nonreward, for example, by changing one's goals, job, or life-style, if necessary.

Hierarchy of Reward and Nonreward: Self-Destructive Behavior

Another way our mind maintains equilibrium is by subjecting our needs to a hierarchical order, ranking them by importance and priority. The term "needs" refers here to wishes and desires, as well as actions and behavior that we engage in to satisfy those desires. The term "needs" also means that if these wishes and desires are not fulfilled, we experience anxiety, sadness, depression, or other aversive feelings. In other words, the needs are linked to the reward system and the order of importance is governed by reward and nonreward or punishment.

This hierarchy is rigidly adhered to, although often we are not aware of it; once we are aware, it appears illogical and counterproductive. Nevertheless, this little recognized phenomenon of the priority setting effects of the reward system on our behavior explains many paradoxical features of human behavior.

An everyday example is the amusing situation when we take on with delight a task that we ordinarily do not like, while there is another more urgent and important task that we like even less. In those situations our mind establishes a hierarchy of nonreward and almost eagerly chooses the lesser "evil."

Sometimes both reward and nonreward are enmeshed in a hierarchical order. A serious constellation of unhealthy subordination of reward to nonreward is found in self-destructive behavior. A typical example is the situation of women who engage in relationships with men who are hurtful and destructive to them, women who are said "to love too much" (Norwood, 1985). These situations certainly do not make logical sense and often result in untold suffering.

Traditional psychological understanding of this behavior, based on Freud's (1924) theories, invokes a wish to suffer, called masochism, as its underlying motivational force. However, this explanation resulted from an attempt to fit all aspects of human behavior into one neat, unifying theory. It is also a reflection of the difficulties psychoanalytic theory has had with situations of self-imposed suffering. Freud did not have the benefit of knowing about the endorphin system and its effects on the dynamics of reward and motivation. If he had, he probably would have embraced it fully.

The powerful control of reward systems on our behavior is evident in the self-destructive engagement of woman in abusive relationships. These women desperately seek the reward of having a companion and belonging, with all its social ramifications. As a result, they forgo other very important rewards of a relationship—to be respected and loved, to be treated fairly—for the reward of belonging.

The partner choice of these women might be determined by the hierarchy of rewards in a still larger sense. This same abusive partner may represent what is considered in our society a successful man; for instance, he may be wealthy or powerful. Or he simply may protect her from her anxieties about dealing with the working world by providing for her financially. While there is nothing wrong with these priorities in themselves, they become highly problematic if their achievement is associated with emotional and/or physical abuse. Then, such a relationship assumes the characteristics of an addiction, in which the immediate gratification of certain needs and goals results in chronic emotional and, sometimes, physical harm to the person. As in all addictions, the reward of highest priority, in this case a "successful" man, is desperately sought after because this reward is thought to constitute the most important ingredient for one's sense of well-being.

The power of this wish becomes apparent when it comes to withdrawal, when after all rationalizations the woman attempts to relinquish this need. A mourning process sets in, marked by depression, anxiety, sense of loss, and attempts to renegotiate the need to give up. It may appear ironic to call this process mourning in view of the abuse suffered by her. However, the woman mourns for the positive aspects of the relationship, which she had to relinquish because of the suffering that went with it. She has put an end to subordinating the reward of being loved to the reward of belonging and being protected. If this mourning is successfully completed, it gives way to a newfound freedom and self-respect.

Nonreward Demands Compensatory Reward: Self-Rescue Behavior

Chronically depressing life situations, as we often observe in anorectics prior to dieting, or major and repeated setbacks in life often trigger the urgent wish for self-rescue. This wish can be viewed as a defense mechanism against the nonrewarding effects of a battered self-esteem and the disequilibrium it creates in the mind. This wish for self-rescue can be a powerful motivator for the pursuit of outstanding achievements. But just as healthy defense mechanisms can become unhealthy, the healthy quest for a rewarding experience to make up for nonreward can have its counterpart in unhealthy behavior.

This is illustrated by the case of a portfolio manager who kept losing money in the stock market because of his high-risk approach to investing, although in the past he had done well. An analysis of his situation revealed that just prior to escalating his risk-taking, he had suffered a major loss in the market, which came as a shock to his chronically low self-esteem.

Many professionals might invoke fear of success or unconscious self-destructive wishes as a way of understanding this man's high risk-taking tactics. In my view, his behavior can be completely understood in terms of the dynamics of reward/nonreward. This man wanted to win big and did not fear success. But he fell victim to one mistake. In his quest for a desperately needed rescue for his crushed self-esteem, he subordinated the reward of achieving modest but respectable returns to the reward of showing big gains. As a result, he failed to use sober and circumspect investment strategies; instead, he engaged in high-risk, sometimes foolish strategies, resulting in devastating losses.

Behavior Linked to Brain Reward Is Primary to Thought

If we reflect on the thinking brain's interplay with reward-mediated behavior we arrive at a novel and surprising theoretical concept: that the action of initiating behavior occurs first, before the ideas, fantasies, and moral values associated with the behavior evolve; these occur only as a consequence. In other words, under these conditions behavior is primary to thought.

We have observed this concept at work in the anorectic who, especially during the advanced weight loss phase, clearly submits her ideational life to the behavior of starving herself. Dieting and self-starvation are initiated with only the social reward of slimness in mind. The elaborate ideas of self-idealization—that she is better and purer than others, a martyr of her own cause—go far beyond the desire for slimness. These ideas evolve as a result of her dependence on endorphin reward brought about by self-starvation.

This concept is apparent in states of dependence to endorphins because these have not been initiated with the pursuit of a special "beneficial" drug effect in mind. But we observe the same phenomenon in substance abuse and drug addictions. First the action of using a drug is initiated; only secondarily do we observe the development of an ideational superstructure that in scope far exceeds the initial desire for a "high" and the denial of the detrimental effects of this behavior—not to mention the massive avalanche of craving fantasies triggered by abstaining from an addictive drug.

These observations raise a question: How much of our thinking and ideational life is *not* primarily motivated by behavior that is rewarding, that works? Even in our everyday life, much of what we think and believe seems to be determined by our means of achieving reward or by justifying these means.

This concept is in direct contrast to prevailing psychological and psychiatric theory regarding the functioning of the mind, which teaches that thought and fantasy are primary and behavior is the consequence of thought, i.e., secondary.

The previously mentioned case of Lola, a married woman in her forties working out of her home as a writer, illustrates this point. She frequently masturbated as a means of coping with her anxiety whenever she had to write a magazine article. She admitted with great embarrassment and shame that she had to use surgical tools to inflict pain on her nipples and vagina in order to achieve orgasm. As is standard practice in psychiatry, I asked her about any fantasies she was having while she masturbated. As expected, her fantasies were images of previous encounters with men in authority, like teachers and fatherly advisers, who told her that she was a bad, naughty girl, that she had to be punished.

This, of course, fits the conventional teaching that Lola's sexual masochistic fantasies were primary and the masturbatory behavior secondary. But did she really masturbate by inflicting pain on herself to act on her fantasies? Of course not. She inflicted pain on herself to stimulate her pain responsive endorphin system, a stimulation without which she was not able to have the multiple orgasms necessary to control her anxiety.

Whenever she masturbated she learned that masturbating by inflicting pain brought her to orgasm. Inflicting pain eventually became necessary. Only secondarily did she develop masochistic fantasies to justify and make sense out of her behavior. She relieved her guilt feelings by imagining "punishing" herself as she was giving herself pleasure and relief from anxiety. Thus her behavior was primary, her fantasies secondary.

The Portfolio of Rewards

We have seen in our discussion of the "archaic" brain that reward-mediated mechanisms are essential for the basic functions of self-preservation of the individual and survival of the species. Life without reward is not possible. And this can be said about the higher functions of the thinking brain as well. The dynamics of reward and nonreward occupy a central role in maintaining homeostasis in the human mind.

If reward is so important to life, it follows that life would be more stable if it were based on a broad foundation of rewards. We know that addictions often are the eventual outcome of using a substance as a last resort method of experiencing reward in a life devoid of rewards. If even a self-destructive substance becomes so irresistible, it suggests that one form of reward or another is necessary to avoid feeling depressed, anxiety-ridden, or worthless—or simply to keep living.

Another regular feature of addictions is the funnel effect, a progressive concentration on one reward mechanism or substance at the expense of other rewards that life has to offer. We observe this not only in anorexia nervosa but also in all other forms of addictive behavior and in drug addiction. Similarly, many people have an inherent tendency to rely increasingly on one reward that works. However, the danger of relying on one major reward is easily overlooked, especially in our society, where the "single-minded" pursuit of a goal is so highly valued. Often one sees this exclusive focus on one form of reward in the life-style of apparently healthy and well-functioning people, such as the exclusive pursuit of a career at the expense of other rewards, such as family, friends, intimate relationships, or hobbies.

Unfortunately, many people in this situation find themselves in deep emotional trouble when they experience a setback in the area of their exclusive pursuit. They have not paid attention to securing a broader base of rewards and have thus left themselves vulnerable to depression and anxiety.

To forestall such setbacks we should apply a well-established principle of financial investing to the management of rewards in our lives. This principle is reflected in the adage, "Don't put all your eggs in one basket." Any prudent investor will diversify his or her portfolio so that a setback in one investment will be compensated for by stability or gains in other investments. Similarly, good management of one's life would call for a diversification of one's portfolio of rewards, with careful attention being paid to the maintenance of a variety of rewards. That way, the likelihood of finding oneself devoid of all rewards is much reduced.

A well diversified portfolio of rewards would include work/school, family, friends, intimacy, hobbies, and some form of spiritual life. The degree of passion we feel about any of these pursuits indicates how adequate our involvement in these areas is. If we conduct our life in accordance with this principle, we implement a form of conscious, deliberate psychological defense of our mind's homeostasis, a kind of mental hygiene that will make the need for excessive physical defense mechanisms less likely.

THE THINKING BRAIN: THE SUPEREGO AND BRAIN REWARD

One would think that humans' superior capacity to think is only an asset in that it guides them to conduct life efficiently. But that is not so, paradoxical as it may seem. It is also the source of many difficulties by which humans distinguish themselves from other animals.

Many of our difficulties seem to stem from the inability of our thinking brain to come to terms with the autonomy and rigidity of the "archaic" part of our brain. It is as if the most recent evolutionary acquisition, the cortex and the function of thinking connected with it, is in conflict with the oldest archaic part of the brain and its functions of promoting homeostasis and survival of the species. Many psychiatric conditions of our times can be traced back to this core conflict and its physical and mental manifestations.

The most prominent players in this conflict are, on the one hand the superego, the standard-setting part of our thinking brain, and on the other, the rigid, limit-setting parts of the "archaic" brain. While we are familiar with the archaic brain from an earlier discussion, the superego requires a brief introduction.

The standards of the superego are established in early childhood by learning what is acceptable, based on the family's and society's values, norms, and morality. This learning process essentially takes place by trial and error, by finding out which behavior is rewarded and praised, and which behavior is not, perhaps even punished. In short, these standards are established by what works, what is rewarding.

While this link to brain reward may sound plausible, it also can be the source of devastating mental dysregulation. Under normal conditions the superego sets the standards for ambitions and aspirations, the achievements a person seeks to fulfill in pursuit of his/her idealized self. The superego also assumes the task of signaling to the person when the goals have been reached and the person should sit back and enjoy. However, in extreme situations, mostly related to an impairment of self-esteem, these standards become excessively harsh and punitive, thus leading to pathological conditions, one of which is illustrated here.

Stretching the Limits

In our society a life of aspirations and achievements is highly valued for good and healthy reasons. But in our world of hyperbole, some teachers and preachers of self-improvement want people to believe that a person "can do anything in life as long as he/she puts his/her mind to it." This, of course, is utter nonsense. Nevertheless, many people are driven by excessive standards of achievement and the promise of "happiness" through success, so much so that their sense of well-being is highly dependent on ever greater success in terms of income, power, and social status. While many individuals are able to pursue this goal without any signs of strain, others become casualties of this obsession.

Let us consider a clinical situation: Myra, a highly capable and successful woman in her late thirties holds excessive expectations of herself as to what degree of accomplishments constitutes sufficient reason to settle down and enjoy the fruits of her efforts. She is obsessed with achieving an ever higher degree of success, despite signs of severe strain on body and mind, such as anxiety attacks, sleep disturbance, nervous tension, and obsessive, morbid fears of illness and death. Although these symptoms are frightening to her and reason to seek professional help, she seems unable to slow her pace.

This woman finds it so difficult to change because she has been caught in a vicious cycle of conflict between her superego and her archaic brain. It began when, as a result of serious self-esteem problems, her superego forced her in a tyrannical fashion to make ever greater efforts towards achieving the impossible. As a result of her unrelenting pace of work, the archaic part of her brain has reached the point at which it no longer is able to adapt her mind and body functions to the ever increasing demands placed on them.

As a last ditch effort to reestablish equilibrium, the "archaic" brain causes the body to run at 150% of normal speed; it has triggered the "fight or flight" response, a self-protective system, which Myra experiences as anxiety attacks. However, no matter how much Myra tries to override these signs of distress and danger, they already signal disintegration of the protective functions of the brain.

These anxiety attacks are the sum total of debilitating, frightening changes in body functions and sensations usually mediated by the autonomous nervous system. These can include irregular heart beats, a feeling of air hunger resulting in hyperventilation, strange sensations in the stomach, restlessness, cold clammy sweating, shaking of limbs, and often very morbid thoughts of hopelessness or imminent death. In other words, the brain has responded by initiating an internal regulatory mechanism very similar to the mechanisms of homeostasis of other organ systems. It is in the patient's interest to recognize these symptoms as signals that she has stretched the limits of her brain's adaptive capacity too far.

Stretching the limits and the resultant anxiety states can be self-imposed, as in the case of Myra, or they can be imposed from the outside. Children and adolescents, in particular, experience stresses from the outside which they cannot escape. These stresses can be the result of parents' direct expectations and directives or, more subtly, the result of parents' values and ambitions that have been incorporated by the adolescent and now powerfully motivate his/her thinking and behavior. Of course, the breaking point of this pressured way of life is reached earlier if the individual has an inherited constitution of greater sensitivity and vulnerability. Similarly, early environmental pressures stemming from peers and teachers can lead to excessively high standards and perfectionism, the precursors of this state of mental and physical dysregulation.

Whatever the avenue leading to anxiety states, the problem here is that the danger signals are emanating from the very organ, the brain, that is designed to respond to danger signals from other parts of the body and to implement protective measures. Who looks after the mind when it is in danger? Unfortunately, nobody and nothing. Rather than properly registering the anxiety attacks as signals of danger to the brain and mind, and accordingly scaling back her work load, Myra responds to these danger signals by intensifying her pursuit of activities that she has used to achieve a peace of mind all along—still higher aims and greater efforts. Thus, the mechanisms of the brain serving homeostasis create a destabilizing momentum once the functional capacity of mind and body is reached, leading to the malignant syndrome of stretching the limits.

Not surprisingly, this situation cannot continue indefinitely.

A person in this situation will eventually experience a so-called nervous breakdown, when the autonomous nervous system is in total disarray and the thinking part of the brain has lost the capacity to see things in their proper perspective, or to determine which perceptions are real and which are not.

The Corruptible Superego

A second characteristic of the superego is that it can change its standards through the influence of reward mechanisms. This should not come as much of a surprise, since these standards were formed under the influence of reward and nonreward. But it is generally believed that once the superego is formed it is quite autonomous and not subject to change. The special conditions under which the standards can change drastically are those of addiction, to drugs and otherwise, especially when the addictive process has been initiated by a dire need to avoid major disequilibrium of feelings and thoughts. Under those circumstances the superego can become outright corrupt.

We have seen this corruption in anorexia nervosa, of which one of the most puzzling features is the transformation of the anorectic personality, from what Steven Levenkron (1978) has aptly described as "the best little girl in the world" to the unrelenting self-starver who defies her parents' most severe admonitions and pleas to eat.

In Chapter 2, we discussed the power of endorphin reward to influence the anorectic's judgment. The key is dependence, the need for an ever increasing flow of endorphins achieved by starvation. The superego has adapted to this dependence not only by suspending judgment and normal values of what a pretty body looks like, the much discussed changes of the body-image, but also by developing a new value system that makes self-starving a virtue, such as, "I am better, purer, cleaner, than those who cannot control their desire to eat."

This phenomenon has been known to some degree from drug addiction, in the sense that every addiction changes the person's values in defense of the addiction, far beyond the well-known phenomenon of denial. It is obviously difficult for addicts to proclaim virtues in the use of self-destructive drugs, no matter how well they temporarily feel. In the case of anorexia nervosa, however, an addiction to natural substances of which the individual is not even aware, we observe an exceptional and persistent tendency to justify self-starvation in most virtuous terms.

This feature of anorexia nervosa represents a unique model of the corruptibility of the standard-setting part of our mind, the superego. Basically, our superego will accept whatever works to reduce imbalance in our minds, i.e., whatever reduces our anxiety, depression, and fear. Whatever works can be behavior, that is actions, such as exercising or self-starvation, or thoughts, such as ideas or fantasies, or adaptations to life such as political beliefs, religious convictions, and life-styles. While under normal circumstances the superego is strongly influenced by family values or societal standards, these standards are irresistibly thrown overboard as a result of addictive dependence.

Once the superego has become corrupt it will subordinate the executive of our mind, the ego, causing it to carry out the commands of the superego like a slave. The result is a fragmentation of the personality; superego and ego no longer work in synergy, as a team with proper checks and balances. Quite the opposite— when influenced by addictive reward the superego disregards the effects of its selfish and tyrannical commands on the total organism; it can destroy the body of which it is part. Just as there is no mechanism to stop the disastrous consequences of drug addiction, there is no mechanism in anorexia nervosa to stop this faulty judgment, eventually leading to coma and death.

The superego, the agency promoting stability and good judgment, becomes in the case of addiction the part of our mind that causes devastating instability. There does not seem to be a higher agency, such as a super-superego, that would preserve healthy judgment in the course of an addictive process. This appears surprising, in view of our belief that nature has built such checks and balances into our system that survival is assured under most abnormal conditions. However, even this very phenomenon is part of nature's wonderful ways.

The reward mechanisms of the brain were not intended to serve as an instrument of humans' addictive coping systems. The problem is that humans with their thinking capacity have taken matters into their own hands and thus run into difficulties with the superego when reward mechanisms get out of hand and become addictive.

Self-esteem, the Measure of Reward

Having come thus far, it seems fitting to ask if the people we have encountered in the case studies have anything in common in their psychological makeup, one particular personality trait that causes them to run into difficulties with their reward system. The answer to this question is yes: the personality feature of low self-esteem.

The term self-esteem refers to sum total of how we view ourselves in relationship to our own expectations, how we measure up against our often idealized standards and in comparison to others. Self-esteem results from two components; one is related to the sum total of our achievements in our lives, our accomplishments and defeats; the other is the value that we attach to these accomplishments and defeats.

In terms of the different agencies of the mind discussed earlier, self-esteem is basically a measure of the interplay between the superego and the ego. Ideally, there is a balance between them. Low self-esteem results from a wide gap between the expectations of the superego and the attainments of the ego.

As we have seen, the superego is closely tied to reward mechanisms. By defining standards for the ego as to what is good and bad, and what works, the superego determines which ego action is rewarding and which is not. For these reasons self-esteem is closely related to reward mechanisms.

On the other hand, self-esteem has very little to do with reality, in that it is not much influenced by natural endowment or actual accomplishments. People with substantial achievements and skills may place themselves at the bottom of the pecking order, while others with few or no aptitudes or virtues may hold themselves in very high esteem.

Where Does Low Self-Esteem Come From?

Low self-esteem can be observed as a symptom of other conditions or can be a personality trait that pervades the life of a person from early childhood on.

As a symptom of other psychiatric conditions it is, observed most frequently in major depressive disorders, in which a previously perfectly self-confident person falls into a deep feeling of worthlessness and self-loathing. However, if we consider the "other" side of depression, observable in people with manic-depressive disorder, also called bipolar illness, we find the same person in a manic phase displaying high self-esteem, riding high on an unrealistic feeling of being on top of the world. These drastic changes within the same person suggest that self-esteem is influenced to some degree by the biochemistry of the brain.

On the other hand, low self-esteem can also be part of the symptom complex of anxiety or panic attacks. Here one observes a rapid deterioration of a person's subjective sense of worth and confidence in him/herself. Typically, this sudden lowering of self-esteem lasts only for the duration of the attack, maybe hours or minutes. While people suffering from anxiety attacks tend to be more sensitive in their general personality makeup, they are not necessarily afflicted by the personality trait of low self-esteem.

Our principal focus here is on the personality trait of low self-esteem, which can be one cause for the symptoms of anxiety and depression that we identified as the principal constellation of aversive feelings that make a person vulnerable to addictive behavior. Other sources for the onset of anxiety and depression, of course, are the many acute or chronic traumatic experiences found in the histories of people struggling to recover from addictive disorders.

Low self-esteem as a personality trait appears to be a remarkably fixed dimension of an individual's psychological makeup; it undergoes few changes during life. Often the basic level of self-esteem can be traced back to early childhood and even to certain behavior patterns in babyhood, so much so that it may well have been determined before birth.

To what degree it is inherited is a question. Several recently published studies indicated that shyness, one of the many manifestations of low self-esteem, is genetically transmitted from one generation to the next. If a person suffers from shyness, we often find that other members of the family were similarly afflicted, often going back for several generations.

Among the factors that influence the basic level of self-esteem, there is the element of nurturing, which determines the outcome of so many aspects of our natural endowment. Many parents do everything in their power to help their offspring overcome the effects of inherent low self-esteem. And, fortunately, many parents—especially those who are guided by their child's needs rather than their own—succeed in raising their child's self-esteem to a tolerable level. Moreover, many children make extraordinary efforts to compensate for their difficulties, many of them successful and healthy. Other methods appear healthy but turn out to be inefficient and prone to break down, as is evident from the case histories of self-rescue in action or ideas and fantasy.

On the other hand, even a child born with a healthy natural endowment of self-esteem can have it destroyed by an abusive, punitive, and debilitating environment. Whether caused by uncaring and selfish parents or by a tragedy in a child's family, such an environment can lead to a life of fear and sorrow, devoid of opportunities to achieve.

Although most people with low self-esteem will readily agree that their unassertive behavior is neurotic and does not make sense, they tend to suffer much anxiety should they try to change. This is so prevalent that one might ask whether our self-esteem level is not an evolutionary residue of the natural pecking order that one observes among animals of certain species.

Once one takes the vantage point that certain members of a

group in fact belong to a lower level in the hierarchical organization of a group, the behavior of a low self-esteem person makes perfect sense: No matter what his actual achievements are, he aims to please everyone around him and find fault only in himself, he does not have a firm opinion even in matters of his expertise, he will not impose on others for the smallest favor. Quite the opposite—every conceivable opportunity is used to show deference to others, as if they were truly higher in rank. A healthy child would not relate this way to his parents, even though he depends on them in a real sense.

Fortunately, there is no natural pecking order in the human species. Granted, we differ in knowledge, skills, and experience, and not everybody can be a leader. But this kind of interpersonal behavior pattern leads to incredible difficulties in a world where among groups of people the emphasis is on equality. Healthy people are not prepared for the self-effacing attitude of the person with low self-esteem and do not respond well to these unhealthy interactional patterns. Some will callously take advantage of such a person; in any case, there are likely to be serious misunderstandings and hurt feelings.

One possible explanation for a constitutional lack of self-esteem is closely related to perception of danger in a wider sense, and social danger in particular. Naturally, the perception of danger is a critical ingredient of our actions in life. What we do or do not do depends largely on whether or not we consider these actions dangerous to our health and emotional integrity. Actions, including the willingness to try something new and to try over and over again if we do not succeed immediately, the readiness to make mistakes, and ability to risk failure in our own judgement or that of our group, are the precursors of accomplishment and success.

A young child with low self-esteem experiences a heightened sense of danger to his physical or emotional well-being in all his endeavors. The child sees danger where there is none at all or none of great consequence. It is as if the system to monitor the outside world for signs of threat to the organism is overly sensitive, or the threshold for the danger signal is set too low.

The perception of danger is in many ways related to the inborn sensitivity of the central nervous system, which has been frequently mentioned as an important factor contributing to the vulnerability to anorexia nervosa or other addictive behavior. We have experimental evidence from two animal studies that the endorphin system may play a role in mediating the perception of danger, as it is evident in the process of separation-individuation of the infant from the mother and in pain tolerance.

Herman and Panksepp (1978) investigated the role of the endorphin system in the ability of guinea pig pups to tolerate distancing from their mother. They tested this hypothesis by studying in several experimental designs how morphine or naloxone affected the pups' ability to separate from their mothers as measured by the number of distress calls and relative distance to the mother. Morphine was presumed to have similar physiological effects as endogenous endorphins, whereas naloxone was given in the assumption that the drug would block endogenous endorphins.

The results were quite remarkable. The distress vocalizations of the pups, called out when in isolation or when not permitted to be close enough to the mother for comfort, were clearly reduced by morphine. On the other hand, naloxone administration increased the pups' distress calls substantially in the same experimental settings. The investigators also found that morphine decreased the amount of time a guinea pig pup chose to remain in close proximity with its mother.

Although we have no evidence that endorphins have the same effect on humans, this experiment is intriguing. It suggests that, perhaps along with other factors, endorphins play a role in the infant's mastery of the developmental task of tolerating separation from his/her mother.

The authors hypothesize that infant-mother attachment is the result of an endorphin addiction process in which the infant becomes dependent on the mother's proximity for endorphin stimulation, and that separation from the caretaker triggers a state of endorphin withdrawal. A much simpler explanation of Herman's results would be the notion that endorphins modulate the perception of danger, such as the danger perceived by the pup prematurely separated from the mother in this experimental design. Giving an opioid receptor agonist, such as morphine, reduces the perception of danger. Interference with the endogenous endorphin system by naloxone increases the perception of danger.

Pain tolerance, the degree to which an individual can tolerate pain, is another parameter influencing the perception of danger. The proverbial "thick skin" refers to the ability to tolerate physical *and* emotional pain, which is what individuals suffering from low self-esteem are lacking.

While pain tolerance depends largely on inborn, genetic factors, it also is influenced by experiential factors during early life. For example, Torda (1978) explored early developmental influences by studying whether exposure to pain would modify the ability of rat pups to tolerate pain in adulthood. She exposed the rat pups to pain-related stress by using repeated electrical stimulation of certain brain areas and by placing them on moderately heated hot plates. She found that only the rats treated with pain stress in early life had a greater pain tolerance as adults. Also, endorphin receptor activity and levels of endorphin-like substances in the brain were significantly higher in treated rats than in controls. Thus, this experiment shows that stimulation of the natural pain control system produces higher tolerance for pain than is achieved if this system develops without exposure to pain.

One might speculate about the role of endorphins in the perception of danger and say that the brain seems to have a natural filter through which all messages from the outside and from inside the brain, such as thoughts, pass. This filter, which evaluates each message as to possible danger, appears to be linked to the endorphin system, since changes in endorphin levels are instantly reflected in the effectiveness of this filter: The perception of danger changes with changing endorphin levels.

Take the experience of many joggers, for example. They will tell you that seemingly overwhelming or frightening tasks of the day appear to loom much larger before they go for their run than afterwards. The endorphins triggered by the run make these tasks appear much less "dangerous"—a most striking observation for anyone experiencing or witnessing it.

It is quite possible that this endorphin-mediated filter has not developed fully in individuals with low self-esteem—and may never develop fully unless trained. As a result, vulnerable children are disadvantaged in two ways: As a result of their lower threshold for danger, they will not try out new things, will not risk something physically, intellectually, emotionally, or socially challenging because they fear pain and embarrassment. Consequently, their pain control system will not be trained, as Torda showed for rat pups, thus leaving them at a still greater disadvantage in comparison to fearless, go-getter children with a "thick skin"; they do not experience the sense of accomplishment coming from mastering new tasks and the sense of reward derived from it that is so important for the establishment of a healthy self-esteem.

What Is It Like to Live With Low Self-Esteem?

Self-esteem is the central factor in determining people's normal behavior. It also leads to many forms of abnormal behavior and thinking. In fact, it is so important an attitude for a healthy mind and body that there are multiple mechanisms for the regulation of self-esteem. These mechanisms come into action whenever there is a lowering of self-esteem. This is not unlike the regulation of other systems of the body that are constantly subject to corrective mechanisms in order to maintain a fairly narrow range of normal functioning. In that sense self-esteem is crucial to our understanding of a person's life in terms of personality development, defensive styles, overall functioning, and symptoms indicating dysfunction and illness.

What happens, then, in the mind of people who have low self-esteem? Ostensibly, they have developed a belief in early childhood that leads them to interpret their experiences as evidence that they are not as good as others.

To illustrate the interplay of mental forces regarding self-esteem, one could compare them to a scale, a pharmacist balance. Normally, such a scale measuring self-esteem would be in balance, in that negative life experiences weighing down the left side, let's say, are sooner or later fully compensated for by positive experiences, resulting in a reasonably stable sense of feeling worthwhile over time. In people with low self-esteem, the scale has a built-in tendency to tilt to the left, low self-esteem side, thus making it very difficult for them to attain equilibrium: It takes only minor negative experiences for the scale to sink even further on the left side, resulting in terribly shameful and self-incriminating feelings. On the other hand, positive experiences, which normally would cause a person to have a feeling of pride, barely manage to elicit a lessening of worthless feelings. In fact, it takes disproportionally big accomplishments to tip the scale towards a positive sense of worth, and then the experience is short-lived; the scale quickly resumes its negative tilt.

It is precisely because of the desperate wish to balance one's self-esteem scale that there are so many different forms of addictive behavior. In other words, the greater the tendency to have negative feelings about oneself, the more the mind yearns for a way of counteracting it. The more persistently one's mind is troubled by the nonreward of low self-esteem, the more it seeks reward to avoid falling into deep depression. Therefore, for the most part even behavior that becomes addictive at some point starts off with a healthy attitude of fighting depression, the consequences of chronically low self-esteem.

One of these originally healthy forms of fighting depression is the self-rescue fantasy. It starts off with the wish to permanently correct feelings of being worthless and unacceptable by accomplishing something extraordinary. But in the person with low self-esteem it soon takes on excessive proportions, as he/she becomes obsessed with accomplishing something so exceptional and noteworthy—albeit often unrealistic and out of reach—that it becomes an ideational form of addiction.

We can observe this self-rescue fantasy in the 13-year-old ballet dancer who dreams of one day making the front page of a major newspaper as prima donna; that way she hopes to get back at her siblings and friends, to show them who she really is. Or the young accountant who obsessively mourns for years over the loss of a girlfriend. Although he did not get along with her, after their break-up she represented everything he ever wanted from a potential wife.

Another way of counteracting low self-esteem can be seen in the phenomenon of "overachieving." To succeed in one's career beyond expectations and to be recognized for one's achievements by peers is one of the healthiest and rewarding goals in life. However, among high achievers there are many who have done so in an obsessive pursuit of accomplishments. For example, Harvey's (1981) study of high achievers revealed that many subjects live with the constant fear of being found out to be imposters. These people fear that they may be judged to be wrongly regarded as exceptionally capable and deserving of the prominent position they occupy. Calling it the imposter phenomenon, Harvey found it to be more prevalent among high achievers than in normal achievers and to be closely correlated with low self-esteem.

This fear may actually function as a motivational force of high achievement—what could be more powerful than that? The driving force behind the success "enjoyed" by these individuals is the need to rescue themselves from some form of inborn or acquired self-doubt. Consistent with the notion of addictive reward seeking behavior, their success is driven by an ever greater demand for accomplishments and the recognition that comes with it. Thus, the fear of being found out is tantamount to the fear of withdrawal from the sorely needed reward of success to counteract low self-esteem.

SUMMARY

To sum up this chapter, I have tried to extract some theoretical implications from our clinical explorations of eating disorders and other forms of addictive behavior. We have seen that brain reward assumes an important role as a motivating force of human behavior and thought, but especially as the substrate governing mechanisms of defense to maintain mental equilibrium. We identified the conditions under which the superego threatens mental homeostasis by setting excessive standards or forcing a person into excessive reward seeking behavior and addiction. Finally, we traced the constitutional and developmental roots of impaired self-esteem, the one personality factor found at the core of depression and anxiety, the precursor symptoms of most addictive behavior.

The observations on low self-esteem might serve as a cognitive conceptual framework for the psychotherapeutic work of the trait conditions leading to addiction. Although it requires hard work, enhancing self-esteem is essential for successful treatment of addictive disorders. It must be done and can be done, especially if one follows the motto: Practice, practice, practice. Let us remind ourselves of the words of the great Greek philosopher, Aristotle, who said as long as 2350 years ago that we feel virtuous by doing something virtuous.

Bibliography

Abraham, H. D., & Joseph, A. B. (1986–87). Bulimic vomiting alters pain tolerance and mood. *International Journal of Psychiatry in Medicine, 16*(4), 311–316.

Allgood, S. C., Gurll, N. J., & Reynolds, D. G. (1988). Naloxone requires circulating catecholamines to attenuate the cardiovascular suppression of endotoxic shock. *Journal of Surgical Research, 44,* 73–81.

American Psychiatric Association (1987). *Diagnostic and statistical manual of mental disorder* (third ed., rev.) (DSM-III-R). Washington, DC: Author.

Atkinson, R. L. (1982). Naloxone decreases food intake in obese humans. *Journal of Clinical Endocrinology and Metabolism, 55,* 196–198.

Bakke, J. L., Lawrence, N. L., & Robinson, S. (1974). The effect of morphine on pituitary-thyroid function in the rat. *European Journal of Pharmacology, 25,* 402–6.

Baranowska, B., Rozbicka, G., Jeske, W., & Abdel-Fattah, M. H. (1984). The role of endogenous opiates in the mechanism of inhibited luteinizing hormone (LH) secretion in women with anorexia nervosa: The effect of naloxone on LH, follicle-stimulating hormone, prolactin, and beta-endorphin secretion. *Journal of Clinical Endocrinology and Metabolism, 59*(3), 412–416.

Benson, H. (1976). *The relaxation response.* New York: William Morrow and Company.

Blumenthal, J. A., O'Toole, L. C., & Chang, J. L. (1984). Is running an analogue of anorexia nervosa? *Journal American Medical Association, 252*(4), 520–523.

Bodnar, R. J., Kelly, D. D., Spiaggia, A., Ehrenberg, C., & Glusman, M. (1978). Dose dependent reductions by naloxone of analgesia induced by cold-water stress. *Pharmacology Biochemistry & Behavior, 8,* 667–672.

257

Boskind-White, M., & White, W. C. (1991). *Bulimarexia, the binge-purge cycle.* (2nd ed.). New York: W. W. Norton & Company.

Boyar, R. M., Katz, J., Finkelstein, J. W., Kapen, S., Weiner, H., Weitzman, E. D., & Hellman, L. (1974). Immaturity of the 24-hour luteinizing hormone secretory pattern. *New England Journal of Medicine, 291*(17), 861–65.

Brambilla, F., Cavagnini, F., Invitti, C., Poterzio, F., Lampertico, M., Sali, L., Maggioni, M., Candolfi, C., Panerai, A.E., & Mueller, E.E. (1985). Neuroendocrine and psychopathological measures in anorexia nervosa: Resemblances to primary affective disorders. *Psychiatry Research, 16*, 165–176.

Brown, G. M., Garfinkel, P. E., Jeuniewic, N., Moldofsky, H., & Stancer, H. C. (1977). Endocrine profiles in anorexia nervosa. In R. A. Vigersky (Ed.), *Anorexia nervosa* (pp. 123–136). New York: Raven Press.

Bruch, H. (1978). *The golden cage, the enigma of anorexia nervosa.* Cambridge, MA: Harvard University Press.

Bruni, J. F., Van Vugt, D., Marshall, S., & Meites, J. (1977). Effects of naloxone, morphine and methionine enkephalin on serum prolactin, luteinizing hormone, follicle simulating hormone, thyroid stimulating hormone and growth hormone. *Life Sciences, 21*, 461–66.

Caldwell, J. D. (1992). Central oxytocin and female sexual behavior. *Annals of the New York Academy of Sciences, 652*, 166–179.

Cantwell, D. P., Sturzenberger, S., Burroughs, J., Salkin, B., & Green, J. K. (1977). Anorexia nervosa: An affective disorder? *Archives of General Psychiatry, 34*, 1087–93.

Carr, D. B., Bullen, B. A., Skrinar, G. S., Arnold, M. A., Rosenblatt, M., Beitins, I. Z., Martin, J. B., & McArthur, J.W. (1981). Physical conditioning facilitates the exercise-induced secretion of beta-endorphin and beta-lipotropin in women. *New England Journal of Medicine, 305*, 560–563.

Carter, C. S., Williams, J. R., Witt, D. M., & Insel, T. R. (1992). Oxytocin and social bonding. *Annals of the New York Academy of Sciences, 652*, 204–211.

Catlin, D. H., Hui, K. K., Loh, H. H., & Li, C. H. (1977). Pharmacologic activity of beta-endorphin in man. *Communications in Psychopharmacology, 1*, 493–500.

Christenson, G. A., Mackenzie, T. B., & Mitchell, J. E. (1991). Characteristics of 60 adult chronic hair pullers. *American Journal of Psychiatry, 148*(3), 365–370.

Cocchi, D., Santagostino, A., Gil-Ad, I., Ferri, S., & Muller, E. E. (1977), Leu-enkephalin-stimulated growth hormone and prolactin release in the rat: Comparison with the effect of morphine. *Life Sciences, 20*, 2041–5.

Croxson, M. S., & Ibbertson, H. K. (1977). Low serum triiodothyronine (T_3) and hypothyroidism in anorexia nervosa. *Journal of Clinical Endocrinology and Metabolism, 44*(4), 167–74.

Csontos, K., Rust, M. M., Hollt, V., Mahr, M., Kruomer, W., & Teshemacher, H. J. (1979). Elevated plasma beta-endorphin levels in pregnant women and their neonates. *Life Science, 25,* 835–844.

Cusan, L., Dupont, A., Kledzik, G. S., Labrie, F., Coy, D. H., & Schally, A. V. (1977). Potent prolactin and growth hormone releasing activity of more analogues of met-enkephalin. *Nature, 268,* 544–7.

Danowski, T. S., Livstone, E., Gonzales, A. R., Jung, Y., & Khurana, R. C. (1972). Fractional and partial hypopituitarism in anorexia nervosa. *Hormones, 3,* 105–18.

Demura, R., Odagiri, E., Yoshimura, M., Jibiki, K., Adachi, T., Shirota, M., Demura, H., Shizume, K., & Oouchi, H. (1982). Placental secretion of prolactin, ACTH and immunoreactive beta-endorphin during pregnancy. *Acta Endocrinologica, 100,* 114–119.

De Wied, D. (1977). Pituitary Adrenal System Hormones and Behavior, *ACTA Endocrinologica Supplement,* 85:214:9–18.

Eckert, E. D., Goldberg, S. C., Halmi, K. A., Casper, R. C., & Davis, J. M. (1982). Depression in anorexia nervosa. *Psychological Medicine, 12,* 115–122.

Elliot, D. L., Goldberg, L., Watts, W. J., & Orwoll, E. (1984). Resistance exercise and plasma beta-endorphin/beta-lipotropin immunoreactivity, *Life Sciences, 34,* 515–518.

Faden, A. I., & Holaday, J. W. (1979). Opiate antagonists: A role in the treatment of hypovolemic shock. *Science, 205,* 317–318.

Farrell, P. A., Gates, W. K., Maksud, M. G., & Morgan, W. P. (1982). Increases in plasma beta-endorphin/beta-lipotropin immunoreactivity after treadmill running in humans. *Journal of Applied Physiology, 52,* 1245–1249.

Feighner, J. P., Robins, E., Guze, S. B., Woodruff, R. A., Winokur, G., & Munoz, R. (1972). Diagnostic criteria for use in psychiatric research. *Archives of General Psychiatry, 26,* 57–63.

Freud, S. (1924). The economic problem of masochism. In J. Strachey (Ed.), *The standard edition of the complete psychological works of Sigmund Freud* (vol. 19). New York: W. W. Norton & Company.

Fullerton, D. T., Swift, W. J., Getto, C. J., & Carlson, I. H. (1986). Plasma immunoreactive beta-endorphin in bulimics. *Psychological Medicine, 16,* 59–63.

Fullerton, D. T., Swift, W. J., Getto, C. J., Carlson, I. H., & Gutzmann, L. D. (1988). Differences in the plasma beta-endorphin levels of bulimics. *International Journal of Eating Disorders, 7*(2), 191–200.

Furuhashi, N., Takahashi, T., Fukaya, T., Fukaya, H., Shinkawa, O., Tachibana, Y., & Suzuki, M. (1983). Human ACTH, beta-lipotropin and beta-endorphin levels in maternal plasma at delivery. *Gynecol. Obstet. Invest., 16,* 269–273.

George, R. (1971). Hypothalamus: Anterior pituitary gland. In D. H. Cluet (Ed.), *Narcotic drugs: Biochemical pharmacology*. New York: Plenum Press.

George, R., & Kokka, N. (1976). The Effects of narcotics on growth hormone, ACTH and TSH secretion. In D. H. Ford & D. H. Clouet (Eds.), *Tissue responses to addictive drugs*. New York: Spectrum.

Gerner, R. H., & Sharp, B. (1982). CSF beta-endorphin-immunoreactivity in normal, schizophrenic, depressed, manic and anorexic subjects. *Brain Research, 237*, 244–247.

Getto, C. J., Fullerton, D. T., & Carlson, I. H. (1984). Plasma immunoreactive beta-endorphin response to glucose ingestion. *Appetite: Journal of Intake Research, 5*, 329–335.

Gold, M. S., Redmond, D. E., & Donabedian, R. K. (1978). Prolactin secretion, a measurable central effect of opiate-receptor antagonists. *The Lancet*, Febr. 11, 1978, 323–24.

Gold, P. W., Kaye, W., Robertson, G. L., & Ebert, M. (1983). Abnormalities in plasma and cerebrospinal-fluid arginine vasopressin in patients with anorexia nervosa. *New England Journal of Medicine, 308*, 1117–1123.

Goldman, M. J. (1991). Kleptomania: Making sense of the nonsensical. *American Journal of Psychiatry, 148*(8), 986–996.

Goldstein, A. (1978, February). Endorphins. *Sciences* (N.Y. Acad. of Science), 14–19.

Goldstein, A., & Lowery, P. J. (1975). Effect of opiate antagonist naloxone on body temperature in rats. *Life Science, 17*, 927–932.

Graber, B., Blake, C., Gartner, J., & Wilson, J. (1984). The effects of opiate receptor blockade on male sexual response. In R. Segraves & E. Haeberle (Eds.), *Emerging dimensions in sexology* (pp. 253–260). New York: Praeger Scientific.

Grevert, P., Albert, L. H., & Goldstein, A. (1983). Partial antagonism of placebo analgesia by naloxone, *Pain, 16*, 129–143.

Guillemin, R., Ling, N., Burgus, R., Bloom, F., & Segal, D. (1977). Characterization of the endorphins, novel hypothalamic and neurohypophysial peptides with opiate-like activity: Evidence that they induce profound behavioral changes. *Psychoendocrinology, 2*, 59–62.

Guillemin, R., Vargo, T., Rossier, J., Minick, S., Ling, N., Rivier, C., Vale, W., & Bloom, F. (1977). Beta endorphin and adrenocorticotropin are secreted concomitantly by the pituitary gland. *Science, 197*, 1367–1369.

Gurll, N. J., Vargish, T., Reynolds, D. G., & Lechner, R. B. (1981). Opiate receptors and endorphins in the pathophysiology of hemorrhagic shock, *Surgery, 89*(3), 364–369.

Gwirtsman, H. E., Kaye, W. H., George, D. T., Jimerson, D. C., Ebert, M. H., & Gold, P. W. (1989). Central and peripheral ACTH and cortisol levels in anorexia nervosa and bulimia. *Archives of General Psychiatry, 64*, 61–69.

Harvey, J. C. (1981). The imposter phenomenon and achievement: A failure to internalize success. *Dissertation Abstracts International, 42*(12), SECB, pp. 4969. (University Microfilms No. ADG 82-10500, 9000).

Hedner, T., & Cassuto, J. (1987). Opioids and opioid receptors in peripheral tissues. *Scandinavian Journal of Gastroenterology, 22*(130), 27–46.

Hendren, R. L. (1983). Depression in anorexia nervosa. *Journal of the American Academy of Child Psychiatry, 22*(1), 59–62.

Herman, B. H., & Panksepp, J. (1978). Effects of morphine and naloxone on separation distress and approach attachment: Evidence for opiate mediation of social affect. *Pharmacology Biochemistry & Behavior, 9*, 213–220.

Holaday, J. W., Wei, E., Loh, H. H., & Li, C. H. (1978). Endorphins may function in heat adaptation. *Proc. Natl. Acad. Sciences, 75*, 2923–2927.

Holtzman, S. G. (1979). Suppression of appetitive behavior in the rat by naloxone: Lack of effect of prior morphine dependence, *Life Sciences, 24*, 219–226.

Jaffe, J. H., & Clouet, D. H. (1981). Opioid dependence: Links between biochemistry and behavior. In H. M. Van Praag (Ed.), *Handbook of biological psychiatry, part IV* (pp. 277–308). New York: Marcel Dekker.

Jirikowski, G. F. (1992). Oxytocinergic neuronal systems during mating, pregnancy, parturition, and lactation. *Annals of the New York Academy of Sciences, 652*, 253–270.

Johnson, C., & Larson, R. (1982). Bulimia: An analysis of moods and behavior. *Psychosomatic Medicine, 44*(4), 341–351.

Johnson, M. R., Bower, M., Seckl, J. R., & Lightman S. L. (1990). Neurohypophysieal secretion to insulin-induced hypoglycemia and its regulation by endogenous opioids in women. *Acta Endocrinologica (Copenhagen), 122*(4), 467–471.

Jonas, J. M., & Gold, M. S. (1988). The use of opiate antagonists in treating bulimia: A study of low-dose versus high-dose naltrexone. *Psychiatry Research, 24*, 195–199.

Katz, J. L. (1986). Long-distance running, anorexia nervosa, and bulimia: A report of two cases. *Comprehensive Psychiatry, 27*(1), 74–78.

Katz, J. L., Boyar, R. M., Weiner, H., Gorzynski, G., Roffwarg, H., & Hellman, L. (1976). Toward an elucidation of the psychoendocrinology of anorexia nervosa. In E. Sachar (Ed.), *Hormones, behavior and psychopathology* (pp. 263–284). New York: Raven Press.

Kaye, W. H., Berrettini, W. H., Gwirtsman, H. E., Chretien, M., Gold, P. W., George, D. T., Jimerson, D. C., & Ebert, M. H. (1987), Reduced cerebrospinal fluid levels of immunoreactive proopiomelanocortin related peptides (including beta-endorphin) in anorexia nervosa. *Life Sciences, 41*, 2147–2155.

Kaye, W. H., Berrettini, W., Gwirtsman, H., & George, D. T. (1990). Altered cerebrospinal fluid neuropeptide Y and peptide YY immunoreactivity in anorexia and bulimia nervosa. *Archives of General Psychiatry, 47,* 548–556.

Kaye, W. H., Gwirtsman, H. E., George, D. T., Ebert, M. H., Jimerson, D. C., Tomai, T. P., Chrousos, G. P., & Gold, P. W. (1987). Elevated cerebrospinal fluid levels of immunoreactive corticotropin-releasing hormone in anorexia nervosa: Relation to state of nutrition, adrenal function, and intensity of depression. *Journal of Clinical Endorcrinology and Metabolism, 64* (2), 203–208.

Kaye, W. H., Pickar, D. M., Naber, D., & Ebert, M. H. (1982). Cerebrospinal fluid opioid activity in anorexia nervosa. *American Journal of Psychiatry, 130,* 643–645.

Keys, A., Brozek, J., Henschel, A., Mickelson, O., & Taylor, H. L. (1950). *The biology of human starvation,* Vol. 2. Minneapolis: University of Minnesota Press.

Kobrinsky, N. L., Pruden, P. B., Cheang, M. S., Levitt, M., Bishop, A. J., & Tenenbein, M. (1988). Increased nausea and vomiting induced by naloxone in patients receiving cancer chemotherapy. *American Journal of Pediatric Hematology/Oncology, 10*(3), 206–208.

Kokka, N., & George, R. (1974). Effects of narcotic analgesics, anesthetics, and hypothalamic lesions on growth hormone and adrenocorticotropic hormone secretion in rats. In E. Zimmerman & R. George (Eds.), *Narcotics and the hypothalamus.* New York: Raven Press.

Krieger, D. T., & Hughes, J. C. (Eds.). (1980). *Psychoendocrinology.* Sunderland, MA: Sinauer Associates, Inc.

Lacey, J. H. (1982). Anorexia nervosa and a bearded female saint. *British Medical Journal, 285,* 1816–1817.

Lang, I. M., & Marvig, J. (1989). Functional localization of specific mediating gastrointestinal motor correlates of vomiting. *American Journal of Physiology, 256,* G92–G99.

Levenkron, S. (1978). *The best little girl in the world.* Chicago: Contemporary Books.

Levenkron, S. (1982). *Treating and overcoming anorexia nervosa.* New York: Scribner's.

Levenkron, S. (1991). *Obsessive compulsive disorders.* New York: Warner Books.

Levine, A. S., & Billington, C. J. (1989). Opioids: Are they regulators of feeding? *Annals New York Academy of Sciences, 575,* 209–220.

Levine, J. D., Gordon, N. C., & Fields, H. L. (1978). The mechanism of placebo analgesia. *Lancet,* Sept. 23, 654–657.

Levine, S. (1976). Stress and behavior. In *Progress in psychobiology, readings from Scientific American* (pp. 143–148). San Fransisco: W. H. Freeman and Co.

Li, C. H., Chretien, M., & Chung, D. (1965). Isolation and amino-acid sequence of beta-LPH from sheep pituitary glands. *Nature, 208,* 1093–4.

Lightman, S. L., Jacobs, H. S., Maguire, A. K., McGarrick, G., & Jeffcoate, S. L. (1981). Constancy of opioid control of luteinizing hormone in different pathophysiological states. *Journal of Clinical Endocrinology and Metabolism, 52*(6), 1260-3.

Lomax, P., & Ary, M. (1974). Sites of action of narcotic analgesics in the hypothalamus. In E. Zimmerman & R. George (Eds.), *Narcotics and the hypothalamus*. New York: Raven Press.

Margules, D. L., Goldman, B., & Finck, A. (1979). Hibernation: An opiod-dependend state? *Brain Research Bulletin, 4*, 721-724.

Margules, D. L., Moisset, B., Lewis, M. J., Shibuya, H., & Pert, C. B. (1978). Beta-endorphin is associated with overeating in genetically obese mice (ob/ob) and rats (fa/fa). *Science, 202*, 988-991.

Marrazzi, M. A., & Luby, E. D. (1986). An auto-addiction model of chronic anerexia nervosa. *International Journal of Eating Disorders, 5*, 191-208.

Marrazzi, M. A., & Luby, E. D. (1989). Neurobiology of anorexia nervosa. In M. Cohen (Ed.), *The brain as endocrine organ* (pp. 46-95). New York: Springer Verlag.

Martin, J. B., Audet, J., & Saunders, A. (1975). Effects of somatostatin and hypothalamic ventro-medial lesions on GH release induced by morphine. *Endocrinology, 96*(4), 839-47.

Mecklenburg, R. S., Loriaux, D. L., Thompson, R. H., Anderson, A. E., & Lipsett, M. B. (1974). Hypothalamic dysfunction in patients with anorexia nervosa. *Medicine, 53*, 2.

Melchior, J. C., Rigaud, D., Colas-Linhart, N., Rozen, R., Fantino, M., & Apfelbaum, M. (1990). Negative allesthesia and decreased endogenous opiate system activity in anorexia nervosa. *Pharmacology Biochemistry & Behavior, 35*, 885-888.

Minuchin, S., Rosman, B. L., & Baker, L. (1978). *Psychosomatic families: Anorexia nervosa in context*. Cambridge, MA: Harvard University Press.

Mirin, S. M., Mendelson, J. H., Ellingboe, J., & Meyer, R. (1976). Acute effects of heroin and naltrexone on testosterone and gonadotropin secretion: A pilot study. *Psychoendocrinology, 1*, 359-69.

Mitchell, J. E., Laine, D. E., Morley, J. E., & Levine, A. S. (1986). Naloxone but not CCK-8 may attenuate binge-eating behavior in patients with bulimia syndrome. *Biological Psychiatry, 21*, 1399-1406.

Moore, R., Mills, I. H., & Forster, A. (1981). Naloxone in the treatment of anorexia nervosa: effect on weight gain and lipolysis. *Journal of the Royal Society of Medicine, 74*, 129-131.

Munson, P. L. (1973). Effects of morphine and related drugs on the corticotrophin (ACTH)-stress reaction. *Progress in Brain Research, 39*, 361-72.

Murphy, M. R., Checkley, S. A., Seckl, J. R., & Lightman, S. L. (1990). Naloxone inhibits oxytocin release at orgasm in man. *Journal of Clinical Endocrinology and Metabolism, 71*, 1056-1058.

Norwood, R. (1985). *Women who love too much*. New York: Pocket Books.

Pahl, J., Pirke, K. M., Schweiger, U., Warnhoff, M., Gerlinghoff, M., Brinkmann, W., Berger, M., & Krieg, C. (1985). Anorectic behavior, mood, and metabolic and endocrine adaptation to starvation in anorexia nervosa inpatient treatment. *Biological Psychiatry, 20*, 874–887.

Palazzoli, M. S. (1978). *Self-Starvation*. New York: Jason Aronson.

Pedersen, C. A., Caldwell, J. D., Peterson, G., Walker, C. H., & Mason, G. A. (1992). Oxytocin activation of maternal behavior in the rat. *Annals of the New York Academy of Sciences, 652*, 58–69.

Philbin, D. M., Wilson, N. E., Sokoloski, J., & Coggins, C. (1976). Radioimmunoassay of antidiuretic hormone during morphine anaesthesia. *Canadian Anaesthesiological Society Journal. 23*(3), 290:295.

Pirke, K. M., Pahl, J., Schweiger, U., & Warnhoff, M. (1985). Metabolic and endocrine indices of starvation in bulimia: A comparison with anorexia nervosa. *Psychiatry Research, 15*, 33–39.

Quigley, M. E., Sheehan, K. L., Casper, R. F., & Yen, S. S. C. (1980). Evidence for increased dopaminergic and opioid activity in patients with hypothalamic hypogonadotropic amenorrhea. *Journal of Clinical Endocrinology and Metabolism, 50*(5), 949–954.

Rampling, D. (1985). Ascetic ideals and anorexia nervosa. *Journal of Psychiatric Research. 19*(2/3), 89–94.

Rivier, C., Vale, W., Ling, N., Brown, M., & Guillemin, R. (1977). Stimulation in vivo of the secretion of prolactin and growth hormone by beta-endorphin. *Endocrinology, 100*, 238–41.

Selye, H. (1936). Thymus and adrenals in the response of the organism to injuries and intoxications. *British Journal of Experimental Pathologoy, 17*, 234–48.

Shaar, C. J., Frederickson, R. C. A., Dininger, N. B., & Jackson, L. (1977). Enkephalin analogues and naloxone modulate the release of growth hormone and prolactin—Evidence for regulation by an endogenous opioid peptide in brain. *Life Sciences, 21*(6), 853–60.

Sharma, S. K., Klee, W. A., & Nirenberg, M. (1975). Dual regulation of adenylate cyclase accounts for narcotic dependence and tolerance. *Proc. Natl. Academy of Sciences USA, 72*, 3092–6.

Sheehan, W., & Garfinkel, B. D. (1988). Case study: Adolescent autoerotic deaths. *Journal of the American Academy of Child and Adolescent Psychiatry, 27*(3), 367–370.

Slade, P. (1985). A review of body-image studies in anorexia nervosa and bulimia nervosa. *Journal of Psychiatric Research, 19*(2/3), 255–265.

Slade, P. D., & Russell, G. F. M. (1973). Awareness of body dimensions in anorexia nervosa: Cross-sectional and longitudinal studies. *Psychological Medicine, 3*, 188–199.

Stark, R. I., Wardlaw, S. L., Daniel, S. S., Husain, M. K., Sanocka, U. M., James, L. S., & Van de Wiele, R. L. (1982). Vasopressin secretion induced by hypoxia in sheep: developmental changes and relationship to beta-endorphin release. *American Journal of Obsterics and Gynecology*, 143(2), 204–215.

Strober, M., Goldenberg, I., Green, J., & Saxon, J. (1979). Body image disturbance in anorexia nervosa during the acute and recuperative phase. *Psychological Medicine*, 9, 695–701.

Tolis, G., Hickey, J., & Guyda, H. (1975). Effects of morphine on serum growth hormone, cortisol, prolactin and thyroid stimulating hormone in man. *Journal of Clinical Endocrinology and Metabolism*, 41(4), 797–800.

Torda, C. (1978). Effects of recurrent postnatal pain-related stressful events on opiate receptor-endogenous ligand system. *Psychoneuroendocrinology*, 3, 85–91.

Van Wimersma Greidanus, T. B., Van Ree, J. M., Goedemans, H. J. H., Van Dam, A. F., Andringa-Bakker, E. A. D., & De Wied, D. (1981). Effects of beta-endorphin fragments on plasma levels of vasopressin, *Life Sciences*, 29, 783–788.

Vigersky, R. A., & Loriaux, D. L. (1977). Anorexia nervosa as a model of hypothalamic dysfunction. In R. A. Vigersky (Ed.), *Anorexia nervosa* (pp. 109–122). New York: Raven Press.

Waller, D. A., Kiser, R. S., Hardy, B. W., Fuchs, I., Feigenbaum, L. P., & Uauy, R. (1986). Eating behavior and plasma beta-endorphin in bulimia. *American Journal of Clinical Nutrition*, 44, 20–23.

Warren, M. P., & Van de Wiele, R. L. (1973). Clinical and metabolic features of anorexia nervosa. *American Journal of Obstetrics and Gynecology*. 117(3), 435–49.

Warren, W. (1968). A study of anorexia nervosa in young girls. *Journal of Child Psychology and Psychiatry*, 9, 27–40.

Winchel, R. M., & Stanley, M. (1991). Self-injurious behavior: A review of the behavior and biology of self-mutilation. *American Journal of Psychiatry*, 148(3), 306–317.

Willer, J. C., Dehen, H., & Cambier, J. (1981). Stress-induced analgesia in humans: Endogenous opioids and naloxone-reversible depression of pain reflexes. *Science*, 212, 689–691.

Yager, J. (1982). Family issues in the pathogenesis of anorexia nervosa. *Psychosomatic Medicine*, 44(1), 43–60.

Yates, A., Leehey, K., & Shisslak, C. M. (1983). Running—An analog of anorexia? *New England Journal of Medicine*, 308, 251–255.

Index

Abraham, H. D., 257
addiction:
  behavioral aspects of giving up, 84–96,
    147–49, 211–23
  learning about, 81–84, 145–47, 205–11
  precursors of, 19
  use of term, 16
  vulnerability to, 19–20, 79, 132–33
  see also specific topics
addictive behavior disorders, treatment
  of, 196–226
  addictive trait and, 223–24
  battle strategy for, 212–21
  behavioral aspects and, 211–23
  indications for, 200–202
  and learning about addictive process,
    205–11
  principles of, 204–5
addictive disorders, obsessive-compulsive disorders vs., 199–200
addictive unit, defining of, 216–18
adrenal gland, 52
adrenocorticotropin (ACTH), 52–53, 56,
  66, 68, 72–73, 144, 166
advanced weight loss phase, 31–41
  body-image distortion and, 37–38
  denial and, 35
  dependence and, 33–41
  funnel effect and, 38–40
  overcoming tolerance in, 31–33
  reverse funnel effect and, 40–41
  self-idealization and martyrdom in,
    35–37
  transition from, 41–43
aggression and hostility, lack of,
  158–59

Agnes of God (movie), 172–73
Albert, L. H., 179
alcoholism, 3, 30–31, 101
Allgood, S. C., 142
alpha-endorphin, 67, 68
amenorrhea, 13, 32, 33, 51, 72
anger, bulimia and, 127, 131, 147
anorexia nervosa, 1–117, 217, 244
  bulimia vs., 118, 122–24, 126, 133, 145,
    150
  case studies of, 1–15, 168
  clinical phases of, 16–48; *see also* ad-
    vanced weight loss phase; burn-out
    phase; early weight loss phase
  college life and, 1–2, 6–7, 13–14, 22
  convent life and, *see* convent life
  defense mechanisms and, 231
  diagnostic criteria for, 18
  diet and, 8–14, 21–26, 85–92
  drug addiction vs., 16–21, 25–36, 41,
    42, 44, 92
  endorphin role in, xii, 17–18, 23, 25–35,
    41, 42, 49–78, 86, 92, 94, 112–13, 155,
    156, 244
  family and, 2–5, 9–10, 13, 14–15, 18–19,
    22, 90–91, 97–109
  hormone abnormalities and, 51–53, 55–
    59, 71–74
  jogging and, 160–61
  in men, 26
  rewards and, 17–18, 20, 23–27, 31, 34,
    36, 39, 41, 44
  sibling relationships and, 2, 3–4, 8, 22,
    105
  as state vs. trait, 79–80, 99
  summary of basic model of, 176